HELPING CHILDREN WITH AUTISM BECOME MORE SOCIAL

HELPING CHILDREN WITH AUTISM BECOME MORE SOCIAL

76 Ways to Use Narrative Play

Ann E. Densmore

Foreword by Edward M. Hallowell, M.D.
Foreword by Margaret Bauman, M.D.
Drawings by Edgar Stewart and Zachary Newman

PRAEGER

Westport, Connecticut
London

Library of Congress Cataloging-in-Publication Data

Densmore, Ann E.
Helping children with autism become more social : 76 ways to use narrative play / Ann E.
Densmore ; foreword by Edward M. Hallowell ; foreword by Margaret Bauman ; drawings
by Edgar Stewart and Zachary Newman.
    p. ; cm.
    Includes bibliographical references and index.
    ISBN: 978–0–275–99702–1 (alk. paper)
    1. Autism in children—Treatment.   2. Play therapy.   3. Interpersonal relations.
I. Title.
    [DNLM: 1. Autistic Disorder—therapy.   2. Child.   3. Interpersonal Relations.
4. Narration.   5. Play Therapy—methods.   6. Social Behavior.   WM 203.5 D464h 2007]
    RJ506.A9D454   2007
    618.92'8588206–dc22   2007016133

British Library Cataloguing in Publication Data is available.

Library of Congress Catalog Card Number: 2007016133
ISBN: 978–0–275–99702–1

First published in 2007

Praeger Publishers, 88 Post Road West, Westport, CT 06881
An imprint of Greenwood Publishing Group, Inc.
www.praeger.com

Printed in the United States of America

The paper used in this book complies with the
Permanent Paper Standard issued by the National
Information Standards Organization (Z39.48–1984).

10 9 8 7 6 5 4 3 2

To the children and families that face the challenge of autism

Contents

Foreword

Every once in a while you get the chance to read something by someone who really knows what they're talking about. I mean really knows. Their work is something that makes your jaw drop, and your eyes widen at the depth of knowledge the author possesses—the detailed, sinewy, complicated tendons and bones and fascia of knowledge that interlock, criss-cross and grow as they combine to constitute a book.

This is such a book. Ann Densmore is such an author. She and I shared a teacher many years ago, the legendary William Alfred, at Harvard. But we did not know each other then. We only got to know each other in the past decade, around her work with children and her desire to send her ideas out into the world in the form of a book. From time to time I would hear from Ann about her latest rejection, and I would urge her to press on. I knew she was a gifted therapist, and I knew her book would be valuable. I hoped she would persevere.

Now, you have proof that she did. I knew the book would be good, but I did not know that it would be great. In my estimation, this book is an instant classic. I have never read anything that is so detailed and spot-on about how to connect with a child who lacks the basic tools of connecting.

Ann is remarkable in her intuitive gifts and her ability to reach someone who is by genetic nature cut off, and for most people impossible to connect with.

But Ann gets into the mind of the autistic child and she helps that child get into the world the rest of us live in.

There is almost no feat of human interaction more difficult than the feat Ann makes available to us in this book. Connecting and communicating with a child who would rather not is difficult beyond most people's understanding.

I have rarely read a more impressive book than this. You hold in your hands a work that will unlock doors heretofore locked forever, a book that will make you laugh and cry, a book that can change many lives, and will live forever as a classic work.

Edward M. Hallowell, M.D.

Foreword

This book offers some approaches and suggestions that may be effective with many autistic children. However, it must be remembered that Autism Spectrum Disorders (ASD) is not a "one-size-fits-all" group of disorders. Strategies that are successful for one child may be inappropriate and/or ineffective for another. Thus, this book should be considered a guide, with the recognition that the programs highlighted herein may meet with variable success, depending on the child. However, the principles described by the author can be applied broadly and may be useful to many families of children with autism.

Infantile autism is a behaviorally defined disorder, first described by Leo Kanner in 1943. While much has been learned about the syndrome over the past sixty years, there remains much to be discovered. It is now recognized that autism is clinically heterogeneous but with a core cluster of features that include impaired social interaction, delayed and disordered language/communication, and isolated areas of interest. Additional characteristics may also include poor eye contact, repetitive and stereotypic behaviors, atypical cognitive abilities, a need for sameness, and sensory modulation dysfunction against a background of a normal physical appearance. Now known as the ASD, there is strong evidence of a genetic etiology at the basis of the syndrome, but environmental factors are also suspected as playing a role.

Imaging and postmortem studies have noted abnormalities in multiple cortical, subcortical, and cerebellar regions in the autistic brain. Consistent microscopic findings have been noted in selected regions of the limbic system, regions responsible for emotion, behavior, learning, and memory. These areas include the amygdala, hippocampus, medial mammillary body, medial septal nucleus, and entorhinal cortex. Histoanatomic observations in the cerebellum have included significantly reduced numbers of Purkinje cells in many but not all cases, primarily in the posterior inferior regions of the hemispheres. In the cerebral cortex, the presence of abnormal minicolumns have been reported, which, if replicated, may be related to dysfunctional information processing. More recent findings in the cerebral white matter have found evidence of increased numbers of microglia and astroglia, the significance of which is uncertain but which may be related to the presence of abnormal brain circuitry.

Since 2001, imaging studies have demonstrated enlarged cranial volume in young children with autism, which appears to disappear by adolescence. These observations coincide with data suggesting that the brains of young autistic children are heavier in weight than those of adults. At the microscopic level, changes in neuronal cell size and number have been observed in several brain regions, which differ between children and adults with autism. These findings combined together strongly suggest that the neurobiology of autism may involve an ongoing process that alters over time.

Complementing these neuroanatomic findings, a number of neurotransmitter systems have been explored in autistic brain tissue including gamma amino butyric acid (GABA), acetylcholine, and serotonin. Preliminary data suggests that GABAergic interneurons are reduced in the hippocampus and may be a particularly vulnerable target in the autistic brain. Additional data indicated that the GABAa receptor system in the cerebellar cortex may be down regulated suggesting alteration in the functional state of the Purkinje cells. Purkinje cells are the brains primary inhibitory neurons and abnormalities in these cells may have important implications for information processing in multiple cognitive and behavioral domains.

The growing fields of basic science research in autism is moving forward in parallel and in association with active clinical research that is addressing the disordered language, social relatedness, and cognitive skills associated with the disorder. Studies looking at early identification have identified a number of clinical "red flags" that raise the suspicion of autism during the first years of life. Early identification can lead to earlier intervention that in turn can result in improved developmental outcomes. Clinical data also supports the need for intensive therapy and services during early life, regardless of the mode(s) of treatment. Interventions that have shown effectiveness include intensive speech and language therapy, occupational therapy, social skills training, pragmatic language groups, behavioral management and developmental (floor time) programs, often provided in combination with each other.

Margaret Bauman, M.D.

Preface

Temple told me she has been able to enjoy spending time with two or three friends. But achieving genuine friendship, appreciating other people for their otherness, for their own minds, may be the most difficult of all achievements for an autistic person.
—Oliver Sacks, M.D., *An Anthropologist on Mars*, 1995, 274, in conversation with Temple Grandin, Ph.D., coauthor of *Animal in Translation* (2005)[1]

My first clinical relationship with a child with autism, who communicated only with gestures, began in the 1970s—her name was Emily.

Emily, a five-year-old with autism, had curly blonde hair, powder blue eyes, and a serious facial expression. She cried, threw objects, and hit others if they were near her. Emily wasn't vindictive, only frustrated because she couldn't talk, play, or enjoy being a child. Her language consisted of gestures and unintelligible words. Each morning her parents woke up hoping that she hadn't escaped the house to roam the neighborhood. Some mornings they found her in the kitchen; she climbed up onto the kitchen sink, opened a cabinet door, and helped herself to granola. She opened the box, poured the cereal on the floor, and then dripped honey on it. Her parents found her sitting amidst granola and honey, licking her hands. Desperate to keep her from hurting herself or others, her parents put her in a small closet with a high open window for part of each day. They kept her dressed well and took her to speech therapy at the local public school twice a week for thirty minutes.

In the 1970s, there were limited programs for children with autism except for hospital-related mental institutions and small, understaffed classrooms for disabled children. During my first year of graduate school in the autumn of 1971, Emily entered a speech clinic where I was interning. She was my first client. I met her and her parents at the door, and her parents followed her as she ran down the long corridor of the clinic, her hair flying and her arms flapping up and down. We entered the small clinic office. She ran to the window and pressed her face against one of the small windowpanes to watch the colorful leaves. She quietly tilted her head, backing away to watch the leaves create shadows on the windowpane.

My first goal was to make a "first contact"—to motivate her to feel and hear the presence of others. Without any contact with another person, the child with autism remains isolated in her own nonsocial world of watching reflections alone. I walked up to Emily and knelt down so we could look at each other as I pressed my hand on one of the leaf reflections. She turned her head to look at me. Then she placed her hand near my hand, covering part of the leaf outline. I smiled at her and nodded my head to say yes. I remained still as we watched the reflections move. As I moved my hand to cover more reflections, she moved her hand in synchrony. Each time I moved, she moved her hand. Suddenly, she turned to watch me. Each time I nodded my head to say yes. Her parents, seated in some chairs nearby, watched in silence.

My office was set up with a rug, one small red toy barn, and two horse figures. I sat on the floor and began to play with the two shiny brown pinto horses. Emily started yelling. I ignored her and talked to the horses. She moved next to me, grabbed one of the horses, and threw it against the wall. I kept playing with a second horse. I ignored her throwing behavior.

She reached for the second horse and I said, "Emily, do you want the horse?" She stopped yelling and began to whimper. She looked up at me. I motioned to her parents to sit closer to us on the rug.

Emily looked at the horse again. "Do you want this horse, Emily?" I asked.

She nodded her head to say yes. She was quiet. I handed her the horse.

I asked, "Emily, I need a horse. May I have the one lying on the floor near the wall?"

Emily crawled across the rug, reached for the horse that she had thrown against the wall, and slid it toward me.

I said, "Thanks, Emily."

I picked up the horse and walked it toward the barn. She looked at me and twirled her horse in the palm of her hand, holding it up so that the morning sun reflected a shadow of the spinning horse on the wall.

I smiled at her and pointed to the horse's shadow. She flapped one hand and held the horse in the other. I pointed to the horse in Emily's hand and then to the shadow. She pointed to her horse, looked up at me, and then pointed to the shadow of the horse on the wall. I smiled at her and she smiled back.

Emily's parents reached to cover a leaf reflection on the window with their hands. Emily turned toward them and giggled. She moved across the rug and handed her horse to her mother. Her mother held it up to make a horse shadow on the wall. Emily pointed to the shadow and her mother's eyes opened wide. Leaning his elbows on his knees, Emily's father watched her and his eyes filled with tears. Emily and her family began my work with children with autism—to help them join others, to work their way out of a mindblindness and become more social beings.

This story demonstrates how mind-reading or understanding other's minds during play is essential to typical toddlers. Children with autism struggle to see what their peers are thinking. A typical child at this age who points to the moon and says, "Moon!" looks back to see if the other person is looking with him (Baron-Cohen, 2001, 132). The child's language is not complex at this moment, but his ability to bring another person into his shared experience and to ask that person to detect and look at a particular thing is connected to the language he associates with the object, the moon.

Linguist and language expert Steven Pinker says that there is a relationship between language and mind-reading. "Human communication is not just a transfer of information like two fax machines connected by a wire; it is a series of displays of sensitive, scheming, second-guessing, social animals" (Pinker, 1994, 229–230; 1997, 330). Baron-Cohen notes that in order for a person to mind read, he must first engage in joint attention that drives the mind reading experience between two people. Baron-Cohen names this skill, "mindreading" and explains a combination of mind-reading behaviors that he calls "SAM (Shared-Attention Mechanism) and EDD (Eye-Direction Detector)."[2] By joining the child, the therapist can increase the child's awareness of the presence of another. As the child notices my actions, words, and presence, he is experiencing SAM, which is based on building a triadic representation between an Agent, the Self, and a (third) Object. Baron-Cohen's model differs from other researchers because the model includes two distinct parts: first, a person has to detect the eyes of another (EDD) and second, he can enter into the SAM—he checks to see if he and the other person are looking at the same thing. He or she has to use EDD cues from the other person's eyes and draw inferences about this person's perception of the shared object. A child needs to learn both parts of this system (EDD and SAM) in order to be able to understand the other person's perspective or to be, as Baron-Cohen writes, in a state of "mindreading."

Children with autism not only lack mind reading abilities, but they are limited in their ability to imitate spontaneously and to solicit another's attention. They lack the ability to use EDD and SAM to draw them close to another person. According to Tager-Flushberg (1993), the child with autism lacks these capacities in both language and in thought.[3]

Baron-Cohen (1991) found that in contrast to normal five-year-old children, children with autism were significantly worse at predicting a story character's emotion that was caused by the character's belief. Rather, he found that they were able to judge the story character's emotion if it was caused by the character's desire. Children with autism recognized the causes of emotion (Harris et al., 1989); however, they had difficulty seeing the "belief-based emotion of surprise" (Baron-Cohen, Spitz, and Cross, 1993). Since children with autism lack these core capacities, they struggle in their social connections with others.

In my experience, the first and most important phase of working with children with autism involves soliciting their awareness that the other participant (the clinical therapist) knows what they are thinking, seeing, and hearing. One of the first goals, then, is to join the child as closely as possible so that I can interpret his or her mental state. I watch his body language, his facial expressions, and what he is watching. If he is watching a leaf fall on the pond's surface and he allows me to be near him, then I can watch the same object in the same way. I can be at the same eye level and move my head the way he does to see the object. I can follow the leaf fall with my hand as he does. I can make appropriate sounds that follow the physical actions of my hand as I watch that leaf fall. The child will see that I am watching with him and I am interested in what he is interested in. The goal is, through imitation, to communicate to him that I perceive the same visual image and hear the same sounds that are in his mind. I am joining his reality and, perhaps, placing myself near or within the same mental state.

Children with autism have difficulty noticing what another person's eyes are doing and what it means when a person refers to a particular object or looks at something with an intense gaze.

Tomasello (1988) showed that eighteen-month-old children are sensitive to gaze as a cue to reference. Baron-Cohen, Campbell, Karmiloff-Smith, et al. (1995) demonstrated how three- to four-year-old children can pick the correct and intended referent when given a display of a cartoon face of a character named Charlie, who is looking at chocolates. Charlie's eyes point toward one of four sweets. When asked "Which one does Charlie want?" the children in this study have no difficulty responding to Charlie's eye direction and making the intended referent. Clinical evidence needs to be studied to show how children can relearn this EDD cueing and can establish a shared relationship.

When I join a child with an object, such as a falling leaf, I am encouraging him to use shared attention and see what I am seeing. I am also giving him a direct opportunity, with a visual object, to draw an inference that I am doing what he is doing. I match his sounds, in rhythm and intonation pattern, and I give him the sound imitation paired with a strong visual image (the leaf flowing up and down with the wind). He can hear sound patterns that are similar to his own sounds. In this whole experience, I see his facial expression change, and he turns toward me. He uses his eye direction to draw an inference that I am joining him. He is participating in a shared experience.

Since the child is seeing me as I watch the falling leaf, he is perceiving that another human being is in reality with him with another object. This reality is one of the most basic of human communications: one person looks at another and then back to a shared object and then back to the person. Both participants share a mental state and join in a shared experience. Of course, the child's thoughts are not apparent. Only his or her behaviors indicate that he is noticing my behavior and may be thinking that I know what he is seeing and imagining. If the child knows that I see him and then watches my hand move and hears my voice, he may be interested in joining me.

I have seen children with autism, children who have only a few gestures and no expressive speech, begin to relate and develop an awareness of others. Like Emily, I celebrate each step a child takes no matter how small toward a greater connection with the social world.

Ann E. Densmore

Acknowledgments

Many people gave me the courage to finish this book. I am grateful for all of them. I thank my family—my two daughters, Kristin and Jennifer—for their many gifts, their tenacity, their courage, integrity, and their drive to help others. My graduate professors at Clark University and the Harvard Graduate School of Education were invaluable—particularly Robert Kegan, who continued to root for my clinical work and who valued these stories. Without his encouragement and help with the design of the model, this book would not have been written.

Some people provided the kind of support a writer gets from a team of experts on life itself: Sherry Haydock, MD, who gave me hope so that I could write; Jesse Jupiter, MD, who gave me the tools to write; Anne Strominger, at Children's Hospital who helped me write about the real child; the late Professor Lawrence Cremin, at Teachers' College and Martin Robbins of Harvard, who were moved by my stories; Stanley Greenspan, MD, who thanked me for my work; Karen Levine and the late Rob Wharton who shared their ideas and listened to mine; Jerome Kagan who listened to my first ideas about how to explain joining children with autism; Margaret Bauman, MD, my wonderful mentor who taught me to respect the complexity of autism; and Ned Hallowell who helped me see my real victory, not this book, but my work with these children.

Many people provided invaluable support to the production of the book itself. My thanks to my special editor, Sharon Hogan, who continued to support my writing throughout—to the end and did a wonderful job editing the book; Debbie Carvalko, my editor at Praeger Press, who believed that this book could be published and who guided me through the process; Julie Silver, MD, for her encouragement at Harvard Medical School; Mary Johnston, Barbara Brown Smith, and Marnie Millington for speech editing; Kristin Bennett for science editing; Caitlin Kuhe who designed the charts for the model; Edgar Stewart and Zachary Newman who created the drawings to enhance the stories; Melissa Daley, my film editor; Rebecca Kahler-Reis who gave me my occupational therapy knowledge; Jinny Hanson who listened to early drafts and who I cherish; Elaine Gabovitch and Kate Hochheiser, both dedicated professionals in the field, for their support and generous help with the text; Donna Popky for her advice on language concepts and research; Morgan Newcomb and Russ Campbell for their technical support; and attorneys, Bob Crabtree and Richard Howard for their legal advice and my excellent copyright lawyer, Bill Strong, for his counsel.

There is not one "best" way to thank all the friends and colleagues who listened to me as I took this journey through the writing and publishing process. They are Diane and Peter Gray, Marjorie Gatchell, Gunnel Schmidt, Phyl Solomon, Sandra Farrar, Jacquie Kay, Susan Zorb, Nancy Holland, Mike Thornton, Susan Scheible, Howard Bernstein, MD, Carol Burt, Nancy Aronie, Sarah Measures, Rachel Bulbulian, Rae Ann Somerville, Sarah Obremski, Kristina Casio, Daniel Reinstein, Bruce Hauptman, MD, Nancy Fuller, Alan Shapiro, Olivia von Ferstel, Bridget Glenshaw, Lauren Alessi, Claudia Kronenberg, Barbara Murphy, Joan Alexrod, Jed Lehrich, Molly Smith, Steve Lessin, Jane Koomar, Rafael Castro, Anne Helmus, Dan Rosenn, MD, Robert Nardone, MD, Janice Ware, Naomi Chedd, Carol Henrichs, Kristie Borges, Nancy Miriam Hawley and Nancy Gray Keyes.

There is another big team that helped these children make progress as much as I did. They are the directors/special education directors—Susan O'Brien, Brenda O'Brien, Moira O'Brien, Jill Green, Maryann O'Brien, Betty Allen, Michael McCord, Michelle Keating and Susan Twombly; the school staffs—Community Therapeutic Day School, Eliot Pearson Children's School, Infant Toddler Children's Center, John Winthrop School, the Learning Project, the Tobin School, Andover Public Schools, North Andover Public Schools, Concord Public Schools, Lexington Public Schools, Newton Public Schools, Nantucket Public Schools, and Maynard Public Schools; the park staffs—Drumlin Farm, Habitat, and Walden Pond.

Finally, I thank my mother, Margaret Densmore, for her wonderful approach to life at age ninety-three and my late father, Ray Densmore, a New Englander, for teaching me about commitment. I thank my two brothers, John and Jim, for their inspiring talents.

The most inspirational motivators for this book were the families and the children with autism who I have treated during the past thirty years. They never lost hope, they continued to try out new strategies, and they told me when things didn't work well or when they did. They continue to be a wonderful driving force for my writing and for my work with children.

Caveat

Some children may have the same diagnosis as the children in these stories, but they may not necessarily respond to this type of treatment. Even with dedicated parents, expert therapists who can engage a child in play, and early intervention, some of these children will not necessarily get better. Some will get better. This is the nature of the highly complex autism spectrum disorder (Bauman, 1985, 1988). New research with advanced technology is showing more precise phenotypes that will reframe this condition as a multisystem disorder with genetic influences and environmental contributors (Bauman, 1994; Bauman et al., 2006; Herbert et al., 2006; Herbert, 2005a, b; Jass, 2005; Murch, 2005; Ashwood, 2006; Vargas et al., 2005; James et al., 2006; Rutter, 2005). These studies show that there are several types of disorders within the diagnosis of autism. Profile studies of different groups, such as Nonverbal Learning Disability, Autism Spectrum Disorder, Fragile X Syndrome, Learning Disabilities, and Attention Deficit Disorder, reveal different neurodevelopmental pathways to the same manifestation, showing many different outcomes with different underlying causes; therefore interventions may vary across the groups (Mazzocco and Ross, 2007, 431).

This book is about socialization strategies that will help some children with autism but not necessarily all children with various types of autism. Some children may need other types of treatment, particular attention to various medical problems, in order to be more receptive to the type of treatment described in this book. When treatment of these or other problems is successful, such children often make faster progress in the therapy approach described in this book.

It is so important for parents to approach all of these methods with caution, to consider how the treatment will affect their child, and to monitor their child's progress on a daily basis. If this play therapy method seems to not make a difference in the child's socialization process, perhaps the method is not the right one for this particular child, or perhaps other treatments may be necessary to get obstacles out of the way. Sometimes a multifaceted approach may be best.

DISCLAIMER

The names and certain characteristics of the children in this book, and other identifying details where necessary, have been changed to protect confidentiality.

Introduction

Many children with autism love to run, pick up objects, and move in the outside environment, although they fixate on these objects, reflections of light, shapes, and motions. The therapist or family member can use that interest to help the child connect socially. By taking the child outside, a play therapist joins him and engages with him where he is comfortable. That can be on a playground, at a pond, on a farm or in a park. When the child notices movement and fixates on a stick, or a leaf, or a pond ripple—that is where the therapy relationship begins, where the child is and wants to be in a natural setting.

For over thirty years, as a speech and language pathologist and play therapist, I have worked with a particular group of high-functioning children with autism who may or may not use expressive speech. They share two qualities: they seek attention from adults and they love the outdoors. Through my experience, I developed a play therapy method, Narrative Play, which utilizes the natural setting to encourage language between children with autism and their peers and siblings. Of course, some children with autism must begin with more structure, because they need the control of a defined teaching situation. Others respond to a therapy model based on the idea that a child relates best to others in a setting that stimulates their sense of pleasure and fun, rather than being confined to a desk, looking at speech and language materials. This method may also help children with Asperger's Syndrome.

There are several current intervention models that are developmentally grounded, play-based therapy methods for treating children with autism: DIR/Floortime model (Greenspan and Lewis, 2002; Greenspan and Weider, 2006),[1] SCERTS model (Prizant et al., 2002, 2003; Wetherby and Prizant, 2000),[2] Relationship Developmental Intervention (RDI) (Gutstein and Sheely, 2002),[3] Integrated Play Groups model (Wolfberg, 1999),[4] Do-Watch-Listen-Say (Quill, 2000),[5] Denver Play Model,[6] and Replays (Levine and Chedd, 2006).[7] The model I developed is called Narrative Play therapy and is a developmental, play-based model. A research-based model, Applied Behavioral Analysis (ABA) (Maurice, Green, and Luce, 1996),[8] is a structured approach unlike the play-based therapy models. Each method has particular advantages and some disadvantages for each particular child with autism. They are all created by experienced clinicians. No particular method is appropriate for all children with autism. Some children require the discrete trial methods inherent in ABA therapy and do not fit into the play-based models. Other children respond to the play therapy approach after they have experienced the ABA therapy first. All of these models can work well together as long as the clinicians communicate and collaborate on goals for the particular child.

In 2002, I met Dr. Stanley Greenspan, M.D., a well-known child psychiatrist who developed "Floortime," a relationship-based model of intensive intervention for children with autism (Greenspan, 1995). Dr. Greenspan and I share the idea that a child's unconventional behaviors may be the best starting point for understanding and finding a way to engage with a child.

Dr. Barry Prizant and Dr. Sima Gerber also agree that "the best starting point for facilitating the language-learning process" is when a child is engaged in his own behavior, interested in something that he likes to do (Gerber and Prizant, 2000, 109). In addition, we all share the idea that peers and parents can serve as language models and partners for social interaction. The Floortime approach fits well into the Narrative Play method, as both Dr. Greenspan and I encourage pretend play, sound production, language development, and social communication.

My own method, Narrative Play therapy, is a developmental, relationship-based approach that incorporates speech therapy and peer relationships into natural therapy settings. It begins with play therapy in a natural situation, similar to the foundation work in the Floortime technique, and moves into a more semistructured speech and language therapy that brings together language, play, and storytelling. In Narrative Play, the therapist makes a connection with the child first by following the child's interest, and then develops a set of specific goals for speech, play, and

language. The therapy becomes an interplay between the child who directs
the play and the therapist who presents planned language tasks or problems
to be solved. Once the child relates to the therapist with gestures of sounds
and recognizes the therapist's actions, the therapist begins the process of
redirecting the child toward a language task. As the child makes progress,
the therapist introduces a peer or sibling, each of whom is a natural language
model. The development of the child's language, play, and narrative become
the goals of Narrative Play. The Floortime model continues to follow the
child's lead to help that child develop social problem-solving skills and to
explore emotional themes through child-directed play. The Narrative Play
model diverges into less child-directed play with more direction from the
therapist to develop language and peer relationships through story themes
in a natural environment.

Both Floortime and Narrative Play are helpful for these complex children with autism and language-based disabilities. Several other models are
designed to help the child with social communication. No one particular
method is best. Some techniques are more helpful at particular moments
in the child's development. Most therapy methods begin by developing a
trusting and caring relationship with the child.

Narrative Play is based on three main ideas. First, children with autism
are interested in a rich visual environment, and, therefore, a natural setting is
best for making connections. Second, when these children focus on telling
real stories with others, and using objects in play, they focus less on their
own repetitive thoughts. Third, when children with autism work with peers
and siblings in natural settings, the therapist does not need to help the child
transfer into the "real world" the language skills he learned in the office.
Rather, the child's emotional connections in therapy take place in the "real
world," where he naturally plays. I have seen that once a child with autism
connects emotionally to others in a particular environment, the child will
want to return to this experience. He will not forget how to relate.

The first idea in Narrative Play is that children with autism are visually
attracted to the features of many objects outdoors, to images, reflections of
light on natural things, and the repetition of motion. My relationship with
a child begins when he knows that I share this world—that I watch what
he sees, that I listen to what he hears. In time, he begins to use language to
communicate ideas and feelings. As he learns to create narratives to express
his ideas through real life actions in play, he emerges from his isolated world.

The second idea is that children with autism can be motivated to
create stories using objects in play. Eventually, these stories, real or pretend,
may interest them more than the repetitive videos and numbers that often
dominate their thinking. By teaching the child to create a story theme, a
narrative, he stays focused on his own play and that of the other participants.

The child no longer retreats to his own mind. Instead, he relates to what is in front of him, a peer or sibling who wants to interact. The child takes another step when he learns to use toy figures and narrate his own actions. Once he gives a toy intentional action that is connected to the meaning of the story, he becomes emotionally connected to the story theme. Eventually, he becomes connected to the other person. He becomes focused on what is happening at the moment in play. The child talks to another about the play, instead of staying "stuck" on his repetitive, "in-his-mind," thoughts.

The third idea is that by doing direct therapy outside the office, the child's siblings and peers can be included. They are often the best models for language. Unlike a therapist, who is limited to a few hours a week, siblings and peers are constantly available. In addition, they have an established relationship with the child with autism, a relationship that is vital to the child's progress. Peers can model such subtle language cues as gesture, eye contact, body language, and voice-tone. These are difficult to teach in an office by asking the child to point to pictures, and feel the emotions that accompany them. Parents, peers, and siblings enjoy being outdoors with the child.

For example, let's say the therapist and her client, a child with autism, and the child's older sibling watch ducks cross a pond. The therapist points to the duck, modeling gesture and language, saying, "Look. It's a duck!" The older child says to his brother with autism, "Oh, look at that baby duck! Isn't he cute?" He accompanies this by pointing toward the duck. The older brother squats down to the level of the duck, like the therapist, shifts his eye gaze to his younger brother, and talks to the duck using a baby-like quality in his voice. The child with autism giggles. His hand follows the duck as the duck swims away. The child has just shared the visual and emotional experience with his sibling, and has related to his brother in this natural situation. Both may remember this experience, and repeat the comments to each other if they return to the pond. Once peers or siblings learn to facilitate language during play, they carry over the therapy to the home, and sometimes to the school playground.

When the child learns in this familiar setting with peers or siblings, the outdoor environment reminds him of what he experienced. He doesn't have to transfer his learning from a picture card in the speech office to the outside world. The child learns in a natural way, in a place where he can use language and practice relating every day.

When treating children with severe disabilities in social interactions, I join them in their experiences. I follow their lead into play to create sounds and simple stories. When possible, I facilitate relationships between peers and siblings in natural settings. In this therapeutic relationship, I work with the child's unique ways of coping with the world in order to bring out his gifts and help him make connections (Densmore, 2000).

Before I introduce the phases of play therapy, I will describe the space, toys, and expectations that set the stage for successful teaching and for building a strong therapy relationship with a child who has autism.

PREPARING YOUR SPACE, YOUR MATERIALS, AND YOUR EXPECTATIONS

The Office Space and Materials

The room setup. Sometimes I begin therapy with a child in my office, but I set up the environment to replicate a natural play situation at school, at home, or outside. My office is a rectangular room with a large window that looks out at the woods. The room has a rectangular, 6- by 8-foot floor mat with a couch for parents on one side and a small table for toddler play at the other. A higher table for speech articulation work or play with objects fits in front of the window.

My desk and three floor-to-ceiling cabinets line the wall opposite the couch; the cabinets contain play sets organized in clear plastic containers. The youngest child's play materials are on the lowest shelf. Art supplies, musical instruments, and the other children's toys are on the higher shelves. A child's guitar sits next to the couch.

Near the floor mat, a small wooden box contains supplies such as sticks, cotton, fabric, and pieces of wood, shells, and rocks. At the end of the room are two small beanbag chairs and a shelf full of books for the children I see each week.

We use a nearby sink to wash hands and paint dishes. A refrigerator in the hallway holds small bottles of water and pretzels for snack time.

As soon as the child is ready, the therapy setting is moved to the natural environment (farms, ponds, woods, playgrounds). Some children are treated only in the outside environment. A natural setting with such items as water, sand, sticks, farm animals, or play equipment become the therapeutic tools for the clinician to work with the child. A tree limb becomes a symbolic toy, or a pond with a duck becomes a center of focus for talking to the child about real life actions.

Stuffed animals and dolls. A large, fuzzy stuffed dog stretches out across the end of the floor mat to help children with sensory needs. They may use the dog to dive under for some "pressure" or when they need to be alone. The dog also has a "vet" kit nearby so that the child can pretend to fix a sick puppy. The cabinets contain two large baby dolls with bottles and doll clothes.

Play sets. I have a set of large blocks that are made of soft but firm material in bright colors. They may be used for constructing pretend cities with a set of large plastic dinosaurs. A wooden tree house with pirate figures, a rope that is used to haul up a bucket, and a small wooden boat sit on the toddler table. I also keep a big dollhouse with a swing underneath my desk. Other play sets that are good for creating stories include an airport, a toy barn, a large plastic castle, building sets, and several tractors.

Toys for speech. I have a red toolbox that holds materials for speech articulation therapy. It contains blowing toys, pictures of children making sounds, and other objects that represent sounds. We practice sound combinations in play with a small handheld mirror while sitting on a floor mat.

Toys for indoor exercise. Sometimes a child becomes fidgety in play, and he wants to bounce on a small therapy ball that I store under the toddler table. We play music and the child bounces to its rhythm. Some children also need to blow whistles and do jumping jacks to become more centered. Then we return to the play set on the floor.

Organization of materials. The arrangement of the room and toys is critical for a child with autism. The cabinet doors are closed and the room is always organized for the particular child in therapy at the time of play. Each child has different needs, and so the play materials change with each therapy session. Some children need a clean mat with one toy, while others need a large play set with figures. Some children need only one or two figures, or they become overwhelmed by the choices or the visual confusion of many objects. Other children want all of the cars with the airport set. I assess each child's needs each day and arrange the toys in the office space accordingly.

The Park or Playground Space and Materials

Some children need to go outside and swing, and then return to the office for therapy. Swinging helps them become calm and focused. The equipment that we use outside varies according to the season, the sport of that season, and the needs of the child.

My bag of tricks. I have a cabinet dedicated to sports equipment, as well as a duffle bag that I take to school playgrounds and parks. This bag includes two soccer balls, three jump ropes, a "Gertie" (spongy) ball, a playground ball, a bat, a baseball and a helmet, three bases, chalk, and several bottles of water.

I also include several language scripts for prompting a child during play. I give key chains that hold the scripts or pictures to parents or specialists to prompt a child if necessary.

More outside toys. I bring a tube sled to the outside session in the winter, and a small wooden boat to float in a pond in the summer. Because children with autism love visual objects, I also take several small kites that are easy to fly in the summer and fall.

I have another bag with a small magnetic dartboard, a few board games, and a large mat for the ground for snack time.

Toys from home. Sometimes I ask the child to bring a favorite dinosaur or super hero from home to play outside with a peer. I may take a video camera to film the work, and give the video to parents to view for practice sessions alone. I ask each parent to bring a mitt for the child if it is baseball season or a sled if it is winter.

Expectations

In the process of preparing for therapy, my expectations depend on the age and the diagnosis of each child. If the child is under three years of age and has a diagnosis of autism, I clear the mat and place one play set on the floor. I reduce the number of items and organize them. A child of three needs some area to play with a clear boundary so they don't run away and pace the room. They need structure to focus on what they are about to do—to play with a purpose and to learn and relate. I use the small therapy ball and stuffed dog if the child needs a break during play. The parents tell me what the child likes to play with so that I can follow his interests. Sometimes I help the child create a plan (a list with photographs or pictures of the sequence of play actions) and we check off each play set as we finish. The child with autism is comforted by the visual support and the order of selecting the toys. Despite the overall structure of a session, I always try to follow the child's lead in play.

When treating a child with autism, I also consider each intervention strategy carefully. If the child is shy and resists having anyone in his space, I move carefully near him. If he is afraid of loud noises, I select quiet toys. If he is easily distracted, I keep the mat clear and toys organized. If he cannot use art materials without overreacting to the feeling of the glue or the shine of contact paper, I use other materials. The sensory needs of the child often determine which materials I use. Current researchers have found that children with autism have serious sensory integration needs (Ayers, 1994; Kranowitz, 2003; Koomar and Bundy, 2002).[9]

With a neutral voice, I also try to set a calm tone in the therapy session and stay alert to the child's needs, and how he processes auditory information. If the child overreacts to moderate noise or has some language processing issues, then I present ideas in a calm, slow manner. I may have to repeat the information to the child several times. In addition, I stay at the child's eye level so that he can see how my facial expressions match the tone of my voice and the intonation pattern of my language.

The therapist and parents must always be aware of the child's goals. As the child develops some routines within the overall structure of play, I create specific goals for teaching language, play, and narrative. I give these goals to the parents and other specialists who work with the child.

During each session, I make sure that the child and the parent know what they are trying to accomplish. For example, a child may need to use more eye contact during his interactions. The parent's goal is to lift an object up to the child's eye level, so he can learn to move his eye gaze from the object to the parent's face and back to the object. The objective for the child's play and language would be to increase the number of "eye-gaze shifts" that he makes during play interactions.

As the child moves from one phase of play to another, and develops more complex language and narratives, the expectations change. Some children learn to play with play sets and use language after a few months of therapy, whereas other children take several years to integrate language, play, and narrative.

How This Book Is Organized

Each of the four phases of the play therapy method is divided into three domains: language, play, and narrative. Each domain includes a number of detailed strategies for intervention for a child with autism. Although these strategies are broken out separately in this book, in my practice I often use several strategies at once.

In the first part of each phase, I talk about the actions of the child and the environment and how I join him in his experience. In addition, I model and use play actions with language to expose the child to language associated with play.

In the second part of each phase, I keep the child engaged in using sounds and words to communicate to sustain an interaction. I guide him toward another child with eye contact, gesture, and language and redirect him away from repetitive language and play that limits his ability to interact and notice others.

In the third part of each phase, I provide direct support with verbal and gesture cues, and language suggestions to the child about how to engage in an interaction with a peer, and negotiate for an object, or a particular play agenda. This last part involves more direct teaching than guiding and requires support for both the child and the peer. (For the purpose of this book, the word "child" means a child with autism and the word "peer" denotes a typical child at the same developmental age.)

The strategies in each phase become increasingly more complex, because as the child moves from phase one to phase four, he uses more complex language, has more interactions with a peer and then two peers, and negotiates with several children as he becomes socially connected.

The strategies of this play therapy technique are arranged in a linear model beginning with phase one and ending in phase four. Each phase may overlap with the next phase. For example, as a child finishes phase one, and makes contact with his family and me, he may just begin to play alongside of another child—a characteristic of phase two.

The main goal of the play therapy model is to help the child with autism use language to interact with reciprocity, to play with peers and family, and to create narratives about life events in a natural situation. Each strategy of this intervention therapy is followed by an explanation that is enhanced by actual clinical cases of real children. The abilities of each child vary; therefore, the therapist must select those strategies that are appropriate for the particular child.

The strategies are a guide to help organize the therapy-child relationship as it unfolds. Along with the therapist, the child and his family endure the tedious, but rewarding struggle to connect with each other. Each phase is a new window into the therapist-child relationship, the child-family relationship in some cases, and in the last two phases, into the connections between a child with autism and a typical peer.

Although the structure of this book is linear in form, the strategies may be used in any order within each phase. Within each phase, the domains of language, play, and narrative are treated separately until the child reaches phase four, when all three areas are interrelated. In phase one, I concentrate on making a connection, a first contact, and the child is focused more on language than on play or narrative structure. Once a child reaches phase four, he is socially engaged and is using language, play, and narrative as one whole unit for expression and communication (see chart on p. 28–29).

PHASE ONE

First Contact

In phase one, a child with autism may rock back and forth, singing endlessly, chanting rhythms, humming, watching lights, following images and
reflections in the outside environment. In order to avoid eye contact and
interactions with others, a child with autism may pace around the playground, spin in circles, and collect objects and place them in a row or
nearby; he allows no one to touch them. The phase one child lacks the
ability to use language to engage and recruit others, produces no language
in full sentences to express ideas and emotions, and uses objects to manipulate without the intention of play with others. He cannot sequence ideas to
create a narrative form that tells a story in play. He is isolated in a limited,
nonsocial world with little access to the world of relationships.

LANGUAGE

Some children in phase one are nonverbal or engage in self-talk, which is
limited to repetitive sounds and noises. They use few meaningful words and
limited eye gaze to others or to objects; instead they fixate on one object
and protest with crying by pushing others away and throwing tantrums.
Language use is very limited in this phase. Without language to produce
simple sentences, the child does not create narratives that associate themes
with play actions. He lacks the ability to use language in a reciprocal way to

engage with others, or to even initiate a conversation; these children have minimal interactions with their own family members. Children with autism have difficulty disengaging from a particular fixation (Bryson et al., 2004) and need continual encouragement to interact with others.

PLAY

A typical child by the age of eighteen months to two years uses symbolic play.[1] He might, for example, use a stick to represent a witch's wand in a story or a small piece of paper to represent a blanket to cover a doll figure. Actions in play are natural for a typical child and a part of the child's own ideas.

In contrast, children with autism in phase one show little to no signs of representing a real life action with an inanimate object in play, and often lack the ability to make associations between the inanimate object and a real life action. With toys collected around them, they play in isolation, keeping others from touching any of their objects. They play with gestures that are unrelated to the toys, often without a purpose in their actions, moving objects or their hands to watch the lines and shapes of an object. Their extensive repetitive actions limit them from interacting with others during play. Expressing emotions of mistrust and anger, their plan for play is to stay alone. They think about favorite videos or repeated images. They may even face the corner and want to stay there until they have to go to sleep at night.

NARRATIVE

By age two, typical children create narratives with a beginning story theme, a sequence of actions, and an ending.[2] There are individual differences and cultural differences in which children within any one culture tell stories. However, many children use these narratives to connect to peers and to play out stories on the playground. In contrast, in phase one, the child with autism cannot create a simple narrative structure using characters or figures in play. Instead, he attends to small details, pointing to a wheel on a train or the corner of a dollhouse, unable to see how these details could be a part of a story. If he uses word approximations, he talks about music, books, and videos that are unrelated to a narrative structure. He is unaware of how to retell an event or how to engage in abstract thought with others. He may face the corner, repeating unrelated sounds and words endlessly with no intention to engage others to listen to a narrative.

In phase one, children with autism are often fearful and are isolated from social relationships; they therefore need intervention strategies that will meet their specific needs.

1

First Contact

JOINING THE CHILD WHERE HE IS

Strategies in this chapter

Strategy 1. Experience what the child experiences.
Strategy 2. Move into the child's play space.
Strategy 3. Listen to each detail of the parents' stories.
Strategy 4. Interrupt the child's fixed patterns of play.
Strategy 5. Assist the child to feel the presence of others by using the environment.

Strategy 1: Experience What the Child Experiences

I join the child in his own experience by listening to and echoing his sounds, as well as those in the environment. I move closer to him in a calm, playful way, making comments about any actions or sounds in the situation. Sometimes I have to move right next to the child and offer a toy or an object like a feather. If he seems anxious, sings repetitively, or exhibits negative behaviors like screaming, I may have to wait to offer him an object. At other times I need to remain more distant and stay silent before attempting to move near the child. In order for him to experience the feeling of being with another person, I observe and wait, watching his gestures and sounds, even if he turns away.

During this first phase of contact, I intervene with caution. Patrick, a two-year-old with big green eyes and curly red hair, is in phase one. His language is limited to gestures, yelling, kicking, and screaming. I met Patrick for the first time when his parents, Paul and Karen, brought him to my office for a speech and language consultation on the advice of a child psychiatrist. During our first therapy session in my office, he faced the corner, allowing no one to be near him or his trains that he carried with him from home. My first strategy was to move slowly into his play corner and listen to him and to the sounds of his trains banging against the wall.

I said, "Oh, Patrick, those trains are loud. Boom! Boom!" My language was associated with his play actions as my experience approached his experience. Patrick stopped for a few moments to listen to my comments. He was aware of my presence.

Strategy 2: Move into the Child's Play Space

A typical child will create a space where he wants to play, move objects, and interact with a peer. The typical child will move his body so that he faces the other child, places his objects in the center or near the center of his play area, and begins play actions toward the other child, or toward the main object of interest. The play space is the area that surrounds the two children and defines where they'll play. One child might move a toy horse toward a barn that he places in the center of the space between himself and his peer.

While a typical child creates this play space, a child with autism will have no idea how to define this area, or where it begins or ends to include others. The child with autism may have sensory issues, may overreact to sounds and to visual stimuli, and become confused in a disorganized area. In contrast to the typical child, his play space may consist of one small area surrounding him; it includes no one else. He will protest if anyone gets too close to him or moves his toys; he doesn't have the concept of how to create a place to play with another child.

One way for this play space to include others is to place a small rug or mat in front of the child, and to set up simple objects that may interest the child. Since children with autism are visual learners, the visual space needs to be clear and not too busy with too many objects—only one or two objects of high interest. Another way to introduce a more flexible play area is to enter his limited play space gradually. I use an object that is identical to the child's object, playing with actions near the child and slowly moving the object closer to him. This act of moving into a play space is complex and takes time; however, it is the beginning of helping the child join and feel the presence of another person. This technique is more effective than taking a child's toy away, which usually causes screaming and tantrums. However, in some cases, touching the object or asking for it is another way to engage with an isolated child who refuses to acknowledge another's presence.

Patrick has frequent tantrums. He doesn't connect with his family or others and he has no expressive speech. He has defined the corner as his own play space and he expects no one to enter this limited area. Patrick clutches the trains to his chest. It is clear that he wants no one to touch the trains. Facing the corner, he unpacks the trains onto the floor. He lines up each one, placing each car parallel to the next in a long row along the wall. He moves the cars back and forth, banging them into the corner.

I sit behind him and ask, "Patrick, can I play?" He doesn't make a sound and continues to move his train cars into the corner. I quietly reach around with my hand to touch a train car, moving into what he perceives as his own play space.

He shrieks, "OOOOOOOh! Nooooooo!"

I jerk my hand back and say, "Oops. I'm sorry, Patrick. But I want to play, too." He shrieks again with a louder voice.

Karen says, "Ann, he won't let you touch the trains. This is what we deal with every day!"

"What do you do?"

"We don't do anything. He plays in the corner all day long. I don't know what to do. We can't get him to move. He has four other siblings and they all want to play with him. He just screams at them. So they go away."

Patrick's language production is limited to "ooooo" and "noooo." He communicates with gestures that don't match his emotional state, limits his eye contact, often shutting his eyes, and places his hands over his mouth when he cries out in protest. Unaware of how to use an object to represent an action in real life, or how to create a story with figures or toys, he retreats, hums, and bangs his train into the wall—the language and play that he uses to cope. He even sleeps with his trains. Patrick's dad explains, "If I took one train away, he'd cry for hours!"

The process of teaching Paul to move carefully into Patrick's limited play space takes hours of tedious work and patience. He has to tolerate his son's constant complaining and crying. This second strategy of moving into the child's play space must be combined with the next three strategies, as I work in this first phase of First Contact. By learning to experience what the child experiences, moving into the child's play space, and listening and working together, the family and I begin to connect to the child.

Strategy 3: Listen to Each Detail of the Parents' Stories

Parents' descriptions of their child's behavior often give me an opportunity to support them as they begin the long and difficult intervention process. By listening to Paul's description of his son's behavior—screaming when someone comes near him, hoarding his trains—I hear both his desperate need to relate to his child and Patrick's efforts to control and preserve his comforting environment in the corner. I understand and openly acknowledge this tension between the father and the son, joining him as he learns how to support Patrick.

In Patrick's second session, he cradles the Thomas train cars in his arms, walks over to the corner, and faces it. Thomas trains are universally loved by children with autism, perhaps because they represent a small object that is nonthreatening, easy to move back and forth, and an object with a kind personality. Patrick got his Thomas for Christmas a year ago and he takes it everywhere. As I watch him, he squats down and lets the cars roll out of his arms one by one. He watches each one fall. Karen says, "Ann, he cries and screams if I suggest that I play with a car. He doesn't want anyone near him. He watches each train fall in order to see the physical details of the car."

"That must be so difficult for you and for his siblings," I say. I notice that Patrick is giggling and moving the train cars again into the wall.

Karen nods and says, "When Patrick tries to use words, he spouts them out fast and looks down. I can't understand anything he says. He screams and yells at us all the time. He never asks for anything. I think he'd go without eating if I let him." Paul folds his arms and leans back in a chair, watching Patrick, who is still facing the corner.

Paul says, "Ann, he doesn't cry for food or anything. He screams if we want to hug him. I was on the Internet the other day and I read that children with autism can't receive love or give love. Is that true?"

I try to comfort him. "I see many children with autism who love and show love to their parents. No one can tell how a child will do once he is in therapy. He could get much better. He is telling you that he doesn't want you near him now, but isn't that communication? He's angry if you move his trains. He's relating to you. We must work hard and we'll see. Just hang on to the hope that he will learn to relate to us."

The parents become the most important advocate and teacher for their child, since they are with their child more than any specialist. Parents often become experts on the methods and they know what methods work with their child. They need respect and support in this journey of helping

their child. The progress of the child and the development of the relationship motivate parents to keep working. Sometimes the progress is slow and
the therapist needs to support them during these times of discouragement.
There will be times of frustration and times when a parent doesn't understand what to do next. The therapist has to be honest about the progress,
explain the goals, and support the parents in every session After I see that
the parents realize that I understand their frustrations and disappointment in
their child, I work on finding the best way to interrupt the child's fixations
on certain agendas, patterns of play, and particular objects. We do this work
together.

Strategy 4: Interrupt the Child's Fixed Patterns of Play

Interrupting a child's obsessive, repetitive behavior is a challenge for any
parent or therapist. The child will not stop these fixed behaviors without
protesting and overtly repeating his play actions. In order for a child to relate
to others, he must be able to use actions with objects that are a part of a
story in play; he cannot be preoccupied with behaviors that reduce his time
for interacting with others.

I watch Patrick move his trains into the wall over and over again,
repeating the same banging noise. I move close to Patrick and move my
hand toward the Thomas train engine. As I slowly pull Thomas away from
him, Patrick continues facing the wall, screaming and banging his fists on
the wall. I hold the engine in my lap. His parents look on with anguish. I
move my finger up to my lips to remind them to be very silent. I smile and
say in a soft voice, "Patrick, I have your train engine. Do you want it? You
can have it. Here!"

I hold it up and tap him on one shoulder and say, "Look!" He stops
crying and he turns around.

He looks at me and shrieks, "Ohoooooooo!"

"Yes, Patrick, you may have it. Give me your hand," I say. He yells
again.

I remain near him on the floor, still and silent. After ten minutes of
yelling, he reaches his hand back toward my hand, his body still facing the
corner. I place the Thomas train engine in his hand. He grabs it, looks
down at it clutched in both hands, and then places it down on the floor
near the other cars. I see his mother and father smile at each other. They
know that Patrick has made his first contact on his own in order to connect
with another person.

"We'll see. We'll work hard," I say.

If a child continues to cry, have tantrums, and refuses to connect, or if he resists any contact, then I try to be sensitive to the basic behavioral principles of rewarding the positive behavior and ignoring the negative. When prompting a child with sounds and words to get him to imitate, I may use a verbal prompt or a reinforcement such as a smile or gesture of approval to the child only if he is just beginning to whine or point or fuss about not getting an object, or if he doesn't have the word or the sound in his vocabulary for the particular situation. In this case, I generally prompt and engage in sound play with positive gestures and play with the child.

However, in some cases, if the child is about to go into a full tantrum or meltdown, I must either leave the child alone or wait and ignore the behavior until he is quiet. Even if the child is only quiet for a few seconds, I may reward him with praise or a positive word at that moment. I try to find the delicate balance between giving the child a word or some positive sound play when he needs it, and ignoring behaviors that are completely inappropriate. As the parents watch, they learn when to reward the child with praise.

Once parents see a tiny successful response from their child, they begin to have hope. They join me and we collaborate. I teach them to observe the child's gestures (such as moving an object with intention); body language (such as moving closer to someone); or sound production (such as giggling)—so that they know whether their child wants to play.

Strategy 5: Help the Child to Feel the Presence of Others by Using the Environment

Being outside where the child is content and comforted helps motivate her to notice another person. After meeting in the office for several sessions with Christine, a nonverbal four-year-old with autism, I determine that she will learn best outside playing in the snow where she is happiest. Christine knows how to play, but she uses gesture instead of speech to communicate.

In our fourth session, we move outside to a nearby park. We grab our plastic tube sleds and bring them over to a small hill with deep powder. Christine climbs into the bright red sled without prompting. I sit behind her, my fingers gripping the sides of the rubber handles as we slide down the snow-covered hill. The trees fly by and snow sprays out from our hands as we soar over the bumps. Christine shrieks with delight as she leans back into my chest, laughing. When the tube sled comes to a halt at the bottom of the hill, we see the snowy hill ahead of us against the dark green trees. We roll off the tube and laugh as we try to get up in the snow.

I watch her face and wait. Waiting allows a child to observe what is happening. She looks at me and laughs. Her delighted facial expression, her sparkling eyes, and her arms lifted upward convey pure joy. She reaches her arms up toward the trees, glances at me, and gazes upward at the tall green pines above us. She says, "aaahhhhhh." I say, "aaahhhhhh" in the exact same sound pattern. In order to engage a child, I imitate any difference in her intonation pattern and listen to hear her response, even if the response is only one muttered vowel sound.

While still sitting in the snow, I pick up a branch with a pinecone. She giggles and reaches for it. I wait and wait, hoping that she'll want to take the branch, indicating that she wants to play. I hold the branch at her eye level. Christine wants the branch in her own hands. I wait. She lunges toward me. I smile at her. Our eye contact is long and we are connected. Timing and listening are delicate skills to use at this moment in relating to the child.

Finally she says, "Oooh?" I hand her the branch. She waves it up and down in the snow, flapping the pinecone against the powder. She giggles and laughs. I wait again. She looks up.

I say, "This is fun! I am having fun!" I try to match what I think she is feeling at this moment with some language that is simple in structure.

She imitates my exact pitch pattern and my gestures and says, "oooo-aa-aa-un; oooo-aa-aa-un!" The wind suddenly howls in the distance. The tree branches sway in the wind, dropping snow down on us. I hold some powder in my hand and extend it toward Christine. She reaches her hand and places it on the palm of my hand. We look at each other. She lifts up some light snow in both hands and throws it upward. It flies into her face as the wind catches it. We both laugh.

We look directly at each other's eyes.

I ask, "Do you want to go down again?"

Christine nods yes. She reaches for the tube and pushes herself up by pressing her hands down on the side of the tube. She waits for me to get up. I push my arm down and it disappears in the deep snow. I push my foot down to get up and it thrusts deeper into the snow. She giggles and pushes the snow off her face. I have a problem to give to Christine, a problem that will require her to engage more with me. I extend my hand. Christine is only four years old. I don't expect her to lift me out of the snow. She turns around, grabs a long tree branch, and extends it to me like a lifesaving buoy. I notice her eyes, her gestures, and her giggles. We burst into laughter at the same moment.

Christine's mother is waiting at the top of the sledding hill, waving at us. Christine waves back at her mom. Her mother holds her face in her hands as she jumps up and down in the snow. As Christine laughs and waves again, her mother waves back. Her mother waves so hard that she falls backwards into the snow. Christine runs up to the top of the hill and tries to pull her out. We all laugh.

Christine yells to her mother, "Get up! Get up!"

Her mother stands up, realizing that she's hearing her daughter's first words. Christine presses her whole body into her mother's arms and they hug for a long time.

After eight months of play therapy, Christine is at the end of phase one. She begins to use meaningful words and phrases to express her own ideas. She imitates gestures and plays with her doll and other objects. Her play, which involves several intentional play actions with more than one figure, is more complex than when our sessions began. Christine's parents learn how to engage her in spontaneous comments about the snow and play. Gradually the communication transfers to the inside situations. As Christine learns to relate, her tantrums and repetitive play disappear. She no longer wants to retreat to solitary play with her doll. She is interested in others.

ENCOURAGING SPEECH

Additional strategies in this chapter

Strategy 6. Show the parents details that indicate a child wants to play.

Strategy 7. Set up a plan for play practice with the family.

Strategy 8. Move to the child's eye level.

Strategy 9. Teach sound combinations and word approximations for speech production through play.

Strategy 10. Encourage the family to use their native language.

Strategy 6: Show the Parents Details that Indicate a Child Wants to Play

Unlike Christine, Patrick learns to express himself first inside, in the quiet environment of an office. Patrick's parents need help in understanding how their son's actions indicate that he wants to play with them. They need support in order to keep a positive attitude about his sounds and his play.

I tell them, "It's hard to predict whether Patrick will begin to use expressive speech or continue to use limited communication. I believe that he has the ability or capacity to talk. He's trying to tell us that he doesn't want us to play with him. He is giving us some message. Right?" Both parents nod their heads.

"I think that Patrick will respond to play therapy and he does want to play. He just doesn't know how," I explain.

"How do you know that?" Karen asks me.

"His crying is lighter and he is less frantic now than he was when he first came to my office. He allows me into his play space for a few minutes. He bangs the trains into the wall with less force and he looks around at anyone who is near him. He moves his trains with intentional action rather than simply manipulating them. Children with autism often hold up an object to stare at the shape or lines on the object or to watch a wheel turn. He moves his train like a train should move, back and forth. These actions show that he can learn to play; however, he isn't motivated to play with others. When he discovers that playing with others is fun, which is a motivation to engage even for a child with autism, he'll want to play with you. Eventually, through more and more interaction, he'll find a bigger vocabulary for play by watching you move your trains across a track to a station. He may like play figures that represent his family. He will want to be with you, and he will get interested in bringing the train to the station to pick you up. I'm sure that it's hard to wait for that first play action, that first two-word phrase, and that first giggle about his own story."

Karen listens and watches Patrick with his engine now in his lap. She smiles at him.

During phase one, the parents' involvement is critical in helping the child move closer to others. My strategy with parents is to explain that their child may not talk right away or learn to play, but they must keep trying to reach him. I describe many ways to connect to him. Once I know that they understand that the process will be both painful and rewarding, it's time for me to help them plan.

Strategy 7: Set Up a Plan for Play Practice with the Family

I talk with the child's family about when they should do their home-based practice sessions with their child. The amount of time needed varies and depends on the child's tolerance for intervention. Some children love to practice and benefit from play therapy throughout the day. Other children resist practice and will need some reward after each practice play session, such as a special time for bike riding with dad or some reading time with mom. One family with six children, including a set of two-year-old triplets, practice everyday for forty-five minutes before bedtime and forty-five minutes before breakfast. Andrew, one of the triplets, has autism as well as delayed language and play skills. His siblings, a boy and a girl, are typical children with no language delay and they talk to him constantly.

We begin our play therapy sessions with the same toys and schedule that the parents will use at home in their practice sessions. In this case, we:

- Use a farm play set and encourage the child to make comments.
- Then we have a snack time and practice articulation and sound production exercises for speech production. The treatment is related to the specific target sound combinations and is "speech-specific" (Lof, 2006, 9).
- Next, we work with play actions that are meaningful within an airport play set.
- Then we move outside to play on the swing or the slide to practice following another person and commenting.
- Finally, we move through a sequence of gross motor activities and practice an exit conversation. For example, Andrew learns to create an obstacle course on the playground with his siblings. They move from the slide to the swings and into a play fort where they have pretend "lunchtime." When their story sequence ends, they practice saying goodbye.

Together, we write out the goals for each week for their practice sessions so that the goals coincide with Andrew's individual speech production goals and his social language goals in his preschool. His goals vary with his progress. As he finishes phase one, he uses word approximations and notices his siblings. The goals at this point are to:

1) increase Andrew's eye gaze shifts (gazes from an object to a person to an object);
2) improve his spontaneous sound combinations and word approximations with his siblings;
3) increase the amount of time for which he allows his siblings into his play space;
4) encourage him to share and give up objects to others;
5) increase his use of sound combinations and words instead of gestures and loud noises when he interacts with his siblings to protest or request.

Setting up a plan for Andrew is different than setting up a plan for a child like Patrick who is not using language at this level, and who will not allow anyone near him in his play space. Andrew follows our plan and learns to make comments with us on the playground during his first play session. Unlike Andrew, a younger child like Patrick needs a different plan that incorporates less structure, less complicated activities, and more time to connect and make contact between the child and the parents.

I remind Patrick's family that they will have to get used to his screaming during the first phase of play therapy. We draw out a schedule so that they can practice with Patrick at home.

I explain, "When Patrick goes to the corner, follow him and sit behind him. Do this for ten to fifteen minutes a day. Then ask him for a train car or a toy that he has stashed in the corner. Slowly, very carefully, pull a train car out from his line up and hold it in your lap. He will scream. Just wait. You may have to wait for a long time. Hold up the train and tap him on the shoulder. Say, 'Look, Patrick!' Wait until he turns to see you and gives you eye contact. Then say, 'You can have your train car. Give me your hand.' Just wait until he reaches out his hand. You may have to wait for only a minute or for as long as an hour. You may have to tap his shoulder and say 'look' several times. Don't give up. When he reaches, give him the car. Even if he reaches with a finger, give it to him."

We write out the goals for Patrick in our plan:

1) to increase his number of eye-gaze shifts from his parent to an object and back to his parent;

2) to decrease his screaming by ignoring it and positively responding when he uses sound combinations and watches his parent;

3) to improve his tolerance for anyone being in his play area.

During each office session, I model and show the parents how to relate to him, how to tolerate his screaming, and how to gradually enter his space. They practice with me in the office and I coach them anytime they need help during the week while they are practicing at home.

Strategy 8: Move to the Child's Eye Level

Paul scoops up Patrick in his arms, cradling him, and then slowly lowers him so that he can dump his train cars into a basket. Paul carries him toward the office door and I ask him to put Patrick down on the floor. Patrick stands facing me. I kneel down at his eye level.

To gain a response from a young child, move to his eye level. If you stay above the child, he feels disconnected from you. I take Patrick's hand, wave it back at myself, and say, "Bye, bye, Ann."

He doesn't respond with any sounds, but he does look at me. He gently pulls his hand away from my hand. I put my hand out, palm up, and say, "Give me five!" He doesn't respond, but his eyes watch my hand and then look up at my face.

I smile at Karen and Paul and say, "That's enough for today. He's looking at me."

Strategy 9: Teach Sound Combinations and Word Approximations for Speech Production through Play

Once a child connects with me, he is ready to learn to imitate sounds during play, imitate words or word approximations that relate to play actions, and to listen to how new sounds are produced. When a child uses gestures with body language to communicate ideas, requests, or protests, I begin to teach the specific sound combinations (consonants and vowels) and early developing words of language.

After ten one- to two-hour sessions of play therapy, Patrick shows some signs of wanting to use sounds to communicate rather than pushing adults away, throwing toys, and screaming. He makes these signs by using vowels such as "ahhhhh—woooo—oooot" and "oooooh" and by using sounds that could be similar to the sounds of a train whistle. He also points to objects and uses sounds to convey protest—he doesn't want me in his play space. Patrick is communicating. Now he needs to learn how to use language to express his ideas and emotions.

Teaching sound combinations with toys

Patrick's body language and his purposeful play actions are other signs that he wants to communicate. He turns away from the corner and falls forward on his chubby hands, still clutching a train in one of his hands. His other train car stands alone behind him in the corner. He crawls toward me, clunking his favorite train on the hardwood floor and looks up at me, smiling. His facial expressions match his vocalizations, all of which show a genuine interest in play. Suddenly, he lets go of his Thomas train, rolls it over on its wheels, and pushes it along the floor to meet my train.

For the first time, Patrick tries to join me in his play. I see the opportunity to introduce and model some sound combinations that are related to the actions of Patrick's trains. I stay with the subject that he is interested in at this moment: trains and moving trains. At some point it may be helpful to sit at a table as it allows for more of a shared focus and maximum use of eye and sound cues, but in the beginning I keep the speech production work in the context of play. Some children do better without a mirror and with a face-to-face modeling approach by the clinician. For some children with autism, a person's face can be distracting and they may be unable attend to either the face or the mirror for more than a glance. Adding a mirror into our play helps Patrick to focus and attend to our sound games for longer periods. Although some children may become overly interested in the mirror and forget about the sound game, Patrick doesn't get stuck on the reflections of the mirror and he likes to imitate sounds with both of us watching the mirror. With Patrick, I use my face to show him some sound combinations and introduce others with the mirror.

I remain calm and persistent as I build my own train track with a bridge and I use my own set of train cars. Using toys that are identical to the child's is a simple strategy for teaching sound combinations in a play situation. Instead of taking the child's toy away, I use a duplicate toy.

I say, "Patrick, look! I have a Thomas and he's going over the bridge! Look!" I repeat these words as I move my train. He crawls closer to me, rolls his train near the bridge, and then he screams as he throws his Thomas train car.

Ignoring his screaming, I keep moving my train car and say, "Patrick, look! Look at my Thomas!" Slowly, he picks up his train and rolls it over toward my bridge. I pat him on the arm. He smiles at me. When he sees the value of including others, Patrick works harder for another pat.

I make the sounds of a train, "whoooo—woot!" with emphasis. Patrick sits still, watching me. He takes a deep breath and imitates my sound pattern, "whoooo-woot!" I pat his arm and say, "Yes! Patrick! I hear you!"

For the next several weeks, I introduce Patrick to direct speech therapy in the context of play with the goal of developing understandable and useful words and/or sound combinations. He begins to imitate my sound sequences of vowels, sound combinations, and finally begins to include the first developmentally appropriate sounds for young infants, the *bilabial sounds* (sounds that are made with the lips together): *p, b,* and *m*. We begin with early developing words, such as "pee," "poo," "pie," "moo," "me," "my," "bye," and "boo." Once Patrick has begun to use these consonant-vowel words, I move to consonant-vowel-consonant words, such as "mom" and "pop," and "pup." Eventually, he learns to use familiar words that he needs to use to request and to talk to his family such as "mama," "papa," "puppy."

Teaching sound combinations with visual models

Eventually, I work directly with Patrick on a floor mat with a small hand mirror for visual modeling. I don't expect him to watch my face for a long period of time. Current researchers are looking at how people with autism gaze at the human face. A recent study found that compared to people without autism, participants with autism show less fixation to the eyes and mouth and an abnormal directionality of saccades (rapid eye movements)

(Spezio et al., 2007). These findings are consistent with my work with young and older children who tend to find direct eye contact aversive. Children with autism, in my experience, look away from a floor mat or a play area if filled with too many toys. There may be many factors involved in causing this distraction. It would be important for future experiments to determine how children with autism treat facial information and whether they report an aversion to direct eye gaze and for how long.

When I prompt Patrick to watch my face, I use a hand gesture toward my mouth and I say, "Just look at me for a second." I model the sound combination and he listens. Then, I face the mirror with him and model the sounds as he watches me in the mirror. It is easier for Patrick to model the sounds by looking at my face in the mirror than to face me directly. If I try to get him to attend to my face for more than a quick glance, he moves his head down, turns away from my face, and begins to redirect our play with an object. While other children with autism may be distracted by a mirror and "stim" (wave their hands or make repetitive movements), Patrick does attend with a small mirror that is hand held. We sit side by side, facing the mirror while we are on a floor mat. He loves to watch his mouth move in the mirror as he practices his *p, b, m,* and vowel sequences. Once he sees that working on sound combinations and practicing how to move his lips to form a particular consonant such as a *p, b, m,* is a "game" and not a "drill," he continues the work. I change the inflection of my voice to keep his interest. He needs many repetitions to be able to produce the sounds adequately to reach his goals. Patrick's first voiced consonant sound is *b* in the word *ball.* I hold up a small ball at eye level. He glances at the object, the ball, then to my face, and then back to the ball.

I produce a long "b" sound. Patrick glances at me and closes his lips in imitation. When I see he is copying me, I move forward into the word by producing the vowel "a" followed by the final consonant "l."

He says a long "b" sound—and screams. He is voicing the sound of /b/.

I say, "Now try this. Listen." I say "b" followed by a with a long "ah"

He looks up at me to match my voicing and says "bah" a "b" with the vowel "ah."

I say, "Okay, Patrick, that's right. Try it again. Listen. Bbbb—baaal!"[3]

He screams, takes a breath, and squeezes the ball, saying, "baaaa!"

I say, "Yeah! Yeah! You did it! You have a ball!"

The sound *bah* is an approximation of the word *ball,* so I reward him by holding up my hand and saying, "High five!"

He holds up his hand and taps my hand with his index finger and giggles.

Paul runs over to him, sits down on the floor, faces him, and holds up his hand, "Hi five, son!"

Patrick lifts his hand and giggles, "Hi!" Patrick and his dad hit hands with a hard slapping sound.

"Watch," I say to Paul.

I say, "Oh, the mommy doll wants to practice with the mirror." I hold up the mommy doll and he reaches for her.

He faces the doll in the mirror and begins some vowels and sound combinations. "ooooo—eeeeee—ahhhhh, ooooooo—eeeeee—ahhhhh." He begins his consonant-vowel combinations, "baa," "boo," and "moo," "mee," "my," and others. He moves the doll up and down as he practices. He watches his lip movements in the mirror and the doll.

Patrick giggles after he says each sound combination. He looks to Paul and me for a smile or a laugh that tells him he's doing a great job.

After Patrick learns fifty to sixty words, he begins to differentiate between voiced and voiceless sounds in word combinations.

The process of learning sound combinations and creating word approximations takes Patrick about six months of work everyday. Patrick needs to differentiate between sounds that are heard (voiced) and sounds that are silent (voiceless). Gradually, he learns to use the voiceless *p* and the voiced *b* sounds in initial, medial, and final positions in words. He learns that when he makes voiceless sounds such as /p/ in the word "pip," he is almost silent as the air flows out of his mouth. He also learns to make a voiced sound such as /b/ in the word "bob."

Children with autism who need help in developing speech learn more quickly and stay focused when the activities are varied and interesting, but predictable. Sometimes we make a list of the activities for the session and the child checks off his accomplishments. Drills with the mirror help, but do not provide enough stimulation to keep the child focused. I often use a small "Gertie" (soft) ball and play catch with Patrick. He can practice his sound combinations as we throw the ball back and forth. This not only improves his speech accuracy but it also helps him when he needs breaks for sensory activities or play.

After Patrick's first word approximation, *ah,* he practiced sounds everyday for twenty to thirty minutes for four months; he is now able to say several words and two-word phrases. Slowly I introduce meaningful single-word activities that interest him in play. As his speech becomes more intelligible and as he reaches his specific goals, I introduce short sentences that gradually increase in length and complexity.

Patrick, who learns to produce sounds, is like many children with autism who have tantrums and no language in the beginning of therapy. Some children with autism learn sound combinations directly from their peers or from others in their environment and don't require the long process of repetitive practice for sound production, while others need to repetitively practice sounds, vowel sequences, and sounds in words in various positions in order to produce speech. Assessment of a child's speech disorder is complex. A clinician must attend to the child's "cognitive, linguistic, motor planning, motor programming, and motor execution that may contribute to a child's speech disorder and to what relative degree" (Strand and Caurso, 1999, 104). This means that when a child with autism has poor speech intelligibility, he needs a full speech evaluation by an experienced clinician to determine if the speech difficulties result from language or motor-based impairments. This is because the design and implementation of therapy will differ based on the findings. In Patrick's case, he doesn't have a motor-speech disorder.

Strategy 10: Encourage the Family to Use Their Native Language

Some children with autism are delayed in language production because they listen to more than one language at an early age according to some studies, while other researchers have found that a child must be exposed to his cultural languages in order to learn and develop language. The current problem for a clinician of children with multilingual families is whether or not the child with autism, with a language delay, should be treated in his primary language or in the secondary language such as English, or in both or several languages.

In the following case example, I chose to treat the child in a particular way. I spoke English in the therapy sessions. The mother, who spoke Greek and the father who spoke Italian, spoke their primary languages in every session. This child had a severe language delay and spoke in sound combinations with gestures accompanied by screams. Her name was Sonia. She was diagnosed with autism and language delay and she was four years old. They came from Europe for six weeks of intense speech therapy training. I worked with the family for three to four hours a day and on several occasions, for five hours a day. The parents translated my words in English to Greek and Italian, the two languages that the child had been listening to since birth.

The purpose of my work with international children who live in multilingual families is to primarily model and teach the parents how to relate to the child through Narrative Play therapy, so that they can return to their own country and continue the therapy in their native languages. Over 50 percent of my work in the therapy sessions is about teaching the family how to facilitate the child's language so that the child's language will develop. There is evidence in research (Gutierrez-Clellen, 1999; Seung, 2006) that a child will do better and learn with a primary language that he knows. In this longitudinal study (Seung, 2006), a child at the age of three was diagnosed with autism and was from a Korean-English household. The speech and language intervention was to provide twice a week therapy in his primary language, Korean, for the first twelve months. For the next six months, the child was transitioned to English. The child made gains in the primary language and then in both languages.[4] This study provides evidence that a child should be spoken to in the cultural language that he lives with and the one he has heard since birth.

In addition, the child needs to be engaged with the person he associates a particular language with or he might become confused. To choose one language and not the other may deprive him in some way. In my experience, I have found that children benefit from learning both languages; the second or third language does not interfere with play therapy or language development, as long as the parents are present to present my words in their primary language. When more researchers find that it is crucial to keep the child's therapy in his primary language, I may refer an international child to a therapist who speaks his cultural language and then transition him to Narrative Play therapy in English after one year, if he is developing language.

I have worked with many international children whose parents are relieved when they can speak to their child in the same language that the child's grandparents speak. Sonia, a four-year-old from India who understands Hindi, lived with her parents who were multilingual. Her father, Renato, spoke German, Italian, French, and English. He preferred Italian since his parents were from Italy. Her mother, Doreena, spoke Greek, Italian, French, and English, and she preferred Greek since her family was from Greece.

When I first met Sonia and her family, she paced in the waiting room and banged her feet against my door. I opened the door and she stood still for a moment, smiling at me. Her brown eyes sparkled as her grin broke into a full smile. She leapt up and dashed into my office, jumped on a cushion on my couch, and bounced up to the back of the couch, landing on it as though she was mounting a horse. She glanced up at me and watched me sit down on the floor mat. I held a set of picture cards. She stretched out her arm toward the box of pictures. I held up one, gave it to Renato, and said, "Renato, hold this up and see if she can name it. It's a vacca (cow)."

Renato replied, "No, she's retarded and she has autism. She doesn't know the name of anything!"

"Try it in Italian, your language. Just see."

Renato wiped his brow and held the card up. Doreena was seated on the couch watching her husband and her daughter.

"Move in a little closer to her."

Renato moved on his knees toward his daughter.

"What is this?" he asks twice in Italian.

Sonia was still sprawled over the back of the couch riding her "horse." She looked at the picture and giggled, smiled, and responded with a whisper in Italian, "Camio (truck)."

Renato dropped the card on the mat and turned to me.

"See. She doesn't know it. It's not a truck."

"But, she is speaking your language!"

"Yes, she speaks—when she speaks—in Italian to me and Greek to my wife."

"That's very smart. You mean that she associates Italian with you and Greek with her mother?"

"Yes."

"That's a very intelligent thing to do."

"Yes."

Doreen said, "Well, I feel so guilty. She was in a special school in Germany for retarded children with autism for almost two years. She had never heard German before she was forced to learn to speak there. So we only spoke German to her at home because we thought that she would not learn if we kept speaking three languages to her. But the school told us that she never spoke a word at school. Then, when we got her out, she started to speak German but she screamed the words. I feel so guilty because she became such an angry child."

"When she speaks Hindi now does she scream the words?"

"Yes, when I hold up a bottle of milk and ask her for a word, she shouts, "M_I_LLLLL_CCCK! (in German)"

"So she really has some emotional response to the German language."

"Right" said Renato.

"Was she happy at her special school?"

"No. She hated it. You see, I didn't talk to her for a year because I was so despondent. It's my fault. I feel responsible for her behavior. I didn't want a child with autism. I didn't want a child who hit everyone, including her mother. I didn't want her."

"No one is at fault. She has a disorder that keeps her from relating to you. She's got the idea that she needs to talk to you in your native language. That's advanced. Let's talk about how to get her more connected with you. It is the relationship that we want more than anything. She is relating, but I think she is teasing you."

Doreena said, "Teasing us? How?"

"Watch. I'll try to show you. I think she knows a lot of words. Watch her eyes and her smile. Listen to her laugh."

I picked up a picture that had a cow on one side and a truck on the other. Sonia was now sitting on the floor mat near me, holding a toy up to the light and gazing at its shape.

"See," said Doreena, "She never plays with toys; she only holds them up to watch them."

"Yes, I know. But, let's see how much vocabulary she has."

I held the two cards up facing Sonia and said the word *vacca*.

Sonia giggled and said, *camio*.

I waved the picture of the truck near her and I asked, "*vacca?*"

Sonia said immediately, "No, camio. Vacca."[5]

Doreena cried as I moved through fifty picture cards that Sonia named correctly.

She looked at her father and said, "car" in Italian and she turned toward her mother and said, "fence" in Greek.

One by one, she watched each card, smiled, and used either Greek or Italian. She never used a German word. I didn't need to ask Sonia's mother and father if she was giving them the correct word. The delight on their faces answered that question.

ENCOURAGING FLEXIBILITY

Final strategies in this chapter

Strategy 11. Create play narrative themes related to the child's interest.

Strategy 12. Identify the methods that a child uses to retreat from others.

Strategy 13. Change the child's narrative to encourage flexibility with peers.

Strategy 14. Be direct and teach the child about the other child's feelings.

Strategy 11: Create Play Narrative Themes Related to the Child's Interest

The typical child can orient his listener by describing the location, time, and characters that suggest where a story begins (Labov, 1972; McCabe and Peterson, 1991).[6] Children with autism have limited experience in creating narratives with structure. They need to be taught this skill because they normally describe one small detail that is in their visual scheme about the story instead of orienting the listener to the whole idea of where the story takes place.

A typical child also follows a simple sequence of actions that leads up to a high point of intensity or a problem in the story. Then he will solve the problem and resolve the story. In contrast, a child with autism will often have difficulty explaining the actions of a character beyond one sequence and may be unaware of how to reach a point of suspense in the story, or how to set up a story problem. The whole idea of narrative structure is abstract and therefore difficult for him.

To teach narrative structure, I suggest themes that will interest the child. If he loves rocks, the narrative can be about geology. If he loves cars, the story can be about racetrack drivers. I know that Christine loves to play in snow.

Fascinated by the light reflections of the snowflakes, Christine stares out of my office window. Her mother and I wonder whether an excursion in the snow might interest her. In the office, we begin by playing with objects related to winter—ski figures and a slanted block that represents a ski hill. We set up a ski race. Christine throws her head back and laughs hard when her ski figure falls off the "slope." The strategy of creating play themes around a child's immediate interest encourages the child to interact.

Some days Christine comes to my office holding a long icicle that she's found on a nearby tree. She holds it up to the light of the window, twirls it around above her head, and smiles as the reflections make light patterns on my wall. Today Christine is so interested in her skier winning the race that she forgets to fixate on the window and the snowflakes. Rather than fixate on one thing, she can enjoy the whole abstract "gestalt" of winter.

Because of Christine's passion for snow, I decide to take her outside to create a simple narrative. She can use some word approximations and some phrases now, but she isn't ready to create a complex narrative. A Nor'easter just passed through our town and a light snow is falling. We grab our plastic tube sled and head out to the nearby hill.

Christine watches me drag my sled across the snow of the parking lot. She is connected and wants to imitate my actions. We pull our sled to the top of the hill that is covered with children, parents, and other sleds.

I say, "Christine, let's pretend that we are big dogs racing in our sled to find a person who is lost in the snow! Okay?"

Christine grabs her sled and nods her head to say yes.

As we reach the bottom of the hill, we roll out of our sled. I point across the field of snow and say, "Oh, look, there must be some lost kids over there. Let's run!" Christine follows me, dragging her sled and laughing. We reach a snowman nearby and Christine runs up to him saying, "Help? Help?"

She understands the idea of a pretend story in play. This is only the beginning, but she is learning that play and narrative are interrelated and she can pretend with another person to create a narrative. Later, in the next phase, Christine will learn how to retell this story about the big dogs finding a lost person in the snow.

Strategy 12: Identify the Methods that a Child Uses to Retreat from Others

Unlike typical children who seek the ideas of others in play, children with autism want the agenda of the play to be what they see in their own minds. For example, if another participant tries to take one toy dinosaur away from a row of dinosaurs, the child with autism may scream or throw the entire line up in a heap and cry for hours.

Like Patrick and Christine, four-year-old Christopher began therapy as a nonverbal child—kicking, screaming, and throwing tantrums. He refused to allow anyone to use his toys or to suggest that he change his own ideas in play. He ignored his peers, paced the playground at school, and gestured to his caregivers and teachers to leave him alone. He created ways of playing in isolation as though he was going to interact in play with his peers. For example, when they tried to play with him, he moved his cars and trucks quickly into the barn and put them to "sleep" by covering them with a pretend blanket of hay. He blocked anyone with his hand if they tried to move a train or one of his cars. He learned to say, "night-night." As he learned to say some single sounds, he'd cry, "uh-uh," push his mother away, and move his trains into the station to be fixed. He immediately removed the objects from the area near the other children. They watched him, convinced that he was going to play out his own story and then return to play with them. They left him alone. After his "pushing gestures" to stay away and crying, he remained alone with his toys.

After one month of therapy in the quiet office setting, Christopher continues to scream, throw toys, and kick the wall. I suggest to his mother that we take Christopher out on a field trip and bring some pictures that I prepared. We pointed to a picture (such as that of a ball), named it, and then showed Christopher a soccer ball on a playground. After four weeks of pointing to and naming objects both in therapy and on their own, the family was exhausted and wanted to stop. I encouraged them to keep going.

Days later, Christopher's mother, Ellen, came to my office and she was beaming. She told me that during the Christmas season, the family went on a car ride after dinner. While Christopher's sister Bridget pointed to the pictures and identified the objects in the environment, he ignored her.

Ellen explained, "She tried to hold his index finger. We all said, 'Look! It's a tree! Look, it's a stop sign!' He just didn't say a word! Then, three days later, the whole family was in the van driving by the town green. We all could see that they were lighting the trees for Christmas. I didn't say a thing. Bridget was quiet, watching. My husband was driving and all of a sudden, I heard, 'Lo-oo-ok, Mom, it's a Christmas tree!' Ann, my husband turned toward me and said, 'Honey, was that Christopher?'"

She continued, "I turned around and yelled, 'Yes, it's Christopher!' Then almost on cue, Christopher said it again, 'Lo-oo-ok it's a Christmas tree!' Ann, you should have seen our faces. We all lit up like Christmas trees."[7]

Christopher responded to the work his sister and parents and school speech therapist had done to associate pictures with objects that he sees every day. But his sudden leap into language use was not accompanied by a desire to socialize and be reciprocal in his language use. He had no concept of how to go back and forth in conversation. Despite Christopher's inconsistent development in expressive language, his parents realized that his intellectual capabilities were underestimated and he understood a lot more than he could express.[8]

Six months later he was still ignoring others and wanted to be alone. I worked on the main goal of phase one in Narrative Play—getting him to connect to others.

During one session, one of Christopher's peers said, "Hey, I want the animals to go down the river and drink water. I don't want them in the barn! We can't play if they have to go in the barn!"

Christopher said without looking up, "Well, they're tired. They need to sleep!" He walked each animal into the barn and placed it on its side. He made a snoring sound.

"Hey, Christopher, that's not fair. What animals can I play with?"

Christopher whispered in a matter of fact tone of voice, "Over there. You can play over there."

Christopher still wanted to keep the story agenda the same, but he was able to use language to express his ideas and make comments to his peer. I could tell he was moving out of phase one because he was making more contact with others and expressing himself with language. He may have used language to manipulate others away from his toys and play space, but he wasn't using gestures to push and shout at them.

Strategy 13: Change the Child's Narrative to Encourage Flexibility with Peers

With a child like Christopher who can outsmart others and keep all the toys for himself, I have to have many ideas to use in the fast pace of play. Christopher wanted the animals to stay in the barn and his peer, who is a typical child, wanted them to move outside the barn so that he could play, too.

A useful intervention when a child wants the agenda to remain the same is to follow his story and then try to change the narrative or add to it—in this case, so that the animals in the barn wake up and go down the river to drink. First, I joined both peers in the play with the barn animals. I accepted the child's agenda at first by using an animal that's asleep in the barn. Then, I found a reason for the cow to need to move out of the barn. This reason had to be interesting enough to engage Christopher so that he would allow me to move the figure.

I picked up a cow and said, "Okay. I'm thirsty now. I'm waking up. Let's go down the river!" I moved the cow out of the barn and started to walk the cow down a pretend river near the barn set. Christopher watched anxiously as I walked the cow. He whined at me. I encouraged the peers in the area to move their own animals down the river with me. We formed a train of animals, marching and making sounds of animals. He continued to watch. Finally, he took a horse out of the barn and *followed* us. He began to make the sounds of the horse galloping down the river and he smiled at his peers as he played.

One of the greatest motivators for an isolated child with autism is to feel the delight of being with a peer in play actions. This method doesn't always work, but sometimes it's clear that the child can learn that joining others is more fun than playing alone with a barn filled with animals that are sleeping.

I try to think creatively and quickly to make these slight changes so that the child accepts them without complaint. It's crucial to be persistent, kind, and sensitive to the child's reactions as he is pressured to change the agenda in play. If the child cries and resists, I must back away and try again at another time or attempt a different strategy. With my support, the peer usually will stay close to the child rather than find another game to play.

Strategy 14: Be Direct and Teach the Child about the Other Child's Feelings

In phase one, it's important to increase flexibility in play by teaching the child with autism about how the other child feels during an interaction. For example, I told Christopher how his peer felt about the animals stuck in the barn, and asked for him to hear that opposing viewpoint: "Hey, Chris, your friend is bored. He wants to play. What can he play with?"

Christopher responded, "Okay, he can have the cow."

"Your friend wants the animals out of the barn. He wants them to go down the river and drink water. Okay?"

Christopher may have said no, but at least he was introduced to a new idea.

Sometimes in my work with Christopher this direct strategy backfires and he throws the cow at the other child. If this happens, I have to intervene and ask him to pick up the cow and give it to his peer. If this request elicits a meltdown from Christopher, I have to keep trying and expect him to respond. There is no "magic" solution when a child is set on one way of playing or one agenda. With the help of the parents, I can be creative about how to get those cows and horses out of the barn.

One father in a play session with his son said, "Oh, I feel so sick. I'm a sick cow! I have to go to the doctor. The doctor is way over there!" Christopher's parents learned to help him see the perspective of others. He learned to see that the cows needed to come out of the barn so that others can play, too. Once most children with autism connect to others, they want to be in a relationship during play. Christopher hasn't experienced that need yet. He is still in phase one and just finding out the others want to join him. The first step for Christopher is to help him experience what it's like to allow another child to change the theme of the story.

By experimenting, parents will find which strategy works best for their child. While working in play therapy with their children, they often become great storytellers and create many options for the objects in play.

A common misperception is that children with autism can't feel what others feel. Look closely, though, and you will see that feelings and re-sponses are evident in a child's gesture, body language, facial expressions, and vocalizations. Peers see these responses in play. Christopher now relates to others and is more connected, but he's not ready to interact or share until phase two, where he'll learn to join others in play. For example, he'll need support in allowing the farm animals to wake up and come out of the barn.

SUMMARY OF STRATEGIES FOR PHASE ONE

In phase one, the most important goal is to make contact with the child by narrating and joining him and experiencing what he experiences. Moving carefully into the child's play space and interrupting the child's fixed patterns of repetitive play make this first contact possible. I include the child's parents and siblings in this phase so that the child will feel the excitement of making a connection with others and feel the need to change his behavior away from his focused, repetitive fixations.[9]

If a child continues to use tantrums and crying to ask for what he wants or resists any contact, then I must be sensitive to the basic behavioral principles of rewarding the positive behavior and ignoring the negative.

To encourage his use of language, I prompt a child with sounds and words to get him to imitate. I may use a verbal prompt or a reinforcement such as a smile or gesture of approval to the child only if he is just beginning to whine, point, or fuss about not getting something or if he doesn't have the word or the sound in his vocabulary for the particular situation. In this case, I can prompt and engage in sound play with positive gestures and play with him; however, if the child is about to go into a full tantrum, I leave him alone, wait, and ignore the behavior until he is quiet.

Nothing is worse for a child than for the therapist to be giggling and smiling at him when he is kicking, screaming, or biting. Such feedback positively reinforces a negative behavior. Even if the child is only quiet for a few seconds, I may reward him with praise or a positive word at that moment. I try to find the delicate balance between giving the child a word or some positive sound play when he needs it and ignoring behaviors that are completely inappropriate.

In addition to narrating and joining the child and prompting only when appropriate during phase one, I work on teaching direct sound production within the context of play. Patrick, for example, learned vowel sequences, consonant production, and sound blending to make word approximations. With some children, this process is a long tedious journey, and with others it is a short experience during which the child talks in full sentences with only exposure to the language expression around him.

In phase one, the child with autism benefits from the outside environment because experiencing nature involves the visual, kinesthetic, and auditory senses that motivate him toward sound play, play with vowel sequences and consonants in a back and forth exchange, and speech production.

The child can experience a simple narrative as Christine did in her sledding experience and the story of the big dog rescue. Even Patrick began to get a sense of a story as he moved his Thomas train over to the bridge to join my train in play. Christopher began to develop a sense of narrative when he took his horse and *followed* me down the river with the other animals in play. Both boys learned to be more flexible and to change their own agenda.

As the child with autism enters phase two, I work on helping him see and feel the perspective and feelings of others in play. In this next phase, I describe, with the help of a peer, what the peer is feeling and why he feels that way. This is one way to help sustain a connection between two children during play.

The phase two child moves into more complex language and learns to play in "parallel"—along side of—another peer. He learns to share play space with another, to share a toy, and to play by making comments about his own actions and those of others. In phase two, the child becomes more connected as well as more interactive and excited about play.

Progression of a Child with Autism from a Non-Social World to a More Social World through Narrative Play Therapy

	Phase I First Contact	Phase II Joint Attention
Language	• Nonverbal • Unrelated gestures • Frequently self-talks • Limited babbling by 2–4 mos. • Uses a few meaningful words • Takes limited vocal turns/eye gaze • Imitates some sounds • Facial expressions to protest/request • Crying/tantrums • Unaware of sharing opportunities • Uses sounds/gestures w/ main caregiver	• Verbalizes words/phrases • Related gestures to protest/request • Limited self-talk • Babbling by 6–9 months • Meaningful words/phrases • Few vocal turns w/ eye gaze shifts • Imitates words/phrases/gestures • Facial expressions w/ ideas • Words for basic emotions • Shares objects w/ prompts • Language w/ familiar peers/adult
Play	• No symbolic play • Plays in isolation • Non-intentional actions • Unaware of others' perspective • Fixates on light, sounds, graphemes • Extensive repetitive actions • No plan/agenda • Uses one to two objects • Expresses irrelevant emotions • Consistent fantasy play	• Simple symbolic play • Parallel play w/ other • Intentional actions • Becomes aware of others' perspective • Limits fixation on light, sounds, graphemes • Limited repetitive actions • Simple plan/agenda • One to two play sets • Expresses relevant emotions • Shifts between fantasy/reality with prompts
Narrative	• No story structure • No sequence • Repeats unrelated details • No retelling • Uses consistent fantasy • No agenda/story • Unaware of a theme/main idea • Attends to details only • No meaningful thought • Unaware of abstract thinking	• Simple story structure (beg, mid, end) • Sequences simple actions • Relates simple details but misses main gestalt • Retells unconnected details • Inconsistent fantasy • Creates & controls own agenda • Wants to create own theme • Formulates details & themes w/ another • Meaningful thought • Inconsistent abstract thinking

28

Progression of a Child with Autism from a Non-Social World to a More Social World through Narrative Play Therapy (cont.)

	Phase III Initiated Reciprocity	Phase IV Social Engagement
Language	• Verbalizes in relevant sentences • Gestures relevant to words • Limits self-talk • Reduces babbling by 12 mos. to use words/sentences • Meaningful sentences in interactions • Frequent vocal turns/eye gaze shifts • Imitates all language frequently • Facial expression w/ intonation • Expresses emotions w/ sentences w/ another • Shares objects without prompting • Uses language with most adults/peers • Verbalizes in relevant sentences	• Responds & formulates relevant language • Gestures match meaning/ideas/emotions • Only subtle self-talk • Eliminates babbling to sentences • Combines meaningful ideas in complex sentences • Frequent vocal turns w/ eye gaze shifts • Limits imitation to develop creative language with actions • Coordinates natural facial expression w/ intonation in negotiation • Expresses emotions to negotiate w/ others • Shares objects, stories, events, & ideas • Engages in reciprocal conversation w/ new peers & adults
Play	• Inconsistent complex symbolic peer • Plays w/ one peer in close physical proximity to peer • Complex intentional actions • More aware of others' perspective • Subtle fixations on light, sounds, graphemes • Less repetitive actions than intentional actions • Plans actions w/ another • Uses several play sets w/ another • Expresses relevant emotions in themes • Differentiates between fantasy/reality play	• Consistent complex symbolic play w/ others • Plays w/ several peers in natural settings • Consistent complex intentional actions • Uses language in play/narrative to interpret others' perspective • Unnoticed fixations on light, sound, graphemes • Few repetitive actions w/ strong intentional actions • Allows others to change agenda/plans • Plays w/ several sets w/ others in many play areas • Combines language/gesture to express emotions • Shifts between fantasy & reality play
Narrative	• Inconsistent complex story structure (beg, mid, end, high pt., resolution) • Sequences more complex ideas w/ high point • Story w/ complex themes & details • Retells story w/ connected details & main theme • Fantasy enhances story theme • Allows others to create agenda • Flexibility w/ others w/ theme • Formulates simple stories w/ themes • Complex meaningful thought • Consistent abstract thought	• Consistent complex story structures • Sequences several events & ideas • Resolves stories w/ complex details/themes • Retells complete meaningful stories • Interweaves fantasy & reality in theme • Allows others to control/participate in forming stories • Consistent flexibility w/ others w/ theme • Creative story formulation w/ several children • More complex inferences from main idea • Abstract thinking about themes

PHASE TWO

Joint Attention

In phase two, the child becomes more aware of others in the play area and initiates play near a peer. He creates simple play actions with objects and includes another child in his play theme. He begins to make comments about his own and his peer's actions in play. He wants to be with a peer in this phase and encourages others by sharing toys, watching his peer, and using facial expression and body language that communicate that he wants to share space with his peer. He no longer collects objects in boxes or in the corner of a play area, turning his back away from his peer. He is more open to sharing toys and offering others his space. The child in this phase has become more social and observes others. He reaches out his hand to peers and moves his body near others. He wants to be connected and seeks out more time with peers. He learns to sustain joint attention.[1]

LANGUAGE

A child is moving into phase two of play therapy when he uses words or phrases to make requests, expresses emotions, makes gestures that are related to what is being said, and uses play to tell a simple story about objects. Language becomes the way to get things, to express anger, and to talk about what's going on with a friend. The language of the phase two child is intelligible and expressed in complete sentences; however, his gestures and facial expressions may not consistently match with what he is trying to say. The phase two child uses some words for the basic language of emotions, but is still limited in abstract vocabulary and reasoning.

PLAY

The main goal of phase two in play therapy is to teach the child to become more flexible in his thinking about play actions with objects with one peer. A child in phase two usually begins in parallel play, using simple play actions in a play set that are separate from another child's toys and narrative. The child with autism plays this way because he is more inclined to express emotions and ideas to adults than to peers. After all, adults have the ability to help him while other children are primarily interested in playing. In fact, children with autism often select certain ways to communicate that protect them from interacting with other children.

NARRATIVE

Children in phase two use simple story structure with a beginning, a middle sequence of simple actions by figures, and some form of ending. Their stories are not complex and usually involve a few figures or one play set. They are able to retell their stories, but with some unconnected details and inaccurate sequences. The child in phase two wants to create his own agenda and doesn't want another child to play with him unless prompted by an adult to formulate a plan with a peer. He often expresses meaningful ideas, but with limited abstract ideas and thought. At times, a child in this phase wants to play only in a fantasy world of pretend play and is unable to shift to narratives about more real-life adventures. He can differentiate between what is fantasy or pretend play and what is playing stories in his own life. A phase two child often misses the main "gestalt," the overall concept or theme of a story, and sticks to the details of the characters in play.

After one year of intense play therapy several hours a week, Patrick, the toddler who would not share his trains in phase one, now looks at me, his parents, and his play figures. He uses words to express himself when he is angry, sad, or disappointed, he even shares some objects with prompting. He speaks in simple sentences with only a noun phrase and a verb phrase, but his adults and peers understand him. His play skills are built around simple play themes such as constructing a tower for his truck, playing with the airport set and the planes, or moving his trains along the train track to a station. He is still limited in his ability to create a narrative with a beginning, middle, and an end; however, he imitates some play and follows simple fantasy stories about characters.

While in parallel play, Patrick uses more eye gaze shifts (i.e., he looks at an object, then at a peer, and then back at an object). Then he verbalizes an idea like "Go train!" while he is using the object with purposeful action (i.e., moving Thomas along the track). In addition, his face and body language coincide with what he means. For example, when he's expressing his delight, his eyes are wide open and he has a big smile; when he's worried, his forehead has a frown and his eyes are closed tight; when he's scared, his entire body retreats to a curled up position. Though he still doesn't let others play with his trains, unless guided to share one, he doesn't mind others tapping them.

At the end of one session Patrick holds out Percy, one of his favorites, and thrusts it toward my hand, saying, "A tap, Ann. A tap!"

I pat Percy's chimney; he giggles, and moves closer to me. He faces me with his arm extended toward me. Percy is perched on the flat of his hand.

"That's Percy. Thanks for sharing him with me. It's fun! Right?"

"Yep. Fun!" he announces in a loud voice.

He jumps up and runs to hug his father.

Patrick has made the transition from phase one into phase two, sharing and connecting with his parents, and now he needs to work on sustaining a closer, more interactive relationship with his friends. Even though he will share a train, he wants the story about the train to be his own or he wants the train to be at a certain place.

Patrick begins to use meaningful sentences and join others in parallel play, but he has problems expressing his ideas to his peers. Patrick watches others, giggles with them. He wants to be with others, but only next to them in parallel play.

The strategies for phase two are explained through Sandy, a five-year old, three-year-old twins, John and Jim, and the continued story of Christine, joined by a peer, Olivia.

2

Joint Attention

FOLLOW CHILD'S INTEREST IN NATURAL THINGS

Strategies in this chapter

Strategy 15. Help a child visualize a new idea to disrupt old patterns.
Strategy 16. Join the child and listen to his complaints.
Strategy 17. Help the child visualize new options.
Strategy 18. Draw on the child's interests in visualizing objects and places.

Strategy 15: Help a Child Visualize a New Idea to Disrupt Old Patterns

The phase two child wants to control the theme and actions of play. He has a fixed idea, usually visualized, about how toys should be arranged or how a teacher should sequence the activities of the day. If a teacher, parent, or therapist rearranges or disrupts the child's agenda, the child becomes upset, confused, and recalcitrant. The child may want to stay on the slide during recess and repeat the same play actions with one figure. Typical children change the theme of their play, rules, and characters of the story—whereas children with autism become upset and refuse to play, often pacing the perimeter of the playground structure—behavior that often alienates them from their peers.

Sandy, a five-year-old child with autism, fixates on a particular part of an object. In addition, he, like Patrick, gets "stuck" on keeping the agenda of play the same. During our fifth session outside on a playground, Sandy gets angry because he wants his "dinosaur" to stand up. The dino keeps falling over because its legs are bent. He throws the dinosaurs across the sand box, flops down on the ground, screaming and pounding his fists, crying, "Go away! Go away!" He jumps up and runs around the perimeter of the playground, screaming and waving his dinosaur with the broken leg. His peers stand still and watch him run.

Though Sandy has complex language and verbalizes with relevant ideas—two characteristics of phase three—he is still in phase two because he insists on repetitive play and can't allow another child to enter his play space. Limiting his play to one or two play sets, he repeats the same actions with the same figures. Unable to create a narrative about his figures, he insists on using the same dialogue. However, when interacting with familiar peers and adults, he uses language to talk about his actions.

Sandy recognizes others, but refuses to play or allow another child to be near his toys or in his play area. Sandy doesn't have the skills of creating a narrative about his play actions because he is set on repeating one theme. If interrupted, he has meltdowns, tantrums, and throws toys at other children.

After a few therapy sessions, Sandy is more aware that others may not want to play the way he plays. However, Sandy sees the figures as his "own" and wants them to look a certain way. I work with Sandy on his feelings about losing the way he thinks the dino should be and how the dino should look.

Strategy 16: Join the Child and Listen to His Complaints

Back in a quiet setting in his school, I sit down on the floor mat next to Sandy. He sobs, covering his face with his hands. I wait and listen to him cry. He takes a long breath. I ask, "Sandy, what happened?"

"I can't make the dinosaur stand up! He falls over every time!"

"Okay, well, maybe that dinosaur is okay on his side."

"No. No. No. He can't be on his side!"

"Why not?"

"Because he needs to stand up to see!"

"Okay, but maybe his legs are bent."

"No they are not! He has to stand up!"

I begin the long process of gaining trust and accept his construction of what he sees has to happen to this dinosaur. If I reject his idea, he will reject our play and leave the situation. I wait for a better time to help him see he has some other options for this dinosaur.

Strategy 17: Help the Child Visualize New Options

"Do you see a picture of him in your head, standing up?"
"Yes. He is standing up!"
"Well, maybe we could prop him up with sticks."
"I don't have sticks!"
"Want to find some?"
"No. That's stupid!"
"Let's see. Maybe he can lean on the other dinos."
"No he can't. He'd fall over! I want to go home!"
"Well, let's try to fix that dino. Want some help?"
"Okay." He stops sobbing and crying.
"Why don't we do an art project about dinosaurs?"
"Okay. I can't look at that dinosaur falling over."
"Okay, that makes you angry."
"Yes, very mad."
"He doesn't look like what you see in your head?"
"Yes. He is standing in my head."
"Okay, let's draw him."
"Okay."

Sitting on the floor near the mat, we pull out some paper and Sandy begins to draw. Sandy has some options of how to visualize the way he sees the figure and how he can be seen as different as compared to the reality of the figure with a bent leg. Sandy needs a therapist with a sense of humor and the patience to wait and listen to his complaints. When a child is stuck on certain images of how something should be, the therapist needs to listen with respect to the child's feelings. The child will listen if he feels that his ideas are being heard and that he might have something valuable to say about his play object. This may take several sessions, over six to eight weeks, to build trust and to help the child realize that you hear his ideas.

Strategy 18: Draw on the Child's Interests in Visualizing Objects and Places

Drawing on Sandy's interest in art, objects, and visual images, I ask him to look at how the figure could be and to think positively that the figure can be changed in his mind, if not in reality. This strategy usually helps a child become less anxious and therefore more comfortable articulating his feelings. Once a child speaks about his honest feelings, he begins to trust the connection he feels with the therapist.

"He's standing up!"

"Right. Like I see him."

"What's his name?"

"Sandy."

"Oh, really? How's he feeling?"

"He's angry and sad."

"I bet he is."

"Yeah, he ran out into the parking lot."

"I know he must have been real angry to do that."

"Yes, he was. He was angry at you!"

"It's okay to feel angry at me."

"Yeah."

"I wanted you to play with the dino even if he fell."

"Yeah and that made me angry."

"That's understandable. He didn't look like the dino you wanted, standing up."

"Right."

"Okay, now we have a drawing of him."

JOINING A PEER IN PLAY

Additional strategies for this chapter

Strategy 19. Reduce the child's distractibility by engaging him in sensory breaks.

Strategy 20. Name the child's feelings of frustration and anger.

Strategy 21. Follow a child's lead toward things of interest in a natural setting.

Strategy 22. Echo the sounds and point out the environment.

Strategy 19: Reduce the Child's Distractibility by Engaging Him in Sensory Breaks

I notice how fidgety Sandy is at the table and move him into a sensory experience such as bouncing on a therapy ball, doing breathing exercises, or taking a walk. Activities such as these help him release his anxious energy before engaging in more narrative work.

"Yeah. Let's bounce on the therapy ball and listen to 'I love mud!'"

He walks over to the ball, sits down, and turns on the music.

"Now I can think about my dino standing up."

"Your drawing matches the picture in your head! Right?"

"Yeah, I can see the picture I made. I'm not so angry now. I'm not mad at you."

"Sometimes you get stuck on wanting something just like the picture in your head. Right?"

"Right. And if it is not the same, I get mad."

"Does your anger sort of 'take you over' and make you feel like running away?"

"Yeah. I want to run away."

"What can we do when you feel that way?"

"I don't know. Maybe you can come and find me."

"Okay. I'll do that. Tell me when you feel that way."[2]

Strategy 20: Name the Child's Feelings of Frustration and Anger

Sandy recognizes and wants to talk about his anger regarding the dinosaur falling over instead of standing up. He also recognizes that he is stuck on this agenda of a "dino standing up, not lying down." As he calms down and draws the dino standing up, he learns that sometimes anger can just "take him over" so that he almost "becomes the anger." This process helps him see the anger as separate from himself. Naming a feeling helps a child identify the source of the child's anger. He begins to see that there may be another way to view the dinosaurs.

Some children with autism become hysterical when anyone introduces new ideas such as a different story theme. Other children with autism follow and stay with their peers, but never really interact or talk with them. There are several strategies to teach children with autism how to notice their peer, how to follow another, changing their own agenda, and responding to the environment that surrounds them.

Strategy 21: Follow a Child's Lead toward Things of Interest in a Natural Setting

When John and Jim, active three-year-old twins, come to my office, they dart from one thing to another. When I first meet them, neither of the twins use language, except to point or to demand some action from an adult, and both of them have autism. They ignore other peers and each other. Five months of working on location with them at a farm helps them move quickly into phase two. In the farm environment, the twins hear the sounds of animals; watch the animals move, jump, and eat hay; and experience the changes in the flowers and the trees as spring arrives. It is through this experience of sharing—listening to a rooster crow or watching a crocus bloom after winter—that quietly moves the twins closer to their mother.

Strategy 22: Echo the Sounds and Point Out the Environment

In our first visit to the farm, John runs over to a crocus. I warn him, "Careful, be gentle. Those flowers are very new. They are babies." John crouches down in a squat position. He watches the purple and white crocus flower that stands tall in the dirt. He gently touches one green stem surrounding the flower. He turns his head around and looks up at me. That small gesture means that he wants to share his experience with me. I am relieved. I pat his shoulder lightly and say, "That's right. Be gentle." He slowly gets up and follows us down the dirt road toward the chicken coop. As we get closer to the coop, the rooster's crow sounds louder. "Cockadoodle do . . ." the rooster says.

Jim, John's twin, says, "Cockadoodle do." John looks at the hens in the chicken coop and says, "plucka, plucka, plucka!"

"My boys are talking!" their mother says as tears stream down her cheeks.

"Wait until their father hears this!" she says, patting away the tears from her face.

After visiting the chickens and the smelly pigs, John points into the horse stall. We all follow him to the stall, where a colt is about to be born. The smell of horses is in the air. Jim scrunches up his nose. John covers his mouth. "It's smelly in here!" I say.

John says, "It's smelly! The pigs are smelly!"[3]

They look at me for several seconds. We share an event. Their mother, who is watching each move we make, and is taping with a video camera so the boys can see the clip after the farm visit. We enter the barn just as the sun streams through the horse stalls. Sorrow, a sorrel mare, stands in the horse stall, dipping her head now and then to sniff the hay. Jim runs toward the horse. He lifts up both hands and yells, "Up!" Again his mother is astonished. The expression on his face and his strong gesture make me think he will say something. My heart races as I focus on his gestures. I want more words. I start to work on his relationship to the horse. "Jim, look! She is moving her nose toward you! You can stroke her nose. It's soft like velvet. Feel it," I say as I pat the horse's nose. He reaches out his hand and pats the horse's nose exactly where I have. He laughs and looks up at me.

CREATING NARRATIVES WITH A PEER

Final strategies for this chapter

Strategy 23. Emphasize to the child the main gestalt and abstract concepts of natural events instead of focusing on all the tiny details.

Strategy 24. Take the child to an event more than once to teach abstract concepts.

Strategy 25. Facilitate language by prompting one peer first and then supporting the other.

Strategy 26. Create a reason for the characters in the two play sets to be together.

Strategy 27. Develop a narrative with an orientation, a sequence of actions, and an ending.

Strategy 23: Emphasize to the Child the Main Gestalt and Abstract Concepts of Natural Events Instead of Focusing on All the Tiny Details

The overall concept of what is happening on the farm will eventually be clear to the child. It takes two farm visits for the twins to understand the overall main idea that horses have babies. With each visit, I talk about the main idea of each group of animals gathered in one pen or pasture. I ask the twins to watch the whole event, such as the "sheep eating their hay" or the "smelly pigs rolling in the mud." A child with autism often focuses on one piece of hay instead of the idea of "who is eating the grass" or they focus on one nose of one pig and forget to see the overall picture that there are several big pigs in the pig pen who smell "awful" and they are all covered in mud. I might say, "Oh, look the sheep are eating grass together!" or "The pigs are so smelly and rolling in more mud!" I would cover my nose and then watch the faces of the twins, hoping to get them to see the whole event and laugh with their mother.

In this first visit, the twins continue to watch and point to the mare, Sorrow. The horse moves her nose through the railing of the stall and nudges Jim who steps back but then runs up to the horse and plants a huge smacking kiss on her nose.

We stand silently and watch until John announces, "Oh, look, the baby foal is shining! He's shining!"

I say, "John the foal is being born into the world. He's not in the mommy's tummy anymore! Right?"

John responds, "Oh, but the foal is so spark-a-lie (the foal's new coat was glistening in the sun)!" John's mother is surprised at the complete spontaneous sentence that John just produced. Often a child with autism begins to talk in full sentences, particularly when they're excited about something in their environment.

"Yes, I know. He's beautiful. But, John, what just happened? Did he come out of the mommy's tummy?"

"Nope. He's just sparkling!"

John is so fascinated by the lights reflecting off of the wet baby foal that he misses the whole idea of birth, the big event. Perhaps the concept of birth is too abstract for any four-year old.

Jim points and says, "Oh, the baby foal is so sparkly!"

I say, "Yes, she is sparkly. She needs milk from her mother now. Her mother will try to get her to stand up. Watch and see."

Holding hands, the twins and I observe the mother pushing the foal to stand; they both squeeze my hands. They giggle and jump up and down, focused on the foal. As she stands, wobbly, they become silent.

John points and says, "Look! She's gonna walk!"

No matter how powerful the event is at the time, both boys fixate on details, but, in this moment, John is talking about a prediction. He's moving from the details of light on the glistening coat on a foal in our first farm visit to the concept of a new mare pushing her filly to walk in this visit. The abstract concept is the whole birth of a foal and the overall main gestalt is that the mother is "taking care of her child because she loves him and she is a 'mother' and that's what mothers do when they have a new baby."

Strategy 24: Take the Child to an Event More than Once to Teach Abstract Concepts

One year later we have the good fortune of seeing another mare take care of a newborn foal. As the twins are scrambling to see the sheep in the pasture, they notice the commotion around the horse stall nearby. I bring them over to the area where a baby foal has been born.

"Let's go over there!" I say. The boys follow me.

We arrive to see the team of helpers and the vet assisting the mare. She delivered a beautiful colt an hour ago and the vet is helping the baby drink from a bottle. The beautiful, glistening colt is wet from the birth. The boys watch intently as the sun shines on the foal. They stand still gripping the side of the horse stall, watching.

After a few minutes, John says, "Mommy!"

His mother runs over to him and scoops him up and says, "John, you called me. I am your Mommy. I am your mother."

John hugs his mother for the very first time. I press his small arms around her neck. Jim watches. After a minute John wants to be down on the ground to watch the foal. I lift up Jim. He looks at his mother. He says nothing.

I say, "Mommy! This is your mommy Jim!" as I press his arms around her neck. She smiles as the tears again stream down her face.

I take John's hand and I point to the mare and say, "Mommy, John, that is the baby horse's mommy!"

Both boys listen and show a facial expression of delight as they touch their mother. Their level of understanding about abstract concepts, such as a birth of a baby horse, a foal, is evident in their gesture, in their attentiveness to the whole event and in their response to their mother.

Both boys hug their mother, patting her face and giggling. I think they see her as a part of their world now. Six months later, they have a new baby sister and they both understand that she "belongs" to her mother who is also their mother and she is a part of the whole family. I'll remember this event and these children.

Fifteen years later, a colorful photograph of Jim and John still sits on my office desk. It is a picture of them standing together smiling directly at each other when they were five, with a background behind them of a big pink mother pig. They are both laughing with their hands stretched outward and their eyes wide open.

Sometimes a pond, the summer wind, an animal's fur, or a flower's sweet scent in summer can calm a frustrated child and be a soothing, calming place for a child with autism. The farm becomes not only a place to teach, but also a place to be, to join others, to quiet one's mind, and to engage. Through their fascination with the horse, Sorrow, the twins pat Sorrow's nose, giggling. They look at each other, instead of darting, running, and pacing. They stay connected as they talk and run.

Unlike the twins, Christine stays close to her mother at the farm and requests that her mother move with her. After two therapy sessions a week in my office for a year—one with me and one with a peer—Christine is ready to go outside to see whether these social skills transfer. Christine is afraid to pat the sheep and flinches when a horse gallops across a pasture. I decide to take her to a quiet pond instead of a farm with animals that are unpredictable. Christine joins a friend, Olivia, another child with autism, at the pond to play and practice social skills. Christine continues to develop more complex language and plays with representational objects at the pond's edge. She enjoys the summer wind and the ducks that make a triangular ripple as they swim across the green water of the pond. Christine and Olivia sit side by side, each building her own castle. I sit between the two children. I bring them rocks, sticks, and buckets to collect water in case they want to make a "drip" castle. They giggle and pack their respective sand mountains without looking at what the other is doing.

Strategy 25: Facilitate Language by Prompting One Peer First and Then Supporting the Other

Both girls scoop up wet sand at the pond's edge and pack it into a big lump to form their own castle. I watch them build and pack sand. Christine looks up at me.

I say, "Christine, I wonder what Olivia's doing?

"Oh, she's making a castle!"

"Oh, how do you know?"

"I just do."

"Maybe you should ask her."

"I don't want to!"

I wait a few minutes and compliment each girl on the creative tunnels and towers on their castles. I ask a general question to both of them, "Will the water come up to the castle?"

Olivia answers, "Of course!"

Christine remains silent and keeps packing sand.

At this point in peer language facilitation, I work on just eye contact between the girls. I take a lump of sand, hold it up, and look at it. I pick up a shell in my other hand and say, "Oh, this would make a great window in a castle."

Olivia responds, "Yes, it would!" She looks up at my shell.

"Where should I put it?"

Christine says, "Here on my castle!"

Olivia, looking at Christine's castle, says, "Oh, it could go there," as she points to a spot on Christine's castle. Christine looks up at Olivia.

I say, "Nice! That's perfect!" Christine, do you want it there?"

"Yep, I want it there." She points to the spot and looks over at Olivia.

Once I see Christine look at the shell, then at Olivia, then at the spot on her castle and finally back to me, I know that she is capable of good eye contact with her peer. I hold up another shell and say, "What about this one? It's beautiful!"

Christine responds, "Olivia can have that one!" She looks at Olivia.

Olivia smiles at Christine.

I prompt Olivia, "Christine that's nice. Thanks."

Olivia says, "Oh, yes, Christine, that's so nice. Thanks!"

Strategy 26: Create a Reason for the Characters in the Two Play Sets to Be Together

The next step in facilitating language between two peers is to create a reason for the two play sets to connect in some way or for a character from a play area to join the other area.

In the case of the two castles, the solution is an easy one.

I suggest, "Hey, let's build a waterway between the two castles!"

Olivia laughs, "Wow! That's great. We can have a boat!"

Christine continues to work on her own waterway. She looks down.

I prompt Olivia, pointing from Olivia toward Christine's waterway, saying, "Christine, how about making a waterway here?"

I point to a corner of her waterway.

Christine says, "Well, okay, I guess so." She looks up at me, then to Olivia, and then to the castle.

I prompt Olivia again, "Olivia, ask Christine if she wants to be the first person to carve out the waterway."

Olivia says, "Christine, do you want to cut the waterway over here?"

Christine says, "Nope. I just want my own."

Olivia looks disappointed. I say, "Olivia is disappointed. I think she wants to join you, Christine."

Christine pouts, "Well, okay, but no boats going to my castle!"

She begins to carve out the waterway. I gesture to Olivia to help her.

At this point, both girls are working together on one waterway that will join both of their castles. I try for some commenting/complimenting between them.

"Oh, Olivia, that's great. You are good at that."

Olivia says, "Christine's good too!"

"Yes, she is."

"Look, Christine, at Olivia's window in her castle!"

Christine says, "That's nice."

"Show Olivia your door," I remark.

She points to her door and makes no comment, but, she does look up at me, at Olivia, and at her castle door.

Strategy 27: Develop a Narrative with an Orientation, a Sequence of Actions, and an Ending

The next step is to create a story about the castles with people who cross the waterways in boats or just walk over a bridge. I pick up a stick and say, "This could be the princess of the castle."

Olivia follows my lead and picks up a stick. "This is my princess."

Christine follows, "This is my princess!" and picks up a stick.

The next step is to suggest an orientation to the story, a time of day or place or a reason for the two characters in the narrative to be together.

I ask, "What could the princess be doing?"

Olivia responds, "Well, she is looking for her children. She can't find them!"

Christine looks up and listens to her.

Olivia says, "She is thinking that they may be making a boat!"

Christine runs toward the water and finds a piece of tree bark and brings it back to the castles. "Here's the boat!" She yells.

Olivia says, "Yes! That's a great boat!"

Christine spontaneously hands it to Olivia. Olivia takes it and tries to make it float in the waterway. By now the tide is starting to come in; some waves are near the castle and the waterways are filled with water and wet shells.

"Look, it floats!" yells Olivia.

"Yes, it floats! Let's put the kids in the boat!"

"Where are the kids?" I ask.

Olivia runs toward the water and finds some small pebbles. She holds up three of them. She yells, "These are the kids!"

PLANNING AND SOLVING PROBLEMS

Final Strategies for this chapter

Strategy 28. Help both children plan a play sequence together.

Strategy 29. Create repetitive problems to solve with options for solutions.

Strategy 30. Describe and model a high point in actions and an ending in the child's story theme.

Strategy 28: Help Both Children Plan a Play Sequence Together

We all look at the tiny pebbles floating in the pretend boat. Both girls are engaged now in creating a symbolic story and making their castles work together. Olivia is not interested in keeping the story theme the way she thinks it should be and the way she has it fixed as an image in her mind; however, Christine says, "I want the princess to ride in the boat with the kids!"

Olivia says, "Nope. There's not room!"

Christine cries, "Yes, there is room!"

Olivia looks at me. I say, "Christine, maybe Olivia wants to tell you what to do with the princesses. That's okay. Next time, you can tell her what to do when they get to the shore."

Christine demands, "No! I want the princesses to be in the boat with the kids!"

She throws the princess in the waterway and runs down the beach. I walk toward Christine, carrying the princess.

I reach her and say, "Christine, maybe the princess can be doing something really exciting when she gets to the shore or maybe she can stand on the top of the castle and see her children in the boat, floating toward her, coming home!"

Christine ignores me but stops running. We return to the castle and decide to come back to Walden Pond another day to finish our story. I know that Christine has had enough language work for today. We leave the castles, knowing that other children will have fun the next day with the waterways and shell windows.

Unlike Olivia, Christine insists on the play agenda being her agenda. In order to get her to see the perspective of the other child, we talk together during the week in my office before we go back to the pond to build more castles in the sand.

"Christine, maybe Olivia wants to have the princess do something else besides get in the boat with the kids." I say.

Christine says, "Nope. She HAS to get in the boat."

Knowing that Christine loves pizza, I say, "What if you have the princess get in the boat and then get out to take the children out for pizza?"

Christine smiles at me. I know that the mention of pizza sounds good to her.

I ask, "Well, they could go out for soup or ice cream? Which?"

Christine says, "Oh, they like pizza!"

One week later we walk down toward the water's edge with Olivia again and build two more castles. This time I prompt both children for comments and compliments to each other. They respond to my gestures and follow my lead to say positive things to each other.

"Olivia, that's a very special castle. Look at those shell windows, Christine!"

I point to the windows in the castle.

"Yes, I love them. I made them just for Olivia!"

"You made them for me?" Olivia grins.

Christine smiles.

"Yes, I made them for you! Look at the great boat that you made!"

I point to Olivia's boat that she made for Christine.

"Nice compliment, Christine!"

"Wow. Thanks, Christine!"

"Here's some pizza!"

"Olivia, do princesses eat pizza?"

"Yes, of course they do. But, they don't eat anchovies."

Christine and Olivia continue to share pizza and shells back and forth with comments. By the end of the second week, they are walking hand in hand to the water's edge and talking about the next castle that they will build together.

Strategy 29: Create Repetitive Problems to Solve with Options for Solutions

The boat is now floating in the waterway. The problem emerges once again. Christine remembers my suggestions and says, "Olivia, the princess can get in the boat and then go out for pizza with the kids!"

Olivia nods her head yes.

Christine smiles at me and then at Olivia. The goal is accomplished for this session at the pond. They are connected and Christine is accepting her peer's idea.

Strategy 30: Describe and Model a High Point in Actions and an Ending in the Child's Story Theme

I walk the princess to the pizza place with the kids and the girls watch.

Olivia says, "Now what?"

"Well, they could play together."

Christine says, "Oh, they see the prince at the pizza place and he asks them to go play in the water!"

Olivia, "Okay, they meet the prince!" I suggest, "Then what happens next?

Olivia says, "Oh, they get married and live in the castles forever!"

Christine smiles, "The end."

Olivia says, "Yep. The End!" and runs into the water.

Christine follows her, laughing and carrying her two sticks that represent a princess and a prince. She plops them into the water and watches them float.

"Look, Olivia, they float!" she says spontaneously.[4]

SUMMARY OF STRATEGIES FOR PHASE TWO

Christine has now entered phase three of play therapy; she is ready to use reciprocal language and to create detailed complex narratives with her peer. In phase three, Christine may even allow Olivia to create a story theme about two castles and many children who all have their own boat.

Child-Initiated Reciprocity

A child with autism in phase three is similar to a typically developing child because they both verbalize in relevant sentences, create space to play, change directions from one play area to another, run and stop to talk, and make eye contact. They use their emotions with meaningful gestures as they act out their stories while they engage in play. While a child with autism in phase three may look like a typical child as he moves with fast play actions and uses language with reciprocity, he needs verbal prompting to sustain his conversation that forms close social friendships. The phase three child also needs modeling and practice with a peer to negotiate and keep friends engaged in play.

LANGUAGE

A child with autism in this phase lacks the skill to formulate ideas with language and to negotiate plans fast enough to keep up with a peer. The typical peer who is socially engaged will negotiate quickly with complex language while playing with a farm set and explain the reasoning underlying his theory. The child with autism in phase three needs help learning how to persuade a peer and to negotiate about anything that is abstract. He needs help in sequencing his thoughts and explaining his reasoning about why, for example, he wants the animals to move in a particular direction. If he's playing with a barn set and the horse is hungry and thirsty, he might tell his peer that the horse is going to eat and then drink water from the water trough. His peer, on the other hand, may want the horse to give the farmer a ride to town first to buy hay. The phase three child has difficulty developing an argument as to why the horse needs to eat or drink before he goes into town. The child may just move the horse over to his side of the barn and ignore his peer, or he might charge toward the water trough without any consideration for his peer, moving the horse with force. This behavior might cause a "grabbing" contest over the horse and a "shoving match" between the two children; the child with autism could be seen as resistant or aggressive. Actually, the child behaves as he does because he doesn't understand how to use language to negotiate.

The phase three child also needs language support because he lacks the ability to shift from the dialogue of his characters in pretend play to a conversation about what is happening in the moment. A typical child in play can talk as if he is the character, create a dialogue within the theme, and shift quickly to talk about when recess is over or what he likes to eat at snack time. A child with autism may continue the dialogue of the characters and ignore his peer's comments about recess, staying focused on his story, whereas a typical peer can shift back and forth between the characters' dialogue and conversation about recess and snack.

The child with autism has a hard time processing the pace of vocal exchanges combined with the quick gestures and changes in body language that are typical of a peer's conversation. A typical child is engaged in an interaction, makes frequent vocal turns with appropriate voice intonation and uses gestures with body language that matches his words and enhances the expression of his emotions. The phase three child is engaged like a typical child, but doesn't make such fast shifts in vocal turns with appropriate emotional cues. He may speak with some gestures, but he is not consistent in using them to enhance the actual meaning of what he is saying. The child with autism struggles to put all these elements of communication together.[1]

PLAY

In this phase, the child's actions with objects are similar to a typical child's actions because the characters move with an intent to be somewhere or do something in the theme of the play. No longer fixating on or manipulating objects in phase three, he drives to get gas for a car or move a horse from a field to the water trough with a purposeful intent. The phase three child plans his play agenda, shares his ideas with a peer, and follows a theme in his narration just like a typical peer. In order for his plans to be implemented, he negotiates with his peer over objects and even demonstrates a few play actions about his proposed play. He often looks like a typical child in play.

Like his peer, he shows his emotions by changing his voice tone in the characters' dialogue and by his own facial expression of concern; he shows a sense of urgency with his actions as he races his car back and forth, pressing it into the ground so the wheels make a screeching noise. At the same time, his wrinkled forehead and his crouched body position over his racecar reveal his concern. If he's playing with a farm set and the horse is hungry, the child whinnies, pounds the horse's hoofs on the ground and looks up at his peer with a worried facial expression that indicates it's time to hurry.

Despite this appearance of looking typical, the child with autism might have his characters speak without affect, causing the peer to become disinterested and discontinue play. Even though the phase three child can express his emotions through play, he is often preoccupied with his own agenda and may attend only to the actions that satisfy his play sequence, ignoring his peer's requests to change. He may keep the figures or the objects to himself when things become confusing and too fast, resisting any change. Then, the peer often leaves the play area to play with another peer.

Another difficult issue for a child with autism is the struggle to be aware of the peer's perspective in play. Even typical children before the age of five or six have difficulty with perspective taking during play interactions.

Unlike the typical child, the child with autism will take a longer time to understand what his peer is thinking. Lack of perspective taking in children with autism doesn't mean that they have an inability to be sensitive to others. In most situations, a child with autism shows concern when another child is crying or hurt. However, a child with autism has a fixed idea that there is only one option to think about, if there is a problem in an interaction. The phase three child has difficulty understanding the thinking and reasoning of a peer who sees several options and has many ideas. The therapist or the parent, as a participating "peer" in play, needs to help the other peer explain his perspective and why he wants the story to be in a particular sequence. At the same time, the therapist also needs to help the child accept his peer's ideas.

The phase three child's lack of perspective taking might lead both children to disagree and misperceive each other in play. Sometimes a phase three child doesn't recognize that he may be hurting his peer's feelings and needs to be reminded that his peer is in distress. Once the child understands the distress, he is the first to help. This part of therapy is tedious because a child in this phase always wants his own agenda and doesn't have the full flexibility of a typical child. The child's lack of flexibility coupled with his wanting things to remain the same make it hard to shift from his own ideas to his peer's.[2]

NARRATIVE

The child in phase three, like a typical child, invents and creates a complex sequence of actions in his story as he moves his characters and persuades his peers to follow his ideas. His peer follows him, commenting and joining him by creating a series of actions and a plan for a high point and a resolution.

Unlike the typical child, the child with autism needs support in using abstract themes for his characters that not only move through a play theme, but also analyze what the characters are thinking. For example, if the horse suddenly runs off into a field, throwing the driver and passengers into the road, the story creator has to resolve what happens to the people. The two children need to discuss, with the therapist's support, what will happen to the story characters and why. Perhaps another horse and carriage will come down the road to rescue them. Perhaps the horse will find a friend, a mare, and stop in the field to smell the flowers and talk to the mare. The driver might retrieve the horse and bring the people back home. All of these details evolve as the children use language to negotiate about how to play out their story. As they talk, they keep the story actions moving forward.

The phase three child needs help with these discussions that are abstract in order to avoid conflicts between both children about the sequence of the story.

Unlike a typical child, the phase three child has difficulty creating a narrative with more than one peer, or formulating a story that interweaves pretend play and play about reality. When a child plays in a pretend world with symbolic figures, he is inventing something from his mind that is fantasy or unreality. When the child recreates play about his family or something that he does everyday, such as going to school, he is playing with themes about reality. He understands story structure and sequences his own ideas but needs the therapist's support using language to incorporate another person's ideas and to plan about the story actions, particularly if there is more than one peer who wants to contribute to the play theme. Once the conversation goes from pretend play dialogue with characters to plans about the theme, the child with autism may become confused and want to leave the group of players. The therapist's role in this situation is to assist the child and the several peers who are engaged in play together. The parents can learn to facilitate language with a group of peers; however, at this point in therapy, the child needs the therapist to fully participate and teach the skills of relating to the whole group. Some parents can learn this skill while others may need to leave this to the therapist. The relationship between the child and his peers forms a bond that allows the peers to help the child as they all talk through play themes and run, winding around a playground, shifting from pretend to real conversation.

The strategies for phase three will be illustrated through the relationship between the therapist and some children who were in phase one and two. In addition, strategies are illustrated through the therapist's relationship with several new children who are entering phase three.

3

Child-Initiated Reciprocity

BRINGING THE CHILD TOGETHER WITH A PEER

Strategies in this chapter

Strategy 31. Connect with the child's peer and engage both children in the ideas of the play.

Strategy 32. Narrate in detail the child's and the peer's actions within the natural play interaction in order to reinforce the child's intentional play.

Strategy 33. Engage a peer to motivate the child to play, and to move the child past his repetitive actions and fixed mental images.

Strategy 34. Model symbolic play with objects that have meaningful relationships in the child's life and that relate to the ideas in the child's play.

Strategy 35. Ask the peer relevant questions directed at finding out the next sequence in the story and the object's destination.

Strategy 31: Connect with the Child's Peer and Engage Both Children in the Ideas of the Play

If a classroom teacher creates a free-choice time in the schedule when children can choose among various objects within a center and can move from one center to another, a therapist is able to work effectively in both the classroom and on the playground with a child who has autism. In a more structured preschool classroom, a therapist might have difficulty incorporating language facilitation in a natural way. The therapist can also work within a structured activity, such as an art project, as long as there are forty-five minutes for the child and a peer to complete the project. I usually work with a child for a two-hour block twice a week in a preschool setting and for a one-hour block once a week during recess time or choice time in an elementary setting. The whole process takes from one to two years of therapy. I follow the child and his peer, participating as though I'm a peer in the play interactions. I work on gaining the child's and the peer's trust. I run up ladders, slide down slides, go through hoops, play in sand boxes, and take the trolley, a ring that slides from one part of the play structure to another. At first, I barely leave the child's side. Gradually, after ten to fifteen weeks of staying close to the child, I fade into the background and become an observer, not a full participant. I enter into the play when the child with autism needs the support. If the classroom is highly structured with no choice-time activities, I consult with the teacher and I see the child at recess or on a playground.

The first step is to find a peer who is interested in the kind of play area that captivates the child with autism. The therapist must observe the play for at least one morning before beginning direct intervention. If the child with autism is using a fire truck, and the peer is as well, the therapist can bring them together more easily than if the peer is playing with a different activity (e.g., play dough) in another area. As the two children play with their objects, the therapist creates a narrative to engage the two children in play. In order to persuade the two children to use their fire trucks together, the therapist must link the play sets together such as she might move a third truck toward a burning building, accompanied by appropriate sounds and body language to model the actions and emotions of the situation. The children and the therapist express their delight as the fire truck saves the people from the building. In Strategy 26, the therapist linked Christine and Olivia's castles together by suggesting that they build a waterway to connect them.

Strategy 32: Narrate in Detail the Child's and the Peer's Actions within the Natural Play Interaction in Order to Reinforce the Child's Intentional Play

As the children move their fire trucks together, the therapist reinforces their play actions by making positive comments, and by joining them with similar actions. The therapist's facial expression, voice tone, and body language must connect with the intensity of the children's movements. The child with autism sees and feels that connection as the therapist not only guides and imitates the actions in the story, but also provides more dialogue for the characters.

To create options during play, the therapist needs to react to the child's dialogue and actions by suggesting new ideas and by narrating the player's actions.

Patrick hugs his fire truck in his lap, saying, "No, this truck is mine!"

I respond, "Patrick, look at your friend. He has a big silver fire truck! Wow! Look at the ladder on that truck. It is so shiny!"

Patrick looks at the truck, then at his own truck, and smiles. I notice that Jason, a typically developing peer is nearby.

I say, "Oh, wow, Jason, can Patrick pat your shiny truck?"

Jason says, "Yep." He hands Patrick the truck.

Patrick touches the ladder and giggles.

This exchange makes a general connection not only between the two children, but also between the two objects in play, the fire trucks.

I suggest, "Maybe we could move your fire trucks together to put out a fire!"

Jason joins me and says, "Yep! We could build a fire station!"

Patrick is still hugging his truck. He slowly moves his fire truck out onto the floor.

I hand Jason a block saying, "Here's a block. This one would make a good fire station."

Patrick reaches with Jason. I hand the block to Jason and give another one to Patrick. They begin to build together.

I continue to narrate details of their actions, "Oh, look at how Jason is building a door to the fire station. It is a tall one!"

Patrick looks up at the door.

I say, "Wow! Patrick that's a great path to the door! Look at that big wide path, Jason. That's great!"

The children continue to build and eventually move both of their fire trucks into the station.

Once the therapist determines some interesting actions for both children, the therapist can help create the story theme. If the story is interesting to the children, both of them will look at each other, touch fire trucks or hand each other a building block. If this critical connection occurs, both the child and the peer will use more spontaneous language following this experience as compared to a parallel play experience. The therapist can talk about their actions and positively reinforce their behavior in play by using gestures or verbal comments to them. As the natural sequence of play with two children takes over, the therapist fades into the background, observing and listening to the sounds of two peers connected to one event by language, play, and emotion. If parents are present, they also need to fade into the background. If this critical experience doesn't happen, the therapist has to shift to other strategies.

If a child hears a continual narration by the therapist about the actions of a peer's car that is going some place for a specific purpose, the child may limit his repetitive actions for a short time. It takes several months of therapy to help a child with autism to pay attention to his peers and see that an object's purposeful actions enhance play. By concentrating on the purpose of the actions, the child will become interested in the theme of the play and lose interest, most of the time, in repetitive play. This new awareness of a theme in play will help him join his peers in their excitement.

Strategy 33: Engage a Peer to Motivate the Child to Play, and to Move the Child Past His Repetitive Actions and Fixed Mental Images

With help from both the therapist and a peer, a child with autism can learn to move beyond his fixed repetitive play. Matching an appropriate peer with the child with autism is critical. The peer, typical or a child with some disabilities, must have the ability to respond with age-appropriate language and be a "model" for the child with autism. This peer must also have some flexibility and an ability to shift to another activity if the current one doesn't work out. A peer with a sense of humor is helpful. Even when the child with autism may appear to ignore the peer, the therapist needs to keep prompting and redirecting the child and the peer; eventually the two children may connect. Often the peer needs as much support as the child with autism. It takes several weeks; sometimes even months to help a child with autism see the advantage of connecting to a peer rather than playing alone.

To the casual observer, Patrick might appear to be a typical child with a typical toddler behavior: dumping blocks off a shelf and letting them fall to the floor. He looks engaged in play as he slowly pulls each block off the shelf. He pulls each block and he carefully spins it to view the corners; his preschool teacher sees that this routine is "visually stimulating to him," an indication that he is intensely watching the shape of a toy. She sees that he needs help to use symbolic and more purposeful play.

Patrick doesn't want to engage in an interaction with a peer, particularly if he is preoccupied with watching objects. In fact, he screams, kicks, and bangs his head on the floor when a peer takes away a toy or changes his agenda. In addition, he does not want to share his toys because doing so would challenge what he is thinking that is "correct" for his objects. Patrick wants to watch a car as he moves it up and down on his chest so that he can see the moving wheels over and over again. He wants to lie on the floor with his face near the long row of lined up cars so that he can see the wheels up close and watch to see the shapes of the various parts of the car. He flaps his hands with excitement, making noises when he has accomplished his goal: to keep the cars all in a symmetrical line up. Patrick's behavior is prevalent in many children with autism and is called "stereotypical behavior." Patrick also doesn't notice his peers because he is focused exclusively on his own agenda.

Patrick has not yet learned to play with intentional actions in a story. Rather than moving cars along a road to a destination, he still manipulates them—running small cars up and down his shirt—viewing only the lines and shapes of the cars. Patrick is in phase three in terms of language, but in phase two in terms of play and narrative.

One morning during a preschool play session, Patrick plays alone in the corner of the block area, rolling a small plastic car up and down the front of his shirt. He moves the car and lines it along the edge of the play mat, looks at it for a long time, and then reaches for the next car from the toy shelf. He pushes the car into his chest as he tilts his head down to watch the car wheels spin. He slowly places the car at the end of a row. Macey, a typical peer at age three, reaches to take one car.

Patrick screams, "No! That's my car! No! No!"

I say, "Patrick, Macey wants to play. I turn to Macey and stand close to her.

"Macey, ask Patrick if you can have a car."

Macey says, "Patrick, I want a car."

Patrick screams and pushes his hand toward her. His face scowls and he shoves his hand back and forth to indicate that Macey must stay away.

I say, "Macey, ask Patrick again."

She says, "Patrick can I have a car?"

Patrick screams again, shoving his hand out toward her face. I move close to Macey and lightly support her arm, keeping her near Patrick.

After three months of supporting Macey to ask Patrick to share and talk about what he's doing in play, I sit back and just listen to their play.

Patrick finally gives in saying, "Well, okay, Macey, you can have this car for one minute." He looks at me as he hands her the car.

Patrick is now more interested in playing with Macey than keeping his car to himself.

Strategy 34: Model Symbolic Play with Objects that Have Meaningful Relationships in the Child's Life and that Relate to the Ideas in the Child's Play

After six months of work with Patrick and Macey in their preschool, I model more symbolic play actions. I continue to capitalize on Patrick's interest, partly because Macey also loves to fly pretend planes.

I pick up a long rectangular block and slowly raise it above Patrick and Macey's eye level; Macey looks up at me. I smile at her, pat her on the shoulder and say, "Patrick watch me! I'm making an airplane with this block!" I model the motion and the voice intonation pattern as I move the block in a pretend plane flight.

I swoop the block down in a pretend flight pattern, near the car that Patrick is holding next to his shirt. I make the sounds, "RRRUNNNN!" like a plane engine. I swoop it near him several times. Macey watches and giggles. Patrick looks up at the pretend plane.

I say, "Right! Look Patrick. It's a plane!"

He continues to roll his car down his shirt, turning it as he moves it downward toward the floor. I shift my tactics slightly again by suggesting that he move his car into a garage built with blocks. I persist in creating a new theme for the objects that he has in his hand and at the same time engage a typical peer in the process.

I say, "Patrick, let's build a garage for the cars!"

He shakes his head no and waves his hand at my face. He screams, "No!"

I point to the blocks on the shelf. He walks over to them and begins to pull all of the blocks off the shelf, one at a time. He takes one block, holds it up to his eye level, and turns it like a spinning rod to watch the reflection of the block's image against the wall.

He doesn't hear me when I say, "Patrick, look at my block." I pick up one block and place it near his row of cars. He reaches over and shoves my block away.

He screams, "No! No!"

I persist and ask Macey to help me build a garage. We build a part of the wall. Patrick knocks it down.

I return to the earlier strategy and say, "Macey, Patrick doesn't want the garage. Let's play airplanes!"

Macey smiles, "Okay, let's play airplanes!"

I continue my play actions with my plane, but I shift again in my strategy and concentrate on asking Patrick questions about the destination of his objects in play. Patrick needs questions to encourage him to think about where his objects are going and why.

Strategy 35: Ask the Peer Relevant Questions Directed at Finding Out the Next Sequence in the Story and the Object's Destination

As I land my plane next to Macey's, Patrick looks at both of us. I hand Macey a long rectangular block. She takes the block and swoops it up and down like an airplane.

I praise her, "Oh, Macey, that's cool! Look at the plane. Where is the plane going?" I look first at Macey and then at Patrick.

Macey replies, "Oh, it's going far away, over there!"

Patrick is watching the plane now and rolling his car on his chest.

I pick up another block and follow her pretend plane. We swoop our planes up and down and move across the room. Patrick is watching.

Macey and I engage in pretend play and fly around the play area, landing near Patrick's cars. He doesn't scream. I leave my pretend plane on the floor. He drops his car and grabs the block. He giggles and swoops it up and down to follow Macey as they both make the sounds of a whirling plane engine.

"Where is your plane going?" I ask.

"Oh, it's going over there on a vacation!" answers Patrick.

BUILDING TRUST BY LISTENING

Additional strategies for this chapter

Strategy 36. Use gesture and body language with meaningful language, pointing out what the peer is doing, and making suggestions to the child for actions that will connect to the peer's actions in play.

Strategy 37. Once a child consistently looks at a peer in a quiet office setting, follows a peer's point toward an object, and watches the actions of a peer, take the child to an outside location to work on joint attention in play.

Strategy 38. Coach the child's parents, teacher, and aides to run with the child, to move in his rhythm, and to point out actions in the environment.

Strategy 39. While watching an artistic event or using art materials, join the child in what he is experiencing by describing the feeling, sounds, and images of the natural situation; encourage the peers to participate in the conversation as well.

Strategy 40. Use child-directed conversation that builds trust by remaining calm and attentive, listening to the emotional state of the child, and suggesting language to validate the child's feelings.

Strategy 41. Listen, wait, and be available to respond in a calm, neutral voice when a child expresses anger and disappointment, offering concrete solutions not only to validate the child's feeling, but also to shift her focus on what to do next.

Strategy 42. Suggest some concrete motor activity that not only encourages eye contact and turn-taking, but also involves a simple skill that the child can perform with ease.

Strategy 36: Use Gesture and Body Language with Meaningful Language, Pointing Out What the Peer Is Doing, and Making Suggestions to the Child for Actions that Will Connect to the Peer's Actions in Play

One of the therapist's first jobs is to help the child notice a peer and listen to another child's comments. As one child plays near another, the therapist leans near the child with autism, points to the other peer, and quietly makes a relevant comment such as, "Look, Macey is building." Then, the therapist supports the child's interaction with the peer by talking about something the two children are doing together. As the child either looks up at the peer or moves closer to her, the therapist makes a comment such as, "Oh, maybe you can drive that car toward Macey's building" to engage them both in conversation. At this point, the therapist needs to narrate a theme that incorporates objects at hand such as, "Oh, Macey has some packages in her building (pointing to smaller blocks) and maybe you can ask her for a package to put in your truck!" This invitation from the therapist to the child might motivate Patrick to move his truck closer to Macey's building. The therapist needs to create a theme that seems compatible with both children and one that makes sense. As the two children move their objects, the therapist and the children talk about the actions of the event, hold up objects, and point toward the shared visual event. Together they feel the emotions of the whole experience and respond to each other with spontaneous language. This experience is the basis for joint attention.

Joint attention encompasses much more than just handing a peer an object in play. It also involves both children reacting to the event together, responding with appropriate body language and facial expression and gesture, pointing out the details of the actions, and sharing. In this process, both children are acknowledging the other's presence. It is obvious to the observer that they either are having a good time, being disappointed, frightened, or excited together.

Across ten months of play therapy four hours a week, four-year-old Patrick joins Macey to use objects as symbols of real-life things, talking, giggling, and looking up at her in parallel with his play.

One place to teach these joint attention skills and reciprocal interactions is at a playground as we will see with four-year-old Jacob.

Strategy 37: Once a Child Consistently Looks at a Peer in a Quiet Office Setting, Follows a Peer's Point toward an Object, and Watches the Actions of a Peer, Take the Child to an Outside Location to Work on Joint Attention in Play

When I first meet Jacob, a four-year-old with Asperger's Syndrome, I observe him in his classroom and find that he watches his classmates and looks at them when they say, "Hey, look at this!" or "Watch me!" or "Over there—look!" He enjoys staying close to them but doesn't engage in their conversation. I begin to work with Jacob and one classmate in a small office near Jacob's classroom. He's delighted to be in a quiet situation with one play set and one peer. Once he learns to sustain a conversation for more than a few minutes, I introduce him to play and interactions on his school playground.

I ask him to play "follow the leader" and stay in the same proximity as his peer, but instead Jacob runs and paces, leaving his peer behind. He runs so fast that his feet barely touch the ground. The summer breeze lifts the sand from the sandbox, throwing it upward in a swirl. He watches the sand turn in the air and land on the slide as it trickles over the edge and falls to the ground again. He giggles, turns to me, and looks up with dancing eyes and says, "Did you see that sand twirling in the wind? It is magnificent!" He runs away, laughing and clapping his hands upward. He stops abruptly and leans down to pick up a leaf and a stick.

He brings them to Diane, his teacher, and says, "Here, Diane! Pretend this is a spaceship. We are going up into a space shuttle together. Watch!"

Children with autism often seek adult attention rather than attention from their peers, knowing that it is the adult who gives them language support when they need help. Jacob zooms around the perimeter of the play structure, barely noticing his peers who are running up and down the ladders and shrieking as they slide down the chutes.

He doesn't move when a peer runs by him and says, "Jacob, come with me. Let's collect rocks!" He just keeps moving, holding his space shuttle upward, running around and around, alone. Every few minutes he runs toward an adult to talk about his activity or to ask for approval.

Jacob's parents complain that he clings to them when other children are around. When they take him to a park, he whines, paces the play area, and then pulls at his parents' hands. I explain to his parents that he will learn to socialize with his peers. He has the capacity to relate to adults; he just needs to transfer these skills to his interactions with peers. We know that Jacob is a highly intelligent young child with a reading comprehension age score of a twelve year old. He reads *Time* magazine and can explain the content. Jacob's parents are surprised by his ability to read and comprehend adult material, and are concerned about his inability to connect with peers and to have a reciprocal conversation.

I ask Jacob's parents to join me in a speech session with Jacob at a playground near their home so that I can coach them on how to facilitate language interactions with peers. At the same time I work with him once a week for two hours at his school playground.

The success of taking a child outside to work on language during interactions depends on the relationship between the therapist and the child as well as the bonds between the family, the child, and the therapist. The next strategy explains how to facilitate language within this close relationship with a child in an outside situation.

Strategy 38: Coach the Child's Parents, Teacher, and Aides to Run with the Child, to Move in His Rhythm, and to Point Out Actions in the Environment

Jacob runs up to me and taps my leg. "You wanna play?" he asks.

I smile and say, "Of course, what shall we do?"

He runs away and travels his familiar route around and around the swing set that is surrounded by a dark spongy area. Other children are laughing as they swing high. Jacob runs as if they are not there. I run with him for a while to move in his rhythm. He turns back to look at me and smiles.

I say to him, "Jacob, look over there! The kids are swinging so high! Look!" Jacob just keeps running! He's in outer space. He skips over pebbles and jumps over the cracks in the black squares that line the swing area. I try again, but this time I run up to his side, tap him on the shoulder, and then try to slow him down to a fast walk. He turns to look up at me.

I ask, "Jacob, let's swing with the kids! Look over there!"

I point toward the swingers. He looks at me and shakes his head no.

I concentrate on how to relate to Jacob and how to get him to move into the same physical proximity as a peer. I suddenly run to a swing, jump on it, and start swinging, calling to Jacob, "Wow! I'm swinging! Look at me!"

Jacob stops and giggles at me. He looks for a minute and then continues on his running path.

I get off the swing and follow him again. "Jacob, there's Michael. He might want to play!" No response. Michael stops and looks up at me. I move next to Michael and bend down to help him push the sand into a mountain.

I ask, "Michael would you help me get Jacob to play with you?"

He says, "Okay."

He yells at Jacob, "Come here, Jacob, and collect rocks with me!" Jacob doesn't respond. He just keeps running.

I tap Michael and say, "Follow me!" Holding a few rocks in his hand, Michael immediately jumps up and follows me. We both follow Jacob around the play structure.

I run in front of Jacob and say, "Michael is here and he wants you to collect rocks with him! Look!"

I prompt, "Michael, ask him to collect rocks!"

Michael says, "Jacob, I want a good rock collector. You wanna help me?" Jacob nods his head yes. Then, he keeps on running. He circles the swings and then goes to the slide structure. He kicks up the sand and laughs loudly. Michael follows him. He tries to catch him. Jacob looks back. He runs faster and Michael gives up. Michael begins to cry. I run to him.

He says, "Jacob doesn't want to play with me, Ann."

As I hold Michael on my knee, I say, "He does, but he doesn't know how."

His teacher smiles at me and says, "He is so cute and he does have great language. Why does he reject playing with other children?"

"It is so hard for children with Asperger's Syndrome to relate to peers. They don't understand the subtle cues like facial expression, tone of voice, and gesture; they can't process all this information when a peer talks to them. They cope by running away or by getting stuck on some routine. That's why they don't stop to talk. They don't know how," I explain.

Once in the classroom, I sit down on the circle rug and Jacob runs toward me. I see his smile. As he laughs, our eyes meet. He throws his small arms around both shoulders and leans his head sideways on my arm.

He says, "Ann is here! Ann is here today!"

I pat his back and say, "Yes, I'm here!"

He suddenly pushes me away and spins around on the floor saying, "Ya wanna play?" He turns around to watch my face. I smile back at him.

The process of helping Jacob separate from his adults and specialists to become an independent child connected to his peers is a long, tedious experience for both his parents and professionals. There is no magic in this coaching process. The therapist needs to be with the child consistently running, talking about the actions, talking to the other peer, and joining the child in the immediate interactions during play. The parents/specialist follows the therapist at first and then intermittently replaces the therapist to practice the method of joining the child and watching the play interactions up close. When the child makes spontaneous comments to peers during play and sustains an interaction for more than ten minutes, the child is ready for the therapist to fade in and out of participating in the play. In about two months, the therapist can "fade" or move into the background on the playground and intervene only when the child needs help negotiating. In parallel, the child's teachers, aides, and specialists need to allow the child to learn on his own and to experience the success and sometimes failure of social communication. At this point, the child is moving into phase four.

If the therapist sees the child each week for at least two hours in a natural context and coaches the parents and assistants during that time, the process of teaching a child to limit his fixations on objects and to join others in play in an outside location generally takes about two years.

A child with autism is not only interested in shapes of objects, but also has a high interest in the visual reflections of images that can again cause a child to focus exclusively on an object's physical characteristics and ignore the main idea of play themes. However, by guiding and redirecting this same visual interest in play, the therapist can help him expand language and think in abstract ways, becoming socially connected as we will see in Justin's high interest in the ice sculpting event.

Strategy 39: While Watching an Artistic Event or Using Art Materials, Join the Child in What He Is Experiencing by Describing the Feeling, Sounds, and Images of the Natural Situation; Encourage the Peers to Participate in the Conversation as Well

When children with autism notice sights in their environment such as the reflection of light on ice, or the beautiful color of a fall leaf, or a long ripple of water on a glassy pond surface, or when they hear the sounds of an ice cutter, the wind rattling the leaves, or the "lapping" sound of the water on a pond's shore, they experience something that moves them to reach out with their hands, talk to their family, or even to cry with joy. It is at this moment, with the therapist pointing out these experiences, joining the child, that the child connects images and sounds to an emotion and both of these to language. One of the best ways to create this experience is to bring artistic events (e.g., musical, performance art, or sculpting) to children with autism. By watching an artist work, a child engages in reciprocal talk about the emotions that connect to the artistic expression before them. The therapist and the child have a safe place to talk about a shared event. As the child is captivated by a visual experience, he feels what it is like to be close to another person.

Justin, a five-year-old with Asperger's, joins his classmates outside on the playground to watch Erik, an ice sculptor, carve a big polar bear from a 300-pound block of ice. As the artist walks toward the huge block of ice with both his chisel and his electric saw in hand, he talks to the class. Justin sits motionless, legs crossed, next to his classmates. I sit between him and one classmate on the playground asphalt.

It is mid-afternoon at the tail end of a New England blizzard, the sun feels warm at the preschool's after-school program. The children are wearing parkas and mittens as they sit on the asphalt of the playground. The sky is streaked with pink and dark gray clouds from the previous storm. It is early spring day in New England that means the weather is unpredictable; the temperature is about twenty-five degrees, with snow or freezing rain expected. Today, the ice is melting and dripping from the school rooftops causing a tapping sound on the rain gutters that circle the school building. The white and purple crocus are showing just above the surface of the wet flower beds. There are reflections on the buildings from the sun shining on the ice and the patches of snow along the street.

Erik's black snow pants are wet from the melting ice and his bare forearms drip with water. He moves his tools slowly. First, he marks the ice with a small sharp chisel that he holds in his right hand, moving it down the side of the block of ice that will become the long leg of the polar bear. Next, he turns on his electric saw that he holds in his left hand. Justin turns to me with a big grin.

"Is he going to cut it?"

"Yes, watch. I think it'll be something big!"

"Is it going to be a big bear?"

"Yes, I think so."

"I hope the saw isn't noisy!"

"It might be."

"Can I ask him?"

"Of course."

"Erik, is the saw noisy?"

"No, it's very quiet," remarks Erik with a smile.

I smile at Justin, patting him on the shoulder to praise him not only for asking a question, but also for anticipating when things might be too noisy.

Erik turns the power saw on; we hear a low hum as he begins to carve out the bear's head. Ice chips fly out from the electric power saw as he starts his first cut. He moves quickly toward the bear's paws. In a few minutes, we can see the beginning shape of a whole polar bear about five feet tall.

I watch Justin as he watches the polar bear figure and moves his head back and forth.

"What is it?" I ask, moving closer to him.

"Oh, see the colors. The sun's going through the polar bear's head. See? Wow! It's a prism. It's a rainbow! Wow! See the light?" he whispers.

I lean my head over from one side to the other. He giggles at me and moves over, motioning for me to sit where he is sitting. He knows that in order to see the sun's reflection on the ice of the polar bear's nose one has to be in the right position. I watch the visual image of the colors that shine through the polar bear's head. The rainbow of colors moves me to tears. I smile at Justin as he looks at me with a serious but caring facial expression. I smile at him and move over. He pulls a peer into this special spot. He points toward the polar bear's head.

"Watch the polar bear's head! Look at the colors!"

"Oh, wow, Justin, that's great!"

One by one, several of his classmates, move into this special place to see the colors that pass through the ice, reflecting onto the blacktop of the playground.

I ask, "Justin, you're sharing the colors with your friends!"

"Yep," he says, "and they see the colors like I do!"

Justin turns to the peer on the other side of him, smiles and gives him a high five.

All of a sudden, Erik spins the ice block around; the bear is facing us. We can see the polar bear's hair, a series of cylinders carved by the chisel. The children sit motionless, watching and listening. The sculptor's soft deep voice, the hum of the electric saw slicing through the ice, and the quick cuts in the ice by the chisel create a feeling of magic as the sun shines through the ice and lights up the faces of the children.

I ask, "Erik, have you carved other animals?"

"Of course, hundreds. I've been carving for twenty years!" he explains. "Yell out an animal and I bet I've carved it."

One child after another yells out the name of an animal as Erik nods his head to say yes to each question. After a few minutes, he laughs and says, "That's all now. That's a lot of animals."

Justin yells, "Have you ever carved a monorail or a steam engine?"

Erik yells back, "Yep. I have. Lots of trains."

Justin often speaks in continuous monologues about what interests him most; trains and planes, a behavior that is characteristic of children with Asperger's disorder. His friends often abandon him because he can't stop talking about trains, train numbers, or plane models. For today, he's fully engaged in ice sculpting and the polar bear carving. He's still fascinated by the reflections and the colors on the pavement, but he's listening to the speaker, joining his peers in the whole experience. The child's language becomes relevant and spontaneous when he sees this connection between a shared event and the visual world in his own mind. The whole experience of watching the artist, asking him questions, and making comments to his peers keeps him centered on language that is relevant and focused. For now he is not repeating monologues about unrelated subjects like trains.

I say, "Justin, you can ask him a question now."

He raises his hand, asking, "How do you see what to carve first?"

Erik smiles, holds his chisel in one hand, lays it on the palm of the other, and says, "Justin, you just cut away what you know you don't want. That's all you do."

"But, how do you know?"

"It's in your mind."

"I have a lot of things in my mind, like trains. Can I carve them?"

"Maybe you can carve a train."

"Wow! I'd like to carve a whole Thomas." Justin smiles, leaning his head sideways to see the bear from a different view.

When there is a tangible object, such as a polar bear out of ice, the therapist talks about how the object feels, and encourages the child to experience the materials of art by touching them. Handling the artistic object and the artistic materials used to create it gives the child more to talk about.

After the bear is finished, the children are allowed to walk up and talk to Erik and touch the bear. Justin is the first. He stretches as high as he can to touch the polar bear's nose. He taps it with one finger. He runs his fingers across the polar bear's face and down his neck, watching his hand move along the carved lines on the bear's legs and paws.

He watches as Mark, a peer, does the same thing.

Mark says, "I feel like I'm inside of the polar bear."

Justin says, "Yes, me too. Look at his eyes!"

Nodding his head, Mark says, "Yeah. They look blue!"

Justin says, "I think they are!"

Mark says, "I wish we could touch his ears!"

I lift them both up, one at a time, to touch the bear's ears.

Both children turn toward each other in front of the bear and hug, giggling.

Justin says, "How cool."

Mark says, "Yeah, how cool." The boys' friendship forms as they engage in clear joint attention.

He motions to Justin with his hand, saying "Come on! Let's play on the playground before the bear melts and gets us all wet!"[3]

Justin reaches for Mark's hand and follows him.

Strategy 40: Use Child-Directed Conversation that Builds Trust by Remaining Calm and Attentive, Listening to the Emotional State of the Child, and Suggesting Language to Validate the Child's Feelings

Children with autism, particularly children with Asperger's, need constant reinforcement that they are valued as human beings. These high-functioning children are aware of how they impact others, how they are perceived by others, and of how they are, in many ways different from others. Often, these children can't see their own gifts: high visual acuity, sensitivity to others, a strong long-term memory, and striking artistic talent. These children may not immediately understand the perspective of another child in social interactions, but they are sensitive and will often cry when they discover that they may have said the wrong thing to a peer. Making social connections with others is the hardest part of their day. They want to relate and be a part of the social group at school, and yet they also want to be alone to pursue their own interests.

Seven-year-old Elsie, like Justin, is fascinated by color, artwork, and by the shape and form of the visual images in her environment. She has Asperger's and attends a special school in western Massachusetts for children with autism and emotional issues.

As I pull into the muddy driveway of Elsie's school, I see a long white building with big rectangular shaped windows that look out over the gray-stone walkways.

I park my car, walk to a huge white gate, swing it open, and walk toward the white building. I've come to see Elsie, who has severe learning disabilities and autism. A tall thin girl appears in the hallway. "I'm Elsie," she says. I look at this young girl.

"I want to kill myself and I am stupid," she says. She begins to walk down the school corridor and pounds her forehead with her fist. Her teacher nods to me that I can follow her. I walk behind her. She is singing to herself as she pounds her forehead.

She chants, "I don't deserve to live. I am a terrible stupid person."

"I'm glad that you're here." I say in a whisper. She stops walking and looks around at me.

Once she continues walking, I watch her slow stride and notice her arms at her side; they don't swing in a natural cross-extensor reflex. Her face is tense and she looks at her feet with each step.

I think to myself that more children die from suicide than cancer, heart disease, or any other illness. In fact, according to the National Institute of Mental Health (NIMH), in 2004, suicide was the third leading cause of death in children ages ten to fourteen years (1.3 per 100,000).

I know I cannot rescue all the children in the world, but I can try to help Elsie. I have to face that I might not succeed. We find her locker, which is next to her classroom. She opens her locker and says, "I want to kill myself. I am stupid." I listen.

I say, "Elsie, do you want to kill yourself right now?"

"No, not yet," she says. She doesn't smile, but she doesn't push me away.

Elsie and I enter her classroom to find her lunch box. When I work with a child who is suicidal, I remain quiet and observe her behavior. As long as she doesn't express the desire to kill herself at that moment and she doesn't explain how she'd kill herself, I continue with the therapy and provide support as much as possible. If she did give details about how she would kill herself and said she would act on those plans immediately, I would send her to a pediatric hospital where psychiatric professionals could address the emergency. For now, I stay in her physical proximity, and I also don't expect interactions or eye contact. I follow her to her desk. I don't look up to introduce myself to her classroom teacher. I watch Elsie.

She grumbles, "Oh, my mother probably didn't give me chicken noodle soup, and she probably gave me chicken gumbo and I hate chicken gumbo!" She grabs her lunch box and sits down. Elsie pulls out her thermos and places her hands on the top. She starts to twist it cautiously as if it might explode. She flips the cover up and on the floor. She winces when it bounces and clangs against her metal chair leg. She looks inside her thermos and screams, "It's chicken gumbo!"

I say, "Elsie, let's see if there is something else to eat. You have an orange. You can eat that."

She stops yelling, pulls out the orange, and starts to peel it. She takes ten minutes to pull out one wedge—holds up an orange slice and looks at it. She watches the orange slice as she pulls off a string, twists it around to see it from all angles, and eats around the edge. She jumps up when the orange squirts her in the face, walks across the room and throws the rest of her lunch in the trash. Her thermos cover still lies under her desk. I say nothing but notice that she sees it. I look at her, expecting her to pick it up. She doesn't. She sits down at her desk and pounds her fist into her forehead.

I say, "Elsie, what are you doing?" She stops.

"I am pounding my head." she says.

"Why?" I ask.

"Because I hate myself and I got chicken gumbo soup!" she cries.

"Have you told your mother that you only like chicken noodle?" I ask.

"Yes, but she wants me to like chicken gumbo! And I don't like it!" she replies.

"Elsie, it's okay to express your ideas. It's okay to dislike chicken gumbo," I say in a calm voice, sitting near her.

"Thanks," she says and sits still next to me.

Strategy 41: Listen, Wait, and Be Available to Respond in a Calm, Neutral Voice When a Child Expresses Anger and Disappointment, Offering Concrete Solutions Not Only to Validate the Child's Feeling, But Also to Shift Her Focus on What to Do Next

I sit patiently. I wait. She finally picks up the top of her thermos and screws it on. She puts her lunch box under her desk and takes out her spelling workbook. I watch her as she prints the letter "l," a task that takes her over five minutes. Elsie has dysgraphia, an inability to form letters or graphemes, and some possible sensory issues. She has difficulty using pressure and modulating her own strength. She clenches her teeth and squeezes the pencil until her thumb and first finger are white. She makes an indentation in the paper as she writes. The paper tears under the pressure of her pencil. She doesn't notice the tear.

I ask, "Elsie, have you ever used one of these?" I show her a rubber pad to slip on her pencil to cushion her grip.

She says, "That's for babies."

"Okay." I say.

She turns to me and says, "You are annoying." I say nothing.

Elsie is beginning to express her ideas and emotions and she is no longer directing her anger inward, toward herself.

Strategy 42: Suggest Some Concrete Motor Activity that Not Only Encourages Eye Contact and Turn-Taking, But Also Involves a Simple Skill that the Child Can Perform with Ease

For the next two months, I see Elsie for two hours twice each week. I also consult with her classroom teachers. During the second month of therapy, I bring Elsie a language and motor activity that involves a concrete object, a spongy ball called a "gertie"; it is something she can catch easily. We begin the session by tossing the spongy ball back and forth. She looks up at me as she tosses the ball.

She makes one comment, "That is easy to catch!" I nod yes. She smiles at me for the first time. I also "clear the field vision." That means that I make sure my play materials are organized and that there is very little clutter. Elsie's language/learning disability compounded by serious emotional issues makes it easy for her to be visually distracted by disarray.

I work on expanding her expressive speech by asking questions that require answers that are more complex than yes or no or short explanations. The questions are more abstract than concrete; however, they don't call for understanding of figurative language or ambiguous words. I don't ask, "What do you think you will do when you get out of school?" or "How do you like the school?"

Instead I ask, "Elsie, what did you do last weekend?"

She says, "I don't know. I can't remember."

When she answers with "I can't remember" I name two activities that she is likely to have done.

"Well, did you play at home with your sisters or go to a playground?" I ask.

If Elsie chooses one of the two options, I can help her organize her answer with appropriate syntax and vocabulary.

She might answer, "Oh, I stayed home."

I ask, "What did you do?"

Elsie responds, "I don't know."

I respond, "Well, what did you do first when you woke up?

She smiles, answering, "Oh, I ate breakfast and then we played cards."

I continue to question Elsie until she gives me a sequence of activities. Children with autism often have difficulty sequencing their ideas and using language to express logical sequences. Many children with autism have language and learning issues like Elsie. Then I ask her to retell the sequence again. In the retelling task, she chooses her own words and expands naturally on the ideas of her day with her sisters.

In addition, I change the activity when she is fidgety and unable to focus on the task. As I walk over to my game bag, I notice that if I step too close to her, she jumps back and blinks her eyes and frowns at me. If I move my hand near her arm, she jerks her arm away from me. If I move quickly, she jumps up and walks away.

I say, "Elsie, are you having a hard day today?"

"Yep. I am so fidgety. I can't get focused on anything! I feel frustrated," she explains.

I have a plastic box filled with sensory materials that Elsie likes to fidget with and it includes several objects such as a "quosh" ball, pretzels, and wind-up toys. These objects help her focus and relax and may relieve her stress. She is also very calm after she blows whistles or does some yoga breathing. We take a break and go back to questions another time.

Additional strategies for building trust

Strategy 43. When a child feels angry at herself, suggest activities that can be accomplished with little effort, stay close to the child, and remain silent at times to allow the child to express her feelings.

Strategy 44. Introduce simple, concrete games that require reciprocity and provide opportunity for language and conversation in close proximity.

Strategy 45. When a child cries, stay nearby and be patient, sensitive, calm, and attentive.

Strategy 43: When a Child Feels Angry at Herself, Suggest Activities that Can Be Accomplished with Little Effort, Stay Close to the Child, and Remain Silent at Times to Allow the Child to Express Her Feelings

In the first few sessions, I move toward Elsie in a slow and steady pace, walking in a slow stride with her walk. I move as she moves. I speak in a neutral tone of voice only after Elsie speaks first. I reply with a comment or a suggestion. My suggestions are only about things that I know she can do. I am silent much of the time. My silence often causes Elsie to look at me. More frequent eye gaze shifts toward me is another goal. When a child looks at a peer, the child is saying without words, "I like you and want to play." The beginning part of the skill is eye contact. The combination of giving a person eye contact and staying nearby is the beginning of connecting to a peer as friend. As I work with Elsie in each session, I aim toward these goals of getting her to use more eye gaze shifts and helping her stay within speaking distance so that we can communicate.

Strategy 44: Introduce Simple, Concrete Games that Require Reciprocity and Provide Opportunity for Language and Conversation in Close Proximity

During the fourth session, I bring an old game in my duffel bag called "Don't Break the Ice." The game consists of a blue plastic frame and about twenty-five small plastic squares of white "ice." The object of the game is to keep the bear from falling off the ice. We place small cubes, the ice, in the frame that holds up a small figure of a bear. Then we take turns tapping the ice, one block at a time, out of the frame until the bear falls. The players tap the ice until the bear falls. The person who taps the ice block out that makes the bear fall loses. I pull out the game and place it on the floor of the multipurpose room where we work at the elementary school. Elsie says, "Oh, I know that game. Let's play!"

Elsie's eyes sparkle and she smiles in a big grin. "I can win!" she says. She puts her hands out and promptly takes the game and begins to set it up. She smiles at me and looks up for the first time. I ask, "Want to be first?"

"No, you can be first." She says.

We play the game five times and she wins every time. I don't try to lose. She just wins.

Calm and pleased she says, "I love pounding the ice blocks down. I love it when each one falls. It feels good!" she giggles.

I laugh with her. I search for games and simple tasks that give a child a sense of accomplishment at the beginning of each session. The child needs to feel a slow steady progression toward success at some concrete activity with a therapist. I never scream, yell, or raise my voice when a child yells out in anger. I calculate the space I can use to move into a child's physical surroundings. From one session to the next, I gradually move closer to Elsie. After two months, Elsie and I can stand next to each other without her yelling a negative comment or pushing me away with objects or asking me to move to the other side of the room. She is beginning to trust my presence. At this point, I increase my commenting about what we are doing. If she makes a basket, I may say, "Great job!" or "Wow. Good shot!" or "That was clever, Elsie!" If she misses, I say, "Good try!" Developing trust with a child who feels unsuccessful takes many small steps.

Strategy 45: When a Child Cries, Stay Nearby and
Be Patient, Sensitive, Calm, and Attentive

I play Don't Break the Ice with Elsie at the beginning of every session for a
year. I can evaluate how our session will go when I watch Elsie hit the ice
blocks. Some days she slams the tiny plastic hammer down hard and other
days she just taps each block. In the third month of therapy, Elsie slams
down the ice cubes and begins to cry. I know the session might be about
using words to express thoughts of disappointment and sadness. My goal is
to find out why she is crying and to help her express her feelings. This may
take a few sessions or a few months or even a year. I never know.

Elsie doesn't want to set up the game for the second round. She plops
down on the floor and cries again. She rubs her eyes and sobs. I don't ask
why she is crying. I hand her a box of Kleenex; she uses up half a box.
The following day she comes to our session and cries again. At the end of
the session, she tells me that Heidi, her dog, was hit by a car and is in the
hospital. We talk about how hard it is when someone dies.

She says, "If Heidi dies, I will kill myself."

I say, "Maybe Heidi won't die."

She smiles, looking up at me with tears in her eyes. "I can't live without
Heidi, Ann," she says.

"I know," I say with tears in my eyes. We sit on the hardwood floor
looking at each other for the rest of the session. We don't know at the time
that Heidi will pass away two weeks later while Elsie is holding her in her
arms.

Several weeks pass. Elsie cries as she remembers how she loved to take
Heidi in the snow and throw tennis balls for her. She is beginning to
remember the good times and her tears are more of joy than sadness. Elsie
also describes the time Heidi ate a whole birthday cake that she baked,
candles and all.

In between sobs, she remembers, "Yes! She at the whole cake and had
chocolate on her nose and didn't even apologize!"

I see her smile through her tears as she talks about her dog with endearing words that make her both cry and smile at the same time.

"I'd get so mad at her, but I loved her so much!" she says sitting quietly
with a pensive look on her face.

Her grieving process is ongoing, but her ability to use language to talk
about her feelings of joy, sadness, and anger are evident. She is content to
use words to express her intense emotions.

In addition to talking about Heidi during the next several months, Elsie
and I work together to talk about her anger toward her classmates. She says,

"Sometimes I just want to break up the whole classroom and I want to beat up every kid and I want to just die."

"I know you must feel angry and really mad at a lot of things." I say. Week after week Elsie sees that I validate her strong feelings of rage and her confusion about wanting to be a part of her peer group and at the same time wanting to be alone and away from everything. I ask her, "Elsie, I wonder why you are angry."

"I am mad because I can't remember things. I forget everything! I hate myself!" she answers. Although her anger about losing her dog is more intense than forgetting things, she is also mad that she sometimes forgets information when she needs it the most in school. Another time, she acknowledges that she is angry that her dog has passed away and that she is now without a playmate.

NARRATING ACTIONS DURING PLAY

Additional strategies in this chapter

Strategy 46. Select high-interest activities that address not only learning difficulties—such as word retrieval problems and memory deficit—but also the child's sensory needs.

Strategy 47. Listen to the child's feelings in an interaction with others, noting ambiguous terms or figurative language that may be linguistically confusing to the child.

Strategy 48. Shift the focus in therapy from asking for direct responses from the child to "narrating" the child's, peer's, and objects' actions and feelings in order to motivate the child to express spontaneous ideas and to notice what is happening in a shared event.

Strategy 49: Observe the child in social interactions and intervene only when needed by suggesting language scripts that include supportive comments to the child while he is involved with peers.

Strategy 46: Select High-Interest Activities that Address Not Only Learning Difficulties—Such as Word Retrieval Problems and Memory Deficit—but Also the Child's Sensory Needs

"Okay, let's figure out how to remember things better." I say. She looks perplexed and stands with her arms folded.

"Oh, we can't do that! That's stupid! I have a brain problem!" she cries.

"Well, we can try." I say. I begin to work on the visualization strategies from Nancy Bell's book, *Visualizing and Verbalizing* (Bell, 1991), and *It's on the Tip of my Tongue* (German, 2001). Gradually, Elsie learns to visualize an object that she can't remember and to describe it functionally, enabling her to retrieve the word. Part of Elsie's language disability is that she struggles with knowing that she has the vocabulary word in her brain, but she can't express it and respond immediately in conversation, and use it in connected speech. This work is difficult for Elsie and requires intense concentration, but it is something that she desperately wants to recover because she understands that not responding in interactions impairs her sense of feeling connected to others. When peers talk at a rapid pace to her in class, she has to listen to her peers, think about her response, and use the right words to express her thoughts. She loses her words as she tries to listen and organize her thoughts at the same time. I make sure that she has some sensory activity to calm her anxiety about these challenging word tasks. She looks forward to playing with some "green gack," a gooey substance that occupational therapists use to calm children with sensory integration issues. When Elsie finds the gack in my speech bag, she giggles and pulls it out. She becomes less fidgety, even calm. We can talk with gack in Elsie's hand.

I start with a "rhythm syllable-dividing" technique (German, 2001) to give Elsie a strategy for remembering proper names. I find a name, such as "Anthony," and ask her to tap out the syllables as we say the word together. Elsie rehearses the name and taps out, "An-thon-ney; An-thon-ney; An-thon-ney." She smiles and says, "I won't forget that name." I use a "visual syllable-dividing" strategy to remember common nouns. Elsie practices the word "drummer." She takes a black marker and writes down the words into two syllables: drum/ er. She practices the word three times, puts it into a sentence, and repeats the sentence three times. Elsie doesn't like the "same-sound cue" strategy, but we practice it anyway. I say, "Think of each syllable as you say the word, "base-ball." She says, "base-ball!"

I say, "What word could remind you of the word base?"

She says, "Oh, I know. The word 'base' can mean a base on the baseball diamond. Right?"

"Right!" I say.

"Okay, what about ball?" I ask.

"Well, ball is the same as a ball in a baseball game," she announces.

"Ann, I can visualize a baseball diamond and also hear the words in my mind," she says.

"That's it, Elsie. You are getting the idea!" I say. We rehearse the strategies with these words in three sentences.

Elsie says, "Okay I've had enough of this practice! Let's play ball!" We both laugh as we shoot hoops in my office basketball hoop.[4]

Elsie, like many children with learning disabilities and autism, is learning to connect to another person through play and to express her own emotions. In addition, she's learning to use strategies that will help her word retrieval and memory problems. She's also developing a bond with me, her therapist, so that learning becomes a natural, comfortable process instead of a drill task at a table.

Strategy 47: Listen to the Child's Feelings in an Interaction with Others, Noting Ambiguous Terms or Figurative Language that May Be Linguistically Confusing to the Child

Sarah, a five-year-old with fluent expressive language, easily articulates her ideas as does Elsie; however, unlike Elsie, she listens and changes her thinking as she begins to understand the multiple meanings of words. Sarah learns from examples, not blaming herself for misunderstanding an ambiguous word or idea, whereas Elsie struggles longer to understand multiple meanings of words and often feels that she is dumb, blaming herself for having a poor memory.

Sarah is talking while playing with her doll in a therapy session. During my first session with Sarah, we work on understanding the connections between language and emotions and idioms. She says that her doll is crying. I reach for the doll to comfort her and to create a mommy and baby dialogue. Sarah pushes my hand away and hugs her doll tight against her chest. We talk about her feelings through the doll's emotions.

Sarah says, "You can't have my doll."

"Why not?"

"Because she's crying."

"That's okay if she cries."

"No, it's not okay to cry."

"You can cry. I don't mind. I'll still like you."

"I don't like my doll when she cries."

"Why?"

"I don't know. I feel mad."

"You feel mad."

"Yes, I feel so mad right now."

"Why do you feel angry?"

"Because I want to go to Jimmy's and eat pizza with daddy and my brother."

"Oh, I bet you feel mad."
"Yes."
"I'm sorry."
"You look sad. Don't cry."
"Why not?"
"Because speech teachers don't cry. Teachers and mommies don't cry."
"Sometimes they do cry."
"They do?"
"Yes."
"My mommy does not cry."
"She might cry sometimes alone. Why don't you ask her?"
"My mommy doesn't cry. Only kids cry."
"It's okay for kids to cry."
"Yes."
"If mommy cried then she couldn't hold me."
"If your mommy cries, she could still hold you."
"I guess so."
"Yes."
"Do people cry all over the world?"
"Yes."
"Are they mad?"
"Maybe. People cry for many reasons. Sometimes they cry because they feel joy and they are happy."
"Really? That's funny."
"Yes. You can cry when you're so happy that you don't know what to do. You cry and 'burst into tears'!"
"Do you burst into a big fire?"
"No, that's an expression, called an idiom."
"Okay."
"When a person 'bursts into tears' they suddenly start to cry real hard."
"You mean they can't stop it."
"Yes."
"You mean you can burst into tears when you're real happy?"
"Yes, or real sad."
"When I did my first jump in ice-skating, I was so happy. I wanted to burst."

Sarah is beginning to understand abstract concepts captured in figures of speech such as idioms and learns to talk about how she feels and to recognize emotions in others.

"Yes, you were so happy you wanted to cry."
"Yes, but when my kitty died, I wanted to cry hard, real hard."

"Ooh, that's sad."

"Do you have a kitty?"

"I know what it's like to have a special kitty."

"Oh, yeah. I feel sad right now."[5]

I nod yes to Sarah as she picks up a stuffed kitten in my office and hugs it.

Expressing emotions with language during play is essential to a child's progress in play therapy. Sarah is moving into phase four as she learns that she has the capacity to understand her own sadness as well as someone else's.

Strategy 48: Shift the Focus in Therapy from Asking for Direct Responses from the Child to "Narrating" the Child's, Peer's, and Objects' Actions and Feelings in Order to Motivate the Child to Express Spontaneous Ideas and to Notice What Is Happening in a Shared Event

D.J. is a three-year-old with autism who loves to play with others but can't express his emotions and thoughts with language when the interactions around him are fast or the least bit confusing. He struggles in his preschool to play with his classmates and he often shoves them because he can't talk in the confusion of preschooler's play. D.J., unlike Elsie, doesn't have word retrieval issues; he fixates on the details of an event instead of seeing what the whole event is about. He gets stuck on the tiny details of objects in an event, as does Patrick on the wheels of cars and trains. He misses the main point and becomes frustrated when he doesn't understand what is happening and his classmates do. Once frustrated, he shoves and pushes other children to be closer to the event or to get their attention. This shoving behavior causes his teachers to reprimand him and put him in a "time-out." He sits in time-out, content to play by himself and happy to be without all the confusion. D.J. doesn't understand that the time-out activity is a punishment or a place to think about why he "made an error," so that he'll stop shoving others. He loves the quiet of sitting in a bean bag in the corner of the room.

My first morning as D.J.'s play therapist begins with a "worm activity." His teacher sets out a pile of spoons and a box filled with mud that has about three dozen worms. D.J., along with three other preschoolers, is holding a spoon and is sitting next to the box. I kneel down behind the children and take a spoon. I move near DJ and another peer. He looks at me and giggles.

"Hey, D.J., do you like worms?"

"No. I'm afraid."

"I am too!"

He giggles. I reach my spoon down into the dirt.

"Oh, watch. I caught a worm. Ooops! It's falling! Oooops! It fell off the spoon! Oh. I get it! Watch out! Yikes. Oh, it's hiding under the dirt. Can you find it D.J.?"

"I can find it!"

"Okay, I'll get this one. This one is big and squirmy! Ooops! Look! It fell into the dirt, too!"

"I found one! Look, Ann! It's a real worm! Look!"

"I see it. Hold your spoon still. Ooops!"

"It fell into the dirt!" D.J. jumps up and down, turns toward one peer and waves his spoon. D.J. is delighted that his worm fell off of his spoon. He is excited to see other worms waiting for him to scoop them up.

"Yes, D.J., it fell into the dirt!"

"Yes, and look at this worm! Let's get it!"

D.J. quickly scoops up another worm; I back away from the dirt box and the worms to watch and listen. He makes a series of comments, in full sentences, about the worms in the next half hour without any prompting.

He says, "Wow! This worm is the daddy worm and he's gonna go to work!" This worm is the mommy worm and she's gonna take care of the baby worm! Look! This worm is a big fat worm. He is so wiggly. Ooops! There he goes into the dirt. Oh, he buried his head in the dirt!!"[6]

D.J. is involved in a joint activity; he's thrilled to be with his peers and to be able to talk about what he's doing.

To teach joint attention in play the therapist needs to *shift the focus* from giving a child the verbal and gesture cues to expecting the child to respond with an imitation, to *narrating the actions* of the objects. The *narration* by the therapist is a way to facilitate language during play.

For example, in D.J.'s case, I could have pointed to the worm on the spoon and prompted him to say, "Look at my worm." He would have given responses that included repeating my words. When he's excited and happy about his own joint attention with a peer, D.J. creates his own natural response with some variation on the idea that he is pleased about the worm. With this more internally driven response, D.J. uses language to express his own ideas. Once he does this spontaneously, he will continue to develop more language. He's using my model of worms falling off his spoon, but I fade out the verbal model to allow him to experience the event with some of his own ideas in his mind as well as to listen to the verbal models of the other children.

After six months of therapy, two-hour sessions twice a week in his preschool classroom, he begins to talk in simple sentences (noun phrase and verb phrase) about his own actions, explaining how he feels about what's happening.

When I first met D.J., he was grasping a piece of bark on the playground and wouldn't look up from the bark, grasping it with both hands, implying that the bark was the only thing in his environment. Looking at the beautiful colorful leaves on the trees, he didn't notice the tree or the leaves or the peers. Today he sees the trees and gazes up at them with his arms spread upward. He says, "ahhhh!" when he sees the puffy white clouds pass by and the tree limbs sway in the wind. He points to and talks about the whole tree, not just one tiny piece of bark that he doesn't want to share. He freely expresses his emotions to his peers with language and he no longer shoves them to pay attention to him during play. D.J. understands the overall ideas in conversation and is no longer confused by his classmate's comments or fast pace of play. He still needs to take sensory breaks in his bean bag chair and read quietly when classroom noise is too loud. He still loves to play with worms. One day, near the end of our therapy, he snapped a worm into two pieces. I ask him why and he responded, "Oh, now he has a friend."

Strategy 49: Observe the Child in Social Interactions and Intervene Only When Needed by Suggesting Language Scripts that Include Supportive Comments to the Child while He Is Involved with Peers

Jamie has brown hair that sticks up like small spikes all over his head. His eyes focused on the ground and his arms swinging back and forth, he ploughs down the hallway like a small tractor. He barely avoids bumping into walls and other classmates. His teachers say that he doesn't want to relate to others like five year olds his age; instead he paces the playground and eats tree bark. He is in a program at Children's Hospital for children with eating disorders; he uses expressive language appropriate for his age and yet, he has autism as well.

As I enter his kindergarten playground, I check in with his teachers and talk to them about the day. They tell me that Jamie has been growling at a tree, refusing to play with anyone.

Jamie's head teacher says, "Oh, he's a puzzle to me! I cannot figure him out. One minute he wants a hug and the next minute he's pacing around the slide structure. He'll try to follow another child but then gets discouraged, stops, folds his arms, and pouts. He won't stick with the kids at all. They ignore him."

I see Jamie by the large eucalyptus tree, near the school's chain-link fence. The tree's slippery leaves cover the ground so I step with care across this area of the play yard. I walk toward Jamie. He's hugging the tree and growling like a dog. "Rahhhrowl" he says. "I'm going to eat you!" "Rahhrowl!"

Instead of speaking to Jamie, I move near him and lean my shoulder on the tree. I watch him as he growls over and over again. He acts as though he's eating the tree. Then he takes a chunk of bark, pushes it in his mouth, and swallows it. He yells "Rahhhrowl!" He looks up at me and says, "Hey ya wanna play?" "Well, I'd like to play, but I don't feel like eating tree bark!"

"Oh, you can just pretend. I'm a T-Rex," he whispers. "Don't tell anyone. I want them to guess!"

"Jamie, maybe your loud growls are scaring your friends away."

"But, I want them to be scared. A T-Rex is scary!"

"But, Jamie, your friends need to be near you to play. How can they play with you, like a dinosaur, if they are afraid and run away?"

"Oh, that's good if they run away. I don't want them to be near me. I want them to be afraid."

"But, my goal is to help you make a friend on the playground."

"Oh, I don't need any friends. I like to play by myself. I get more done that way."

"Well, maybe you can play alone some times and play with a friend other times."

"I don't know how to play with a friend. I don't know how."

"I'll show you. It's not easy, but you can do it."

"I don't think I can talk and run and follow them. They talk fast and run fast. How can I do that? I'm so slow."

"We'll start with the talking part. What do you say when you see a friend on the play ground?"

"Oh, I just say Hi."

"How about something like 'What can I do?' or 'What are you doing? Can I do that too?'"

"The kids will say no."

"Okay, so you try again until you find a kid on the playground that says, "Okay."

"Oh, but what if everyone says no?"

"Let's try it."

"Now?"

"Sure. Why not?"

"Because I don't know what to say!"

"How about—Hey, can I play that game?"

"Oh, okay. I'll try it once."

Jamie and I walk around the trees surrounding the play yard and watch other kids. He spots a pal and says, "That one. Let's try with Jim."

"Okay, now ask him what he is doing. I'll be right there if you need help in the conversation. Okay?"

"Okay, here goes."

Jamie walks up to Jim, pats him on the shoulder and then he moves away, swinging his arm at Jim.

I remain still, near him.

"Hey, can I play that game?"

"Well, no we have enough players."

"Okay, I'll find someone else."

Suddenly, a large handball rolls across the play yard in between the two boys. They both watch it roll toward their feet. Jamie reaches for the ball.

Jim says, "Let's play catch!" Jamie scoops up the ball and Jim backs away to receive it. He stretches out his arms. Jamie throws it hard and Jim catches it. He laughs. Jim throws it hard back and Jamie loses the ball. It rolls out into the play yard where two other boys run for the loose ball.

"Oh, no! Oh, no!" cries Jamie.

"Here, I'll get it, don't worry," yells Jim as he runs after the ball. All three boys collide and land on the ball. They all fall to the ground and laugh.

Jamie giggles. "Can I play now?"

"Yes. Let's play kickball!"

Jamie's face becomes serious. He asks, "Will you show me how?"

"Sure," I say.

I coach him on the side as he kicks the ball from a homemade plate. He runs toward first and he is put out easily. He looks down at his feet.

Jim says, "Oh, Jamie it doesn't matter. We are all having fun! Who cares who wins!"

Jamie returns to the bench and his teammates pat him on the back.

I work with Jamie twice a week for two hours at his preschool for over a year. During that time, he learns to connect to his peers and becomes a part of his class. He makes one good friend who loves dinosaurs and asks him over to play at his home once a week.

His mother tells me that he's eating more at home now and probably because he's not filling up on bark and sand.

During one of our last sessions at his school playground, he and I sit next to his favorite tree. I talk him into going to the cafeteria to buy his lunch. He buys a PB&J sandwich, potato chips, an apple, and chocolate milk. He wants to eat his lunch outside. I sit with him as I balance a small umbrella between us, listening to the rain tap his boots as he eats his sandwich and potato chips.

He shrugs his shoulders and asks, "Why does my mother want me to eat all the time?"

"Food is better for your health, than eating trees and sand!"

"But, I like pretending to be a Tyrannosaurus Rex! You tell me I can pretend to be ANYTHING!"

"That's true, but I don't expect you to eat the trees, only to pretend to eat them."

"I'm experimenting. How DO dinosaurs stand that stuff?"

"I don't know. I've never tried tree bark."

"Well, I don't eat tree bark anymore. I like kickball better."[7]

As Jamie approaches phase four, he learns that playing with a peer is more fun than chewing on a piece of tree bark and that using language to ask others to play, to protest, and to negotiate in play is better than pacing and being alone on the playground.

BRINGING LANGUAGE TO SPORTS ACTIVITIES

Final strategies for this chapter

Strategy 50. Teach language skills—idioms, figurative language, word retrieval, retelling, and sequencing—through sports activities on the playground or at parks with visuals called "floor maps" to support the child's understanding of rules as well as abstract reasoning.

Strategy 51. Model the relationship between tone of voice and the meaning of the words in an interaction for the child with autism so that he can experience how his tone of voice affects the meaning of language; first, use play figures inside in a quiet setting, and then role play outside with a peer on a playground.

Strategy 52. Model the relationship between the loudness of a voice and the distance between the speaker and the listener for the child so that he can experience how intensity affects what a listener can hear in various situations.

Strategy 53. Minimize the number of objects in a play set with two peers and organize play activities with high interest, simple themes, and concrete action.

Strategy 54. Use concrete activities such as a "Gertie" ball to teach language reciprocity and to acknowledge the child's need for physical activity.

Strategy 55. Assist the child and a peer to negotiate over tangible objects in play and share play sets.

Strategy 56. With the child and a peer, create and practice social scripts, called "Options," which are language-based and solutions to social problems that occur in the child's home or at school.

Strategy 50: Teach Language Skills—Idioms, Figurative Language, Word Retrieval, Retelling, and Sequencing—through Sports Activities on the Playground or at Parks with Visuals Called "Floor Maps" to Support the Child's Understanding of Rules As Well As Abstract Reasoning

Children with autism have difficulty learning the different ways that words shift in meaning from one situation to another. Many words that are spoken or written in English are either ambiguous or figurative. In addition, many words can be both nouns and verbs. For example, a child might learn that an object that looks like or represents a table is called a "table." However, the same child may become confused if a person uses the same word in another way: "We will table that for now."

As a child develops language, the meanings of words can expand. For example, a child may say, "Go break a leg," meaning to "have some good luck." An adult may say "Give me a break," meaning "Don't bother me right now or don't blame me for whatever happens." Most children need some help learning these idioms, particularly children with autism.

Eddy, an eight-year-old boy with autism, sees the last day of school as a relief. He has had all he can stand of school pressures and peers who want to play their own game their own way. Eddy wants to pace the schoolyard at recess and play alone in the classroom. His teachers want him to use his social skills and join his peers, but Eddy wants to be by himself. He doesn't want to talk to his peers and definitely doesn't want to play a game of baseball.

For most children, New England summertime means longer days and more fun. They play outside in the warm summer breeze, taste the salt from the windswept beaches on the Cape, pick blueberries on Nantucket, fish in crystal green ponds, and play baseball on town greens. For Eddy, doing all these things is scary. He seeks ways to avoid unpredictable situations that are open and free, especially if he is asked to play a game like baseball.

Eddy's teacher and parents agree that he needs to participate in a language/sports group on Saturdays with another seven-year-old, Tim, who has some language disabilities. The purpose of these modified sport activities is to create a meaningful context for two peers with language issues to learn language in a safe and highly motivating environment. It is in this safe context that Eddy begins to understand figurative language and idioms, as well as the abstract rules of baseball.

One Saturday, Eddy talks to Tim about the rules of baseball and Tim asks, "So what happens to me if I break a rule?"

Eddy followed, "Break? What? Is that like 'break a leg'?"

I respond, "When a player breaks a rule, he has a penalty. Remember? He hasn't broken anything physically. He didn't follow the rule."

"Okay, I get it. But, my friend was watching me run to my classroom and he yelled at me 'break a leg.'" Eddy explains.

Tim laughs. "He didn't mean to really break your leg. He meant good luck in running fast enough to win!"

"Yes, Tim is right. The phrase, 'break a leg' is an expression called an 'idiom.' It means something different than what it sounds like. That's to make the conversation sound more natural. It means to hurry up and go fast," I explain.

Tim turns toward Eddy and places his hand on his shoulder. They laugh.

Eddy says, "My dad told me to 'break a leg' and good luck!"

Tim says, "Yeah! Good luck in getting it done!"

Eddy responds, "Yeah! Why didn't he just say that?"

Eddy and Tim lean their heads back and laugh together until their baseball hats tumble back on the grass.

After several Saturdays of language/sports group, Eddy learns some abstract concepts of a game, what is a "rule," what is the difference between a "forced out" and "tagged out," and why does he have to remain on the field. I use a "floor map" and some figures to play out the rule and make the concepts clear for both boys.

"I don't get it. Why do you have to stay on the field?" I realize that Eddy is frustrated. He mumbles, wiping away his tears with one hand.

I pull out a small 3″ × 5″ white card from my pocket and I draw a baseball diamond and bases. Sometimes I use an 8″ × 10″ Poster board to place on the ground. I call these "floor maps." Eddy turns to look at my drawing. He pushes himself up to sit on the slide. He leans over the card to look at the diamond.

"Yeah, but why aren't there goals?" he asks as he points to the field.

"Eddy, in baseball you score points not by kicking the ball through a goal but by running around all the bases—first base, second base, then third, and—"

Eddy blurts out, "Fourth?"

"Right. But fourth is called "home," I explain.

"Every time a person gets to home base, after running all the other bases, in order, the team gets one point. That point is for the team," I continue.

"Why don't you get a point for hitting the ball?" Eddy asks.

"Because in baseball you win a point by running all the bases, after you hit the ball," I explain. "That's the rule."

"What is a 'rule'?" Eddy asks.

"Oh, we talked about that once, Eddy. What is a 'rule' again?" I ask.

"Yep. I can't remember," he announces as he sits upright with a straight back, legs crossed, and his arms folded across his chest.

"Baseball rules are hard," I begin. I sit on the end of the slide. Eddy faces me, sitting now with the 3″ × 5″ card in his hand.

"A rule is like an agreement. Every player has to agree that the rules are important to follow," I say.

Rules give some structure for children with autism and they make the game of baseball a place that is more predictable than the fast movement of children on a busy playground. Once the child learns the rules, he relies on them to give him that predictability. Sometimes rules are unclear and abstract. The therapist must explain each rule and make sure the child understands how it works in the whole game.

The idea of a "rule" is difficult for children like Eddy. There are rules about how to play a sports game, rules about how to run a country or a particular organization, and rules tacitly created by two friends about how to be with each other. Children with disabilities need weeks of repetitive examples to understand concepts about fairness, teamwork, winning, and losing. A baseball field is a good place to reinforce some of these concepts, especially with a good friend.

"Oh, okay. A rule is something you're supposed to do. Right?" asks Tim.

Eddy replies, "Right. You have to do it or you'll be out."

"Well, you can be out other ways, too. There are 'force outs' and 'tag outs,'" I say.

Tim asks, "What's a force out?"

"Let's work on this rule when we go back to the office next week. Okay?" I say.

"Okay," Eddy and Tim say in unison.

"One of the rules of baseball is that you can't have two guys on base at once. Remember that rule and then we'll talk about force outs and tag outs," I say.

I bring out the floor map again to explain the whole idea of how a player can be tagged out or how he can be forced out because there are other players on base. It takes several weeks in a play context to teach these concepts. Then, once the game itself creates either a tagged out or a forced out, both boys learn the concept.

Eddy says, "I'm out! I have no choice but to run! I'm out!"

Eddy no longer falls to the ground and cries for an hour because he's out. He walks toward his team bench, saying, "Next time I'll hit a homer!"[8]

Eddy's ability to accept change, to allow others to win and change the game, and to negotiate in play through language rather than pouting, flopping on the ball field, crying and dropping out of the game show that he is developmentally moving into phase four. His parents report that he is getting better marks in school and he's starting to venture out at recess with peers. He's more content and better able to manage changes in the daily classroom schedule. He understands that things change and that he cannot predict every second of what is going on in his life.

As Eddy's mother leaves him at school one morning he teases her, saying, "Okay, but I'll be coming home today—I mean I'll be coming fourth today! See you after school!"

Children with autism have a sense of humor and are ready to accept their own mistakes when they learn in a trusting relationship with a therapist.

Strategy 51: Model the Relationship between Tone of Voice and the Meaning of the Words in an Interaction for the Child with Autism so that He Can Experience How His Tone of Voice Affects the Meaning of Language; First, Use Play Figures Inside in a Quiet Setting, and then Role Play Outside with a Peer on a Playground

After two years of intensive therapy, Jacob, the little boy who used to run around the play structures pretending to be a spaceship, gradually learns to connect with his peers. Now he returns again to work on the more subtle cues of language in communication. His mother reports that he isn't monitoring his volume and tone of voice when he speaks to peers and adults. He needs to practice the subtle cues of language; voice tone, volume effect, and body language.

Unlike Eddy who learns first in the outside sport setting, Jacob needs to learn specific language concepts in his classroom—a less confusing situation. His mother complains that he yells at her when he's a few inches away from her and that he whispers when he's in another room. I learn that he is listening to a peer and then shouting out his responses in a "gruff" voice as if he were not only angry at his classmate, but also as if the peer were a block away. His classmates are playing quietly at centers; he and a peer are playing with a farm play set in a small corner area. The peer covers his ears when Jacob is about to talk. I kneel down near Jacob to be at his eye level. I move his body around to face his listener. I model a natural pitch and a normal volume for the distance between Jacob and his listener.

I say, "Do you want to play with the horses?"

He immediately responds, "Do you want to play with the horses?" in a shouting voice.

I move him away from his friend, saying, "Look, Jacob you are too close to shout. Use a normal inside voice, a friendly voice."

I show him drawings of faces that represent various emotional tones. He watches my face and looks at the drawings. I point to "a little happy" face visual.

really angry   frustrated   I feel okay   a little happy   really super great!

He smiles, "Okay, a happy friendly voice."

I shout to him, "Hi Jacob!" He laughs at me.

"Is that a friendly voice? I ask.

He covers his ears and says, "No!"

I whisper to him, "Hi Jacob!" He laughs.

"Is that a friendly voice?" I ask.

He says, "Yes."

I ask, "Is my voice loud enough?"

He says, "No."

I use a moderate level voice in a friendly manner and say, "Hi Jacob!" He giggles. "This is a friendly voice for talking to a person who is next to me as you are."

Strategy 52: Model the Relationship between the Loudness of a Voice and the Distance between the Speaker and the Listener for the Child so that He Can Experience How Intensity Affects What a Listener Can Hear in Various Situations

During the next session, Jacob is in my office playing with a tree house set that has family figures. I take two dolls and give him one doll.

"Let's pretend. You place your doll here. I'll be here," I say as I gesture to show the places for each doll and the distance between them. The dolls are close to each other.

"Now, let's talk to each other in an easy, friendly voice," I say.

"Hi, do you want to play?' I say in a calm voice.

"Hi, yes I want to play," Jacob says in a similar calm voice.

"That's great! Now listen to how loud my voice is while my doll is close to your doll. Okay?"

"Okay."

"Do you want to play?" I say in a loud, almost screaming voice.

"That hurts my ears!!"

"Yes, my voice is too loud. Right?"

"Now listen. I move my doll across the room."

I repeat, "Do you want to play?" with the same intensity level.

Jacob responds, "Yes, I do!"

Then, I ask him in a soft voice and he yells, "Louder!"

Jacob gets the idea of how to modulate his voice intensity and intonation pattern for a close distance. He has more difficulty with the longer distances. We practice this each session every week. I try to use a Sound Level Meter, an instrument that measures decibels (the intensity of sound). He picks it up and shouts into it. When I point out that the red needle on the sound level meter means that he is too loud, he doesn't understand the increments of loudness. The concept of gradation is too abstract and the explanation doesn't help Jacob understand intensity level. He thinks it is like his microphone that is attached to the radio boom box in my office.

Many children with the disorder of Asperger's Syndrome do not understand the subtle adjustments that two speakers must make when they are talking to each other at various distances even though they are functioning at a high cognitive level as compared to age level peers. In addition, a child with this disorder has to be taught the appropriate voice intonation patterns that match the meaning of the content of the words that are expressed at each moment in a conversation.

In one session at Jacob's school, I introduce the idea of matching facial expression, loudness level, and voice intonation to what I am saying. I engage his peers into helping me teach these subtle cues of language in conversation.

"Michael, will you help me teach Jacob how to use a really mean voice?" I ask. Michael says, "Yep. I'll show you!!" he shouts.

"Okay, but use a mean voice with a happy face. Can you do that?" I ask. Michael looks puzzled. Jacob laughs. Both boys are confused.

"Watch me. I will show you in the mirror," I say.

I walk over to a classroom mirror. Several preschoolers follow us. I lean toward the mirror. I show a happy face and say, "I don't like you!" in an angry tone of voice and a flat pitch pattern. Jacob, Michael, and their classmates laugh. Jacob tries and leans over toward the mirror.

With a happy face he says, "I don't like you!" and laughs. He laughs so hard that he falls backwards on the rug. All six preschoolers try to imitate the same voice. They giggle and fall on the rug. Teaching voice intonation patterns can be both challenging and amusing.

Several weeks later Jacob is at the mirror practicing the various voice intonation patterns and facial expressions. His friend Michael is at his side, imitating his voice.

He says, "Watch my face! I'm disappointed."

Michael says, "You look happy!"

Jacob says, "No! I'm disappointed. Look!"

Michael says, "Okay, better. Watch me!"

Jacob watches and giggles.

When I approach them at the mirror, I smile. They both make a "disappointed" face and say, "We want to do this alone!"

I use a happy face and say, "Okay! Great!"

Jacob laughs, saying, "Watch this! I'm going to be sad first, then happy, and then use an 'excited' face to get you to play with me!" He makes the face with his eyes wide open and his hands reaching outward. His face matches his gesture.

Michael says, "Okay, first one to the slide wins! Come on!"

Jacob responds, "That's an exciting face!"[9]

After two and a half years of therapy, Jacob consistently uses the subtle cues of language and "reads" his peers well. He is in phase four of play therapy, ready to negotiate and to understand the more abstract concept of planning and talking to his friends.

Strategy 53: Minimize the Number of Objects in a Play Set with Two Peers and Organize Play Activities with High Interest, Simple Themes, and Concrete Action

A child with autism needs to learn how to play with more than one peer. At first, the child needs a structured activity that is concrete, but fun and interesting. An obstacle course is a good way to keep the toys organized, to define the play space, and to keep concrete action in the activity. It can also be a source for teaching the language of commenting and giving compliments.

After one year of therapy, Sandy, now age six, is in a regular kindergarten and functioning with one aide who helps two other children in class. Sandy has learned to share concrete objects such as dinosaurs and has limited his impulse to keep all objects lined up and in a particular line of vision. He no longer cries if a dinosaur falls over and is able to express his emotions with language to one peer in a quiet setting.

Once a week, I come to Sandy's kindergarten class to help him relate to his peer during choice time in the classroom. One way to organize toys in a small play center in a classroom is to create an activity that the child loves and introduce a simple story theme. One morning in class I suggest to Sandy and two typical peers that we set up a simple obstacle course in the corner of the play center. All three of them cheer, "Yeah!" I use three small padded round circles that teachers use for children to sit on at circle time and place them at three spots in the center. The boys—Sandy and two peers, Doug and David—are sitting and watching. I place a small plastic container at one spot with a few beanbags.

"What should we do here?" I ask.

"Oh, let's stand on one leg and talk about what we did last weekend!" Sandy says.

"Wow! That's a lot! Now what do we do at the third station?"

"I want to shoot hoops!" says Sandy.

"Sandy, maybe your friends have an idea."

"I want to shoot hoops, too!" Sandy's friend, Tom answers.

I place a small plastic hoop and a small rubber basketball on the one station. The hoop is hooked over a chair.

"Okay, now let's name the whole sequence of events. This is an obstacle course. Sandy, tell us what we should do." I say.

"Okay, well, first we have to throw beanbags in the bucket. Then we have to go to that spot (points) and stand on one leg and talk about our weekend. Then we go here (points) and shoot the hoop. Yeah!"

"Yeah!" shout Tom and Doug.

The boys cheer as each one finishes the obstacle course. The goal for the boys who are not running the course is to make comments and give compliments to the boy who is running the course. Sandy is running the course.

Tom says, "Nice shot, Sandy! Nice going!"

Doug says, "Yeah, you're a good shooter."

Sandy says, "That's too hard to stand on one leg and talk. I can't do that!"

Tom says, "Yes, you can. You're a good athlete!"
Sandy gets to the end of the course and says, "I'm great!"

Strategy 54: Use Concrete Activities such as a "Gertie" Ball to Teach Language Reciprocity and to Acknowledge the Child's Need for Physical Activity

Another way to keep a child focused on his peers and to encourage reciprocal language is to start a ball throwing game with a "Gertie" ball. I set up three children in a circle and toss the ball to one peer. I list several different categories of nouns at first. Then, I ask the child to choose a category. The back and forth movement of the ball keeps all of them concentrating on their peers and allows them to fulfill some sensory need, if they have the need, by squishing the ball before they throw it. In order to throw a ball, the child has to look up and make eye contact with a peer. Sometimes, the medium size therapy ball can be used in the same task but instead of tossing the ball they roll or bounce the ball. After a few weeks of practice, I ask the child a question as I throw the ball such as, "What did you eat for breakfast?" or "What's your favorite movie?" or "What's your favorite book?" Ball throwing can also be used to help a child gauge the distance he is from the listener. He can practice voice intensity in relation to the distance.

John and Jim, the twins who learn from being in the outside environment, love to use the ball for conversation. They are both in phase three and learning to negotiate with each other and their peers. Their parents use this technique to practice conversation every day for twenty minutes. The twins struggle with syntax and have difficulty formulating sentences that are grammatically correct. During one session, they practice sentence formulation and negotiation about one object, a spaceship.

"Hey, Jim, my space?"
"Jim, you mean that you want that spaceship from John?"
"Yep. Spaceship?"
"Jim, ask your brother—'Can I have the spaceship?'"
"Okay, John, can I have the spaceship?"
"No, Jim! No!"
Jim asks him again.
"John, spaceship?"
"Jim, try again—'Can I have the spaceship?'" I prompt with a calm voice.
"John, can I have the spaceship?"
"No, Jim, busy."
"John, tell your brother in a full sentence—'I'm busy playing with this now.'"

"I'm busy playing with the spaceship now."

The therapist rephrases the phrase, "spaceship" and expands on the idea of the sentence, using correct word order as a model for the boys. The therapist has to slowly rephrase several times to help them formulate a full sentence in response to a question. Often these children are so preoccupied with other thoughts in their minds that they don't take the time to create full, meaningful sentences about what is happening in the moment.

Strategy 55: Assist the Child and a Peer to Negotiate over Tangible Objects in Play and Share Play Sets

In addition to working on syntax with the twins, the therapist can also teach simple negotiation skills by helping the two children share objects during play. The twins share with prompting but lack the language to limit each other in play. They are both learning to say that they need more time to play with a particular object and that the adult will support this time for them to keep the object longer. The idea of waiting is always hard for the other child, but with support they will wait, knowing that next time they will have the object for a long period of time. The therapist can also facilitate play negotiation by giving the children visual scripts that help them talk to each other instead of allowing them to tug at a toy or to push each other away. Some sample scripts that are on laminated key chains for each child might be:

"You can have this in a minute."

"I don't want you so close to me. I need more room."

"Okay, one more minute and you can have it."

"Can I play with it after you're done?"

"I'm very busy. You can have it soon."

"Can we play with this together?"

"Do you want it now or can you wait a minute?"

"Let's find another toy like this one."

"Stop. I'm using this now."

The twins practice these scripts every day at home with their parents and eventually begin to use them spontaneously in interactive play.

Strategy 56: With the Child and a Peer, Create and Practice Social Scripts, Called "Options," Which Are Language-Based and Solutions to Social Problems that Occur in the Child's Home or at School

Children with autism need time to practice and think about the social issues that they encounter not only on the playground, but also in play situations with peers. One way to encourage a child to practice is to place the social encounters by typing them on the computer, with pictures if possible. The therapist talks with the child and a peer about the various options that could be used to solve troubling situations. A similar method, "Social Stories" outlined in her books, *The Original Social Story Book* (Gray, 1994a) and also in *The New Social Story Book* (Gray, 1994b) is very successful with children with autism. Carol Gray's work in training teachers and specialists to use social stories to solve problems that children encounter in school has contributed to the socialization of these children. Over the past thirty years, I've collected many social problems from children with autism and they have created the many options that are relevant to the specific situations. They love to create one of the options as a "ridiculous" solution because it provides a contrast to the more relevant and helpful solution. A child with autism sees the correct solution to a problem when they are given or have to think about the opposite idea first. This is one of the differences between Gray's Social Stories and the "Options" technique in Narrative Play; however, they are basically the same technique, except that in "Options" the child is asked to find a "silly" solution to the problem first. Perhaps this "silly" option developed because I work with very young children. With the older children, Social Stories is more appropriate because the "silly" options become "too silly." Carol Gray's Social Stories are used worldwide and are very helpful to all children with social issues.

During a dyad session with Christine and Olivia, in the office, we practice the "Options" technique to reduce their anxiety over their current social difficulties at school.

Problem 1: My friend asks me to come over for a play date. Another friend is standing with me. What do you say?

Options:

A: Say, "Sure, I'll ask my dad to drive me over to your house."

B: Ignore your friend's request and pretend that she didn't ask you.

C: Whisper to your friend that you can't talk now and point to your friend who is standing next to you.

Problem: 2: A boy is teasing me and telling me that I'm dumb.

A: Run away and don't get near that classmate again.

B: Say, "I'm going to tell my teacher!"

C: Say, "I'm angry. I feel hurt when you say things like that!"

Problem 3: My friend is cheating in a game of four-square. What do I say?

A: Run to the teacher and say nothing.
B: Cheat back and say, "I'll get you for that one!"
C: Tell them, "Hey, that's not fair. Let's play this point over again."

Problem 4: My friend wants to steal a toy from the story shelf. What do I say?

A: Say, "No way! That's awful!"
B: Say, "I don't feel good about taking something that doesn't belong to me."
C: Agree to steal one toy with her only.

Over a period of a year, Christine and Olivia generate over fifty social problems and options for the various language scripts or behaviors that they might choose. Many of the social issues seem to be easy to solve, but they both talk about how hard it is to come up with a clear, kind statement to their peer that is organized and helps them feel comfortable. Christine says, "I can't think that fast. Everyone talks so fast! I just can't do it."

Olivia says, "Oh, I just blurt out something to give an answer. I don't care if it is kind. I just say what's on my mind! But, then I get into trouble and my friend walks away!"

After working together for two years on these social problems both in a quiet office setting and at school for one hour a week, they both agree that they now know how to create a good response to their peer when there is a difficult social issue. However, they also know that most of the time, these social scripts are helpful for practicing, but they are not always appropriate in the actual conversation. They now create their own, internally driven responses to social issues.

During our last session on social issues, Christine reports, "I'm thinking of what to say when I talk to my friends. Sometimes I say the wrong thing, but that's okay. Now I have lots of ideas."

During a consultation in a third-grade class at a public school in Massachusetts, I presented the "Options" method to the whole class with the purpose of helping a child with autism and his classmates. The teacher and I worked together to help these children collaborate on various solutions to the social problems they all faced in the classroom. The child with the disability participated at the end of the forty-minute lesson. Not all children with a diagnosis of autism can learn in this inclusive setting, that is, within a class of twenty students. This particular student, the boy in phase two, Patrick, did learn. The teacher presents the concept of "Options" and goes over the technique of defining a problem, finding a "silly" solution first, then a solution that might work, and, finally, a "best" solution. The following dialogue is taken from a transcript from a film clip I recorded in an elementary school classroom with twenty students and the head teacher. We cotaught the lesson. Many children with disabilities, like Patrick, learn in the inclusive classroom setting through peer imitation (Garfinkle and Schwartz, 2002). (Transcript from film clip 1.15.07).

(A=my discourse; T=teacher's discourse; C=class discourse; S=student discourse)

A: When people are too noisy when you're working—is that a general problem for everybody?

C: Yeah.

A: So, the problem is people are too noisy and I can't do my work and concentrate.

C: Yeah.

A: Okay. I bet you can think of some silly options for this one. Let's pick someone new. Rachel?

S: Yell over them.

A: Yell louder than they yell.

C: (Everyone laughs and turns to classmates to giggle)

A: Someone else had his hand up. Yes. (points to a student.)

S: You can say "Be quiet" or "I'm telling!"

A: Okay, how about an option that would be possible, but not the best one to come up with.

S: You could just go (puts finger up to mouth) and say "Shuuuussss"

A: So that's a good idea. . . . but, might make them be more noisy . . .

S: You could write "be quiet" in bubble letters on the board.

A: Now that's a really neat idea. You can go up and write in a bubble "be quiet" on the board. If it were a group of kids, you could turn and say, "Could you please stop talking, I'm trying to concentrate." Maybe your teacher has an idea.

T: One idea that we've talked a lot about this year is that if you were one of the people talking, if you stopped talking so that other people could work, and you were doing your work . . . so if we are taking care of ourselves . . . so we know that we're doing the best thing to be doing, then perhaps other people would learn from you that they need to stop talking.

S: Well, if it's a friend, you can tell them to stop talking.

T: What are some strategies you can use to give them the message?

S: Well, you could ignore them and they would know to stop talking.

T: Jimmy, is there something you want to say about this (problem) of not talking?

S: Give them a glare.

T: Yes, a facial expression.

A: Body language is very important. (The class practices different body language positions to say, "I don't like what you're doing" by role-playing). Gestures help a lot to give some one a message to stop talking. Can anyone think of a time when you've use gestures . . . ?

S: My friend . . . he talks a lot and I just do that (puts his hand up) because he always talks.

A: So you just do this (puts hand up) because he goes on and on and that's not a bad way to do it. (I lean toward the student who has autism) Patrick, have you ever tried to get someone to stop talking?

S: Yep.

A: What do you do?

S: Interrupt.

C: (laughs)

S: No, I don't. I just raise my hand.[10]

Patrick learns how to use his gestures and facial expressions in the particular problems presented in class by watching and listening to this discussion and by watching the role-play with his classmates. The class discusses the use of voice tone and body language to give a classmate a message. The "Options" technique leads the class into a discussion about how the subtle cues (facial expression, voice tone, body language, gestures) of language help create meaning. In most classroom discussions, the students develop their own ideas and bring up problems that are real for them everyday. The strategy of Options is only a guide and a way into this type of discussion. When I use Carol Gray's Social Stories, which is a very similar technique, I find this also happens. The class adapts the method to their needs. The class ends up in a new discussion about some social language skill. The child with autism benefits from watching others practice thinking about social problems and also learns to engage in discussions about subtle language cues (body language, gestures, facial expression).

Helping children think about various ways to respond to social problems is an essential part of the language work in phase three. This practice gives them the confidence to know that there is something they can say when they are anxious and can't immediately organize their thoughts. Christine has had four years in therapy, one year in phase one in individual therapy, one year in phase two in peer therapy in a dyad and two years in therapy with one to two peers in her kindergarten classroom. She is now moving on to phase four, social engagement and the more demanding social constructions of first and second graders.

At this phase three in therapy, some of these children show signs of progressing on a more appropriate developmental path; in fact, their disabilities don't impair their ability to communicate unless they are confronted with a confusing environment.

SUMMARY OF STRATEGIES FOR PHASE THREE

Phase three is illustrated by several children who are moving into a more reciprocal conversation with peers whether they are playing in a "worm box" in a preschool, or watching a sculptor like Erik carve out a polar bear from ice. Each child in this phase moves through the most difficult phase, the phase in therapy when he talks more, uses more spontaneous commenting, and actually has a conversation with others during play interactions.

One child, Elsie, struggles with learning disabilities and her feelings of suicide; she copes with her learning issues through visualization methods and grieves the loss of her dog, Heidi. She uses language to express her emotions, to sort out her own feelings, and to handle her own anger with her classmates. Elsie moves onto phase four because she is able to express herself and her intense emotions to others through language and through her play. Elsie accomplishes more than any therapist might expect from a child with her complex issues and autism.

D.J., a preschooler who loves worms, also begins to use language to express his emotions. At the same time, D.J. recognizes that when he participates in a play interaction, he must be aware of the whole main idea of an event in order to join his classmates. He can't shove them over to see a particular worm; he must talk to them while they share the worm box event. When he smacks his worm into two pieces, he creates a metaphor for the therapist—that a friendship is a partnership and two friends can become separate but "close." A child with autism can learn to be separate, but form a bond with a peer.

The twins, John and Jim, do not move into phase four and remain in phase three. Both boys are using language, but with prompting and relying on scripts that they have memorized or associated with in each situation. The twins' parents are struggling with their behavior at home and are considering a residential placement for them during the week where they will receive continual one-to-one support in a structured setting.

Eddy, the child who learns through sports, begins to grasp the ideas of figurative language and ambiguous terms by relating them to the game of baseball. He learns with visuals and struggles to understand the abstract rules of the game. While Eddy learns in baseball, Jacob learns to practice his tone of voice with play figures and role play on his playground. He also sees that there is a relationship between the loudness of his voice and the distance between himself and his listener.

Christine, the child who is nonverbal and learns to talk playing in snow in phase one, who learns to negotiate over sand castles with her peer Olivia in phase two, learns to write out social problems at school and to solve them with her peer in phase three. Her relationship with Olivia is a lifelong friendship that develops into many years of building sand castles.

Many phase three children move forward to phase four with more reciprocity in an interaction. Whether they are watching ice carvings or worms in a box or participating in baseball where fourth base is called "home," many children with autism move into phase four to become socially engaged. There are some children with autism who remain in phase three and yet, they continue to join and interact in play with one peer. They may not become comfortable interacting on a playground with many peers.

Social Engagement

LANGUAGE, PLAY, AND NARRATIVE

Like a typical child, a phase four child brings a rhythm to movements in his play and talk that creates a special kind of music to the playground, filling it with laughter, drama, and noise. The phase four child is socially engaged and excited about using language in play to express his opinions and feelings. He frequently communicates with facial expressions and eye gaze shifts, both of which are an integral part of his play. Play becomes a medium that allows him to relate to others as he narrates actions in his play. Both a child in phase four and a typical child are constantly moving with several peers, talking to others, and arguing for their own agenda during play. As they plan the agenda of a story theme, they move across a playground with gestures, facial expressions, and language that enhance the meaning of their words. They also use reciprocal language faster than a child in phase three. Language expression, emotion, and telling stories become an integral part of the back and forth exchange in play.

Teaching children with autism to see the interests in another child's *play* and *language* is the main goal of this final phase four of play therapy. A second goal is to teach the child to look for shared interests between both children. A third goal for the therapist is to teach the child to read facial and body language cues and to see the perspective of other peers as they join in story themes in natural settings.

Unlike a typical child, the phase four child is still learning to process the subtle cues of language—gestures, facial expressions, voice tones, and body language—all of which help him make sense of fast-paced social situations. The phase four child who is interacting with more than one peer at a time intermittently needs the therapist's support to read these cues quickly and to respond appropriately.

The therapist's task is to facilitate language within the context of interactions, supporting the child's capacities to use the appropriate timing of comments, to process auditory information accurately, to limit long monologues, to negotiate abstract concepts, and to see shared interests that lead to sustained social relationships.

In addition, the therapist intervenes in most interactions when the child with autism lacks the ability to see the perspective of a peer during play. The therapist teaches perspective taking as a part of the therapy process; this skill is critical to the child's acceptance of another's ideas and direction during play.

The strategies for phase four are illustrated through the relationship between the therapist and some children we have met phase one, two, and/or three. In addition, strategies are illustrated through the therapist's relationship with several new children, including one international child, who are all entering phase four.

4

Social Engagement

HELPING THE CHILD FIT IN

Strategies in this chapter

Strategy 57. Validate and acknowledge a child's feelings by listening attentively when she is disappointed by inappropriate comments from others or feels isolated from peers.

Strategy 58. Join the child in reflecting back on her initial therapy sessions to understand the progress she has made.

Strategy 59. Recognize the child's awareness of not fitting in with a peer group; talk alone with her about new conversation strategies as well as subtle gestures she can use to signal the therapist that she needs help.

Strategy 60. Understand the difficulties and characteristics of the language disabilities that accompany autism and impair a child's social interactions, writing, and perceptual motor skills.

Strategy 57: Validate and Acknowledge a Child's Feelings by Listening Attentively When She is Disappointed by Inappropriate Comments from Others or Feels Isolated from Peers

Even though Elsie, in phase three at age seven, learns to express her own thoughts more consistently, she needs help dealing with her emotions and understanding how her emotional outbursts impact her social engagement with peers. By the end of the second year of therapy, Elsie, now almost nine, is using language to express her emotions. Entering phase four, Elsie is able to articulate her emotions immediately and is willing to be comforted. During art class, Elsie gets frustrated and crumples up her painting.

Her teacher calmly asks, "Elsie do you want another piece of paper or do you want to unfold that one and fix it?" Giving choices seems to work with Elsie. She carefully unfolds the artwork. Her painting is abstract with red and orange lines reflecting off a bright yellow sun.

I ask in a whisper, "Elsie, where is that sun?"

"Oh, it is in my head." she says.

I say, "That's great. Artists carry ideas in their head all the time." She keeps painting. I help Elsie justify her own artistic talent and acknowledge her visual ability that fills her mind with images—a talent needed by an artist.

In another art class the next day, Elsie is working on a small sculpture. She takes her fist and smashes it to a small ball of clay. I look at her teacher. Her facial expression indicates that she is shocked. I smile at her and put up one finger. The teacher knows that I'm signaling that I will manage this reaction.

I say, "Elsie, are you disappointed in what you created?"

"No! I just hate myself! I can't do anything right! I am dumb! I want to kill myself!" she screams as she runs out of the classroom. I follow her toward a tree in the green field. She sobs. I sit with her on a small wooden bench. I say nothing.

She talks to me about the fight she had with her sister that morning before school.

Elsie cries, "She told me that I was dumb and stupid and that I'd never get out of a special school."

I listen. I don't give her scripts to say to her sister.

She cries, "I am really hurt by her comments! I am really mad at her! I am going to tell her right when I get home! My sister has no right! She doesn't know how hard it is for me to talk to anyone. She doesn't get it! I am mad, mad, mad!"

I answer, "I know you're angry. It's okay to be angry." We watch a big bumblebee land on a white morning glory on a vine that twists around the white fence railing in the field. She watches the bee as we sit together, silent for ten minutes.

She says, "She must be searching for honey. She needs to go over there where there are more flowers."

"Yes. Are you okay?" I ask.

"Yes. I'm okay. You didn't leave me," she says.

"I'm here. I'm not going anywhere," I say.

A therapist's calm presence can help a child feel less lonely, even when she's angry. Children with Asperger's often feel that anger isn't a good emotion to feel. When they sense that the therapist respects and acknowledges their anger, they are relieved. It is in this place of joining that a "magic" transformation happens—the loneliness is replaced with a desire to be present in the moment. Exactly why this happens is a mystery. The timing of the therapist's silence is crucial to the child's feeling of comfort. The therapist needs to be aware of the child's facial expression, body language, and voice tone that communicate the degree of discomfort. Unfortunately, the child with Asperger's in phase three may not show these subtle language cues that relate to emotions; the therapist has to rely on intuition and experience to know when to offer encouragement and advice as I did with Elsie's mouse and when Elsie smashed her art project (see next strategy 58). A child in phase three is less likely to express her emotions and is also less able to accept a therapist's suggestions than is a child in phase four who may even ask for advice or comfort. Children feel their self-worth and see that understanding and expressing anger are important. Children with autism need a therapist to accompany them in this process.

Strategy 58: Join the Child in Reflecting Back on Her Initial Therapy Sessions to Understand the Progress She Has Made

In phase four, Elsie is willing to talk about her feelings in the past and in the present and reflect on how she made the transformation to a more content young person; her emotions and language are an integral part of her communication with others. She no longer blames herself for becoming angry. Her anger is an emotion that she can control and express with words.

One morning in an individual session after several months of therapy, Elsie sits quietly and looks out the school office window where we work.

"Elsie, what are you thinking?" I ask.

"Oh, I'm remembering when I was so angry in art," she says.

"Elsie, why did you smash your art projects?"

"Because I thought I was a bad person."

"A bad person? Why?"

"Oh, because I thought that my friends hated me and laughed at me. I thought my work was dumb!"

"How did you change? You're proud of your work now."

"Well, I believed that you really liked my art work."

"How did you know I really did?"

"Because you took time looking at me as I did my work. You saw the tiny things I saw. You saw my feelings as I worked on a project. I knew that. It really helped me stay focused on my work."

"Really?"

"Yep. Remember when you liked the nose on the clay mouse I made?"

"Yes."

"You said that the face of the mouse was so real that you wanted to run and hide!"

"Yes."

"I laughed at you. That felt good. You really liked my mouse. You thought it was real. I felt like an artist. Then, I didn't feel so lonely. I didn't want to die."

"You are an artist."

"I know. But, I didn't think I was anything then. I hated myself and whatever I made in clay. I smashed every project, tore up papers, and I even screamed at everyone."

"Remember that clay flower I smashed?" she says as she moves closer to me.

"Yes."

"Here, I made you another one for you. It's a flower. You can keep it."

Elsie hands me a clay flower and uses her fingers to pretend that she is a bee seeking honey.

Strategy 59: Recognize the Child's Awareness of Not Fitting in with a Peer Group; Talk Alone with Her about New Conversation Strategies As Well As Subtle Gestures She Can Use to Signal the Therapist that She Needs Help

Children in phase four talk and negotiate with vigor but are anxious about the mistakes they make in conversation. Any comment made by a therapist may be perceived as critical. One way to avoid offending or embarrassing a child is to make suggestions subtly and then talk to the child about the social problem away from the group. After a difficult social situation is over, the child and the therapist can meet alone to discuss some ideas about reentering the group of classmates. This activity helps the child organize her thoughts and gives her a place to practice using language that will allow her to fit in the group of classmates.

Anna, age nine, is a third grader at a private school in New York. I am visiting the school as a consultant. She is reading at her classroom desk and looks up through her round, green-rimmed glasses. She pushes her short blond hair back and flips it behind her ears.

"You know, no one likes me. Some days I feel like I want to just be dead. But, I don't really. It's okay to play alone. I like to play alone," she reports to me.

Anna suddenly twirls and spins on her toes across the room. She stops and looks at me and says, "Turn the key and watch me dance. Abigail wants to watch me dance." Abigail, another student, sits at her desk reading, ignoring Anna. I make a slight turn motion with my hand, wondering what she is getting at. Anna twirls around like a robot. Her classmates laugh and look at me.

Abigail says, "Oh, Mrs. Burns doesn't want us to dance in class." Anna keeps turning.

I watch Anna's face as she looks at the light streaming through the window over the tree-lined brick patio. As she twirls, the light reflects off the glass windowpanes and creates rainbows on the classroom walls. I realize that Anna is stuck on a visual image and can't change her focus. She creates a whole story.

"Abby, turn the pretend key in my back so that I can dance!" she says. Her classmate keeps reading. I motion to her to move outside of the class into the hallway where we can talk privately.

I say, "Anna, your friends can't talk to you if you're dancing. Let's get a drink of water and talk."

We walk out into the hallway. I say, "Your friends are still eating lunch. If you read, you won't be able to talk to your friends." Anna reads to avoid peers.

Anna says, "I know, but they don't want to talk to me anyway."

Anna walks back to her desk, sits down, and pulls out a book. Abigail turns to talk to two classmates next to her and ignores Anna. Anna begins to read. I watch her for a moment and sit next to her. She looks up at Abigail. I say nothing.

I say, "Let's go in the hallway and talk."

We return to the drinking fountain.

"How do I get Abigail to notice me?" she asks.

"Lets figure this out. What do you think you could do?"

"Well, I could say, 'Hey I'm here!'"

"Yes. What else?"

"Well, I could ask her what's she reading?

"Yes. That's a start. Try it. I like your idea."

"Okay," she says with hesitation. Anna walks into class, taps Abigail on the shoulder and asks, "What are you reading? Oh, that's a great book!"

Anna turns to me and smiles.

Abigail smiles at Anna saying, "Oh, you read this? It is a great book! What was your favorite part?"

Anna responds immediately, "I like the part when the king announces his marriage to a princess."

Their conversation goes on for over five minutes about the book.

Children with autism need continual support to sustain an interaction and practice initiating many conversations until they are comfortable developing a close relationship with a peer. During this subtle phase of using language to connect to peers, the therapist needs to listen to the child's conversation, and give her support when needed. The phase four child can also cue the therapist when she needs help. She may look over at the therapist or smile or even walk over to the therapist. These cues need to be discussed before the child is in the interaction. This strategy of using a gesture to signal a therapist for help also helps a child feel safe when she is experimenting with new conversation.

Strategy 60: Understand the Difficulties and Characteristics of the Language Disabilities that Accompany Autism and Impair a Child's Social Interactions, Writing, and Perceptual Motor Skills

Anna's class consists of eight seven- and eight-year-olds who are busy talking back and forth at a rapid pace with a complex vocabulary. Anna is usually not aware of the conversation rate or the content. She prefers her own world of reading books, and dancing to light rainbows on the walls of her classroom. Anna has a diagnosis of Non-Verbal Learning Disability (NVLD), a language disorder that is placed on the spectrum of autism by some neuropsychologists and not by others.[1] Some children with this disorder cannot read social cues, gestures, or facial expressions; they also cannot process the humorous side of language. In addition, peers' layers of responses and the quick timing of comments they make to each other confuse them.

In contrast to the Asperger's child who usually writes well, has excellent fine motor skills, and is able to engage in motor activities moderately well, an NVLD child has trouble with gross motor movements as well as fine motor movements that affect writing. Spatial problems and visual-perceptual difficulties are also typical in the NVLD child. The term "nonverbal" includes communication that supports expressive language such as gesture, facial expression, and body posture. It also includes understanding the appropriate distance between the speaker and the listener. Children who carry a diagnosis of either Asperger's Syndrome or NVLD, may have particular characteristics that may differentiate them from these labels or these groups of disabilities. For this reason, the intervention must be customized and planned for the particular child in treatment. The therapist takes time to develop a trusting relationship with the child and then plans intervention.

Anna, for example, confuses ambiguous terms, figurative language, and language that is abstract, all difficulties that a child with Asperger's faces. What differentiates her NVLD diagnosis from Asperger's is a fine line. Anna talks constantly and her expressive language is complex. She has difficulty with fine motor skills and her writing and drawing is developmentally delayed. She also has balance issues and problems with gross motor activities. Anna doesn't recognize faces that should be familiar to her and dislikes anything novel or different. The combination of having difficulty running as fast as her peers, writing as well, and keeping up with her third-grade peers' jokes places Anna at risk for social problems in school. The particular social difficulties are often invisible to most teachers and even some parents. Teachers and parents do see that a child with NVLD or Asperger's takes words literally.

Despite this diagnosis, Anna is extremely bright; she reads two years above her grade level, has a memory for detail above her grade level, and loves to sing, dance, and perform in dramatic presentations. She is a talented young girl who just doesn't fit in socially. Anna makes inappropriate social remarks that embarrass her family. Sometimes she has difficulty transitioning from one activity to another because she has visual-spatial disturbances and cannot predict the sequence of directions.

LIMITING A CHILD'S MONOLOGUES AND ENCOURAGING LISTENING

Additional strategies for this chapter

Strategy 61. Join the child at lunchtime or recess time to help her practice social skills with peers by introducing simple, concrete conversation topics.

Strategy 62. Stay close with the child on the playground; as she interacts with her classmates, function as both a "peer" and a conversation "coach" and then fade back to observe.

Strategy 63. Model language facilitation for specialists and teachers by joining the child, making comments, and using gestures as needed in an outside situation.

Strategy 64. Practice with the child with autism and one peer the technique of using an "A B C Conversation" to limit monologues and help her to respond with relevant conversation.

Strategy 61: Join the Child at Lunchtime or Recess Time to Help Her Practice Social Skills with Peers by Introducing Simple, Concrete Conversation Topics

I join Anna during lunchtime with the goal of facilitating one conversation between her and a peer that is beyond the simple requesting and two to three vocal turns in an interaction. During lunch at Anna's school, each student sits at his/her desk. Four desks are placed together so that the four children who face each other can talk. After listening to the children's conversation, I suggested talking about a subject that is something that Anna can handle and talk about easily. Even though I know that Anna can handle complex information, I want to create a social conversation that is simple at first.

"Anna, Adrian has a peanut butter and raisin and celery sandwich! Wow!" I say.

Adrian smiles at me.

I say, "I think I'd like to make one of those when I get home." The three children at the desks near Anna smile at me.

Anna finally makes a comment, "I love P&J. Look, I have a sandwich with jam and peanut butter." She holds up her sandwich. Anna's statement makes an initial connection to a classmate. The conversation is simple, concrete, and very direct. Anna uses eye contact, takes turns, and enjoys her brief exchange. This is a start.

Strategy 62: Stay Close with the Child on the Playground; as She Interacts with Her Classmates, Function as Both a "Peer" and a Conversation "Coach" and then Fade Back to Observe

It is recess time. Children are running fast, climbing play structures, moving across the sand, hanging by a trolley bar, and jumping off high bars. Anna slowly walks over to a ladder, climbs up, and sits on the top bar. Her classmates are moving underneath her, swinging from rung to rung across the bars, not noticing Anna above. She smiles down at them.

Abigail comes up to me and asks, "Wanna play tag? I am real fast."

I smile back and say, "Sure, but let's ask Anna too."

Anna says, "Nope, I can't run that fast. And I don't want to be it." I reach out my hand to Anna. Abigail is watching.

"Anna, why don't you and I become one team and try to tag Abigail. We can run together!"

Anna smiles and says, "Okay."

Suddenly, Abigail taps me on the shoulder and yells, "You're it!"

I take Anna's hand and we run together. She starts to smile and then laughs hard when she realizes that we have an advantage: we can trap Abigail from both sides of a play area. She gets the idea and runs as fast as Abigail through the bushes, up the slide, around the sand area, and tags her. I fade back and allow Anna to be in her own game with her peers.

She turns to me and says, "Did you see that?"

"Yes, I saw you run fast! You are quick!" I say.

"Yep, I can run when I want to!" says Anna. She grins at me.

As I'm leaving, Anna runs up to me and grabs my arm, pulling me toward the slide.

Then she picks up a ball and asks, "Come on and catch it and throw it to me one more time, please. Please." I catch the ball, and toss it to her.

Abigail comes running up to me and says, "Ann, come and play with us again!"

I say, "Of course!"

As I write my notes about our work on the playground, I think about Anna's smile, her laughter, and her need to be a part of the whole, the world of play at recess. Anna wants to be a part of her peer group. She immediately takes my suggestions and tries them out with her peers. She is willing to risk failing and she's willing to ask questions about her social interactions.

Strategy 63: Model Language Facilitation for Specialists and Teachers by Joining the Child, Making Comments, and Using Gestures as Needed in an Outside Situation

I work with Anna at her school once a week for another year. I run across the playground, encouraging Anna to connect with her peers. I use visual scripts and cue her about what she might say to a peer. I draw social stories with her each week and talk to her about what she is learning. She learns to look at a peer, to make a comment, and to join a peer in short conversations. But the real work is to help her make a best friend so she can experience the relationship of a pal who sticks by her, who watches her, and who wants to be with her in a social group. The hardest part of this work is to help

Anna see how another child really feels. Her teachers ask me each week, "Ann, how do you get Anna to understand her friends? She doesn't seem to get it. She is so left out."

I answer, "Watch me on the playground and try to follow me. I can't tell you as well as I can show you."

I run and the teacher runs with me. I follow Anna across the playground to the trolley. A peer jumps up ahead of Anna and grabs the trolley handle. She swings across to the other side. I prompt Anna with a gesture and smile at her, pointing to the other child. She knows what I want and yells at her classmate, "Hey, wait for me!"

I help her grab the handle of the trolley and she swings across. Her peer, Susan, runs fast and goes on to the high structure, climbing above the sand. Anna looks back at me. I nod to tell Anna to follow Susan. She says again, "Hey, wait for me!" Susan turns and looks at Anna. "Up here, Anna!" she says.

Anna smiles and climbs up. I follow them and sit on the top bars with them. The teacher stands below. I wait. Anna looks at me.

She initiates the conversation, "Hey, let's pretend that we are in a school of wizardry, like Hogwarts, and we are about to fly on a broomstick!!"

"Okay, that's an idea!" her classmate responds. Susan motions for Anna to follow her. Anna sees the gesture and hears the response. They both run across the top bars and I swing down to follow them underneath the bars. They shoot down the ladder and toward the slide embedded in the wooden play yard structure. They jump up and sit down at the top. Anna goes first as she twists and turns down the fast slide into the lower section of the wooden structure. She winks at me as she flies by me. I know she is proud of her work with a physical therapist. Anna needed help with upper body strength and agility so that she could grab a bar and swing fast. The metal sides of the slide glisten in the morning sun. I see Anna watch the sun's reflection on the slide, but she keeps on sliding. She knows the value of keeping up with her friend. It is more important to her now than watching a reflection. I use my arm in a gesture that means to follow me. She imitates the motion and turns toward her friend. Her friend follows her. They run across the play area. Anna turns toward me and smiles.

The teacher turns toward me and says, "I see you give her gestures and comments in the middle of the running. That is a trick! How do you do this work? Aren't you exhausted?"

"I just keep running and talking!" I say to the teacher. "This is the best way for Anna to learn to relate to a peer. Over time she will do it naturally. Just wait a few more months!"

"Okay, I'll try it. Run and talk and watch her and give her gestures and suggestions for conversation and stay with her all the time until she is doing it alone. Right?"

"Yes. And don't give up. Keep helping her. She may look as though she's engaged. Observe carefully to make sure she is really connected and using relevant comments and having fun. Her laughter will tell you how she's doing. Read her facial expressions. Her body language will also tell you how she's doing and how you're doing as her play coach. If she's sitting alone on top of the bars too long, you'll know. She's the barometer. Join her, follow every movement she makes, do what she does—grab bars, swing up, and climb high. Remember to always listen to her and her peers, watch her, and respond. That's all."

Anna's teacher smiles and says, "I think I'd better start by practicing myself. Could you help me climb up on the bars?" We laugh together.

Now in phase four, Anna immediately sees the therapist's role as only "a supportive coach" to call into action when she has difficulty with the interactions that are confusing or difficult.

Strategy 64: Practice with the Child with Autism and One Peer the Technique of Using an "A B C Conversation" to Limit Monologues and Help Her to Respond with Relevant Conversation

When children with autism communicate with complex language, adults feel that these children can automatically understand when to use simple, short responses to a question and when to use more detailed descriptions or when to use a monologue. This conclusion is not always the correct assumption to make. Children with autism, particularly with Asperger's, prefer to give long descriptions in a conversation, but as they exercise this right to monologue, they miss the quick back and forth exchange of ideas with another. Conversations don't build into a mutual understanding about a subject and instead the interchange is one sided with the Asperger's child speaking as an "expert" about details and the peer listening, sharing limited comments.

Nathaniel and Ethan, both ten years olds with a diagnosis of Asperger's, practice social language in a dyad speech session in my office once a week. In most contexts their difficulties do not surface; they use complex language, speak in compound sentences, and use the basic pragmatics skills of taking turns, sharing ideas, planning with a peer, and creating narratives with others. However, they feel confused when their peers are talking at a fast pace and use figurative language or jokes. They avoid these interactions either by leaving or by using monologues to substitute for reciprocal language and social engagement.

I work with both boys on the basic review of speech pragmatics skills in this social dyad for one year. After the two boys spend a year, once a week for one hour in a dyad, working on turn-taking, listening, and timing a response, using greetings and exiting conversation, and responding with eye contact to their peer, they are ready for the A B C Conversation practice that helps them determine when to use (A) a short conversation, (B) a simple response to a question or (C) or a more detailed explanation. Intellectually they both know that they need to limit their longer, more complex answers that turn into monologues about their favorite subjects. I give them a visual cue card that presents a simple explanation of the three types of responses that might be appropriate in particular situations. I explain each type by role playing. The boys listen.

"Sometimes I want to talk about my favorite subjects, like how to make Vermont maple syrup and I know that my friend is bored. I'm telling him too much detail. He looks at me and I know he wants me to stop. If my friend asks me to talk about Vermont maple syrup I can tell him a long monologue and it would be a "C" conversation—one that involves a long response. But, if my friend just passes me by and asks, "How are you?" I know that he'd want me to give him an "A" conversation that is short like, "I'm fine." He doesn't really at that moment want to understand my whole health history. Sometimes he might ask me to explain how to get to a certain hobby store to buy paper airplanes. I can tell him that because I live near that hobby shop. I can give him a "B" conversation that is long enough to explain how to get there, but not so long that I explain every detail of what I see along the road when I ride my bike there. I will carry my three cards in my pocket to remind myself whether I should choose an A or a B or a C conversation when my friends ask me questions."

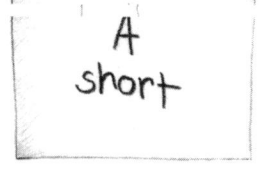 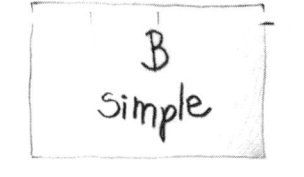 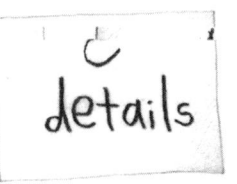

A
short

B
simple

C
details

During a practice session with Nathaniel and Ethan, I review the "ABC Conversation" technique and they make the three cards.

I ask, "Nathaniel, give me a situation when you are asked a question and when you know that the person wants you to tell them a long, long story about something with details."

"Well, if my dad wants to know everything I know about space and the astronauts, I can give him a long, detailed story. But, I remember to ask him first, like you teach us in practice."

"Okay, Ethan, when would you give someone a short answer?"

"Well, when the doorman of a hotel asks, 'How are you?'"

"Right!"

"Nathaniel, can you give me one situation?"

"Yeah, when my friends ask, "How are you doing?"

"Right. You answer, 'Fine thank you.'"

"Yes, but I really want to tell them all that I know about NASCAR car races!"

"You don't do that. Right? How do you control yourself when you really want to talk about that subject?"

"Well, I remember our practice and I see that big "A" in my mind that reminds me to keep it short."

"Does that help you Ethan?"

"No. I forget and I keep talking. But, I see how tired my friend gets. Then I know to quit."

"Is there anyway that you can remember sooner?"

"Yes. I'll practice."

Nathaniel and Ethan practice creating several dialogues about social encounters at school. They have written over fifty social situations when they need to monitor their ideas and think about what kind of response to give to each situation. They have excellent memories and can often remember how to respond; they also carry a small A B C card in their pockets or backpacks that reminds them when to limit their conversation and when it is okay to describe something in detail.

Since Nathaniel and Ethan are ten years old, I teach them these strategies directly with visuals and practice. Five-year-old Luka, a child with Asperger's, also uses monologues instead of reciprocal language. He needs to be reminded with a more direct reinforcement strategy. Each day Luka's teacher gives him five small cards with the word "ticket" written on it and a photograph of a train. He can use a train ticket to talk about trains. When he gives his ticket to his teacher, specialist, or peer, he can speak about his favorite subject. However, once he has used up the five tickets, he can't talk about trains for the rest of the day.

CREATING VISUALS TO REDIRECT REPETITIVE THOUGHTS

Additional strategies for this chapter

Strategy 65. Through role-play and visuals, practice listening for "Key Words" with the child and one peer.

Strategy 66. Create small books with photographs and/or the child's drawings; add dictated writings (child tells the therapist what she needs to write underneath the photo/drawing) to help the child redirect and eliminate invading thoughts about unrelated subjects.

Strategy 67. Develop visual materials to preteach a child about the sequence of an event or field trip; use these materials later to develop a narrative about the trip.

Strategy 68. Help the child watch others interact on the playground by pointing out the peers' behaviors in the interactions; later create drawings with the child to talk about how to read subtle language cues such as facial expression, gestures, and body language.

Strategy 69. Teach the child about a peer's perspective in an angry interaction by creating a visual list of the peer's feelings as well as the child's feelings.

Strategy 70. Teach the child with autism to interpret a peer's discomfort and pain by comparing the painful or sensitive situation to the child's feeling in a similar incident.

Strategy 65: Through Role-Play and Visuals, Practice Listening for "Key Words" with the Child and One Peer

Nicky, an eleven-year-old boy with autism, comes to a dyad language session to practice his social skills with Chad, a classmate who attends Nicky's school. Chad is a typical ten-year-old who loves to talk and who doesn't have any language or learning issues. He enjoys playing with Nicky at home and at school and his parents agree that he can accompany Nicky to his social language session each week.

Both boys are wearing winter boots, parkas, snow pants, and a ski hat. They throw their hats off onto the floor and sit down to pull of their boots. They look at each other and laugh as they both struggle to get their big boots off. They practice the initial greeting of "Hi, how are you?" and the other child answers and returns the same question. They walk to the table where we begin our first conversation about what they both did during the week.

Nicky asks, "Chad, what did you do last weekend?

Chad replies, "I went to Vermont with my dad!"

I use this opportunity to ask Nicky to practice his "Key Words" strategy. I pull out our practice cards.

I say, "Let's practice key words today! Nicky, what are the key words in Chad's statement?"

Nicky responds, "Well, Vermont and he went there."

I say, "Okay, that's right. The key words are 'I went' and 'Vermont.' Dad could be a key word too."

"Right."

"So, now what could you ask Chad about his trip?"

Nicky looks at Chad and says, "What did you do there?"

Chad responds, "Oh, I went skiing."

I say, "Key Words, Nicky?"

Nicky says, "Vermont," "Dad," and "skiing."

I say, "Nicky, try to draw something that reminds you of those three words.

Nicky says, "Okay." He draws a picture of the Vermont mountains, a pair of skis, and his dad.

I say, "Now you know that he went to Vermont with his dad and went skiing. There are many ways you could respond back to him. I can think of three ways: You could ask a question. You could compliment Chad or make a comment about either Vermont or skiing. What do you think?"

Nicky says, "Oh, yeah I get this."

I say, "Now remember to stop your thought and think about your response before you say anything back."

Nicky says, "I bet you're a good skier!"

Chad smiles and says, "Yes! Can I tell you about this big mogul I skied?"

"I remind Nicky, "Key Words. Think of them."

Nicky looks at me and says, "Big" and "mogul."

I say, "Right!"

Nicky looks at Chad and says, "Wow! I bet you had to jump it! What happened?"

Their conversation about skiing continues on for over five minutes. Nicky is pleased and smiles at me, holding his thumb up as if to say, "I get this!"

Many children with autism need the practice with one peer first and then in a group of peers in a less structured situation. They can learn to see not only another child's perspective, but also the key words in their statements, enabling them to respond with relevant comments or questions. With this practice, they can become one of the group and sustain a conversation.

Strategy 66: Create Small Books with Photographs and/or the Child's Drawings; Add Dictated Writings (Child Tells the Therapist What She Needs to Write Underneath the Photo/Drawing) to Help the Child Redirect and Eliminate Invading Thoughts about Unrelated Subjects

Abby, an eight-year-old with Asperger's, loves to talk about any subject that has details and numbers. Fascinated by the subject of space and space shuttles, she hopes to be an astronaut one day. I have seen Abby in a weekly, hour-long session to help her with social problems, and to help her with the invading thoughts that interfere with her ability to interact with peers. She loves her friends but becomes easily agitated when she can't concentrate on her own ideas that relate to her peers; instead she focuses on some irrelevant subject that invades her mind. She has a secondary diagnosis of Obsessive Compulsive Disorder (OCD) and is on medication for this condition. Despite the medication, Abby still is plagued by these thoughts and wants to be able to calm herself and make these thoughts leave her mind. For example, when her peers want to talk about who is the cutest boy in class, her mind wanders to the subject of a space shuttle and how many flights the U.S. astronauts have taken this decade. She drops out of the conversation and jeopardizes her connection with her peers. Practicing the skills that help her redirect her thoughts in a calm, supportive setting helps Abby feel confident that she can control her thoughts.

"Abby, what's happening this week?" I ask.

"Oh, I want to be on the soccer team at recess and my friends ignore me. They are avoiding me. I don't know why!" she cries.

"Well, let's figure out what happened in one conversation."

"Yeah. Well, I'm talking to Bethany and she is talking fast. She wants to be the leader of the soccer team and tell everyone what to do. I need to listen and to follow her so I can stand up for myself."

"Okay, what do you say?"

"It doesn't matter what I say, she won't listen to me. When she ignores me, I start thinking about space and other things and I can't keep my argument going!"

"That's so hard."

"Yes, it's awful!"

"So, let's take a photo of you talking to your friend, Bethany. Then, in my office, you can practice and role-play a conversation with her; you can experiment with ways to control your own thoughts. First, let's talk about those thoughts and then write them down on paper."

Abby talks about her thoughts. "Let's see. Hmmm. I can see the new space elevator that will orbit the earth 300 miles above the earth's atmosphere, tethered and sliding along twisted carbon nanotube fibers that are light as a feather and stronger than steel. I can see it. Imagine! It's a 66,000 mile-long cable to take people for hundreds of miles into space. I can't get it out of my mind."

Abby writes down her thoughts:

Twisted carbon nanotube fibers

Sliding in space

300 miles above the earth

A new space elevator tethered

Abby draws a small picture of the space elevator tethered along carbon nanotube fibers. She crumples it up and puts it in a box that I keep in my office just for Abby. Abby knows that writing down these thoughts makes them less intense. She's making them an object that exists outside of herself and that she can control rather than be controlled by.

I give Abby a small Polaroid camera to take to school. She takes pictures of her friends at recess and asks one friend to take a photo of her with Bethany. Her teacher even takes photos of Abby with her friends playing soccer. At the next speech session, Abby brings the photos and places them carefully on a table in front of me.

"Bethany looks just like you!" I say.

"Yes. We are alike, but she doesn't have those thoughts!"

"I know. But, that's not her struggle. She probably has other ones."

"Right."

"Okay, now put this photo of you and Bethany in a small photo book that can fit in your pocket. We'll add to the book as we create more social situations with other friends."

"But, what do I do?"

"When you feel those invading thoughts get into your head, pull out the photo and look at the picture of you and Bethany. See if it works."

After four weeks of writing down the thoughts about space and practicing with the photo book both in the office setting and outside at recess, Abby has the social situation under control. She leaves her small photo book on her desk at school and no longer carries it around. Her peers love to look at their pictures. After one year of therapy, Abby is now only occasionally plagued by invasive thoughts.

Maggie, a young first grader with autism, also struggles with obsessive thinking; however she is only six and is unable to write long sentences about her ideas. We divide an 8×10 inch piece of paper into fours and on each square she draws a picture that describes a social situation that she needs to be part of in order to connect with peers. We create a small book together from these four pages. She dictates to me and I write the text of her book. Maggie is good at drawing, as many children with autism are, and she draws the concepts in each section. The goal is for Maggie to visually see what she is doing physically in a real-life social situation. In addition, we draw another small four-page book about the repetitive thoughts in her mind that interfere with her focus on the reality of the situation. Maggie continues to draw and dictate to me both the reality of a situation and the unreal thoughts about it. We talk about how they are different and how hard it is to think about the real situation.

Sometimes a child with autism will hold onto an old video in his mind for days, weeks, even months. One child, Sage, a six-year-old with high-functioning autism, was in school and he wanted to go out for recess. The teacher said that is was too cold that day and the class was not going out for recess.

He immediately responded with a comment, "If you're going to do that, I'll slug you!" He put up his fist and waved it at his teacher.

His teacher heard the remark and reprimanded Sage for talking back to her and said, "Sage, you are going to see the principal."

Sage, confused and crying, walked to the door. He was accompanied by his assistant teacher to the principal's office.

In social skills group, Sage talked with me about this incident. Once a week, I went to his school and facilitated language for a small group at lunchtime.

I asked him, "Sage, were you thinking of a video when you got mad at your teacher, today?"

He giggled and put up his fist and said," If you're going to hold my hand, I'll slug you!"

I asked, "Sage, who are you?"

He giggled again and said, "I'm Sally in Charlie Brown!"

"Sage, what was Sally doing in Charlie Brown?" I asked.

"She was talking to Linus," he answered.

"What was Linus doing?" I inquired.

"He was pouting," he said.

"Why?" I asked.

"Because he wanted to hold Sally's hand and she said she would hit him if he did," he said.

"What did Sally say?" I asked again to be sure that he understood what Sally said.

"If you hold my hand, I'm going to slug you!" Sage giggled again and put up his fist.

"Sage is that what you were thinking about when your teacher said that you could not go to recess?" I asked.

"Yes, I was mad. I was mad like Sally!" Sage looked serious.

"Sage what might be a better way to talk with your teacher? She's not Linus. She's not in the video. Were you in your inside thoughts?" I said.

"Yes. I forgot to tell those inside thoughts to go away. I couldn't help it!"

"Okay, try to remember next time. When you feel angry, be sure that you are not in your inside thoughts."

"Okay." Sage smiled. He understood the difference between being in an unreal or pretend role in a story in his head and responding to a real-life situation as the person, Sage.

I developed a visual technique to assist a child with autism who has invading thoughts called "Inside thoughts/Outside thoughts." This is a simple visual technique: use a 3 × 5 inch card with the words "inside thought" on one side and "outside thoughts" on the other side.

Place the card in the middle of the table or near the child on the floor and explain how everyone has both kinds of thoughts. Some children understand the word "inside" if they are told that it is like "daydreaming." Ask them for examples. A child with autism will explain inside thoughts as "streaming videos" of movies, or Disney characters dancing, or trains running on tracks, or revolutionary war figures in battle or a super hero rescuing someone or pretend stories. Once the child sees these as "things" in his mind, he can talk about them, and then practice strategies to shift to his outside thoughts. I define "outside thoughts" as thinking about what is happening in the present—thinking about what a person is saying at that moment or what a person is doing or what event is taking place at that time. The child needs examples to help him define the places and the actions of people in the real-world environment. The therapist can help the child create a list of what are inside thoughts and outside thoughts. Once the child watches the actions of others and talks about those actions, he understands how "outside thoughts" can be differentiated from "inside thoughts."

In addition, the therapist needs to ask the child when it is a good time or a "not so good" time to be listening to and watching inside thoughts. One child said, "Oh, I can't have inside thoughts when my teacher is teaching at circle. I can't hear her because I'm too busy!" He learned instead to make a shift to his outside thoughts by using the strategy of asking himself (self-talk) a question: What is my teacher saying? This simple change in thought process kept him more focused and he learned to monitor his own thoughts. A young child can ask: What is my teacher doing? By listening to the teacher talking or by watching her actions, a child may be able to shift into the outside thoughts, to what is happening at the moment and limit the invading inside thoughts. This method is helpful to some children.

Strategy 67: Develop Visual Materials to Preteach a Child about the Sequence of an Event or Field Trip; Use These Materials Later to Develop a Narrative about the Trip

One morning in class Maggie gets "stuck" talking about balloons and all the colors of balloons during circle time in class. She can't concentrate on what her teacher is saying about a scheduled field trip. I bring her to a small speech office at her school and we begin by drawing balloons—her invasive thoughts. She talks about them and then gives the drawings to me. She watches me as I place them in my briefcase. Then, we make a second book—the class field trip to an apple orchard. Maggie draws pictures about her trip on the four sections of an 8 × 10 piece of paper that is folded twice. We number each drawing of the upcoming field trip to make the sequence clear.

We read and look at this book both before and after the field trip.

Maggie points to the first drawing, "First, we're going to get on the bus to go to the farm. Then, second, we'll get out of the bus and line up. Our teachers will give us apple bags and then we walk into the apple orchard and look at the trees. Then, we pick apples that are close to us, ones we can reach. Then, third, we put them in our bag. Fourth, after we have lunch at the orchard, we go back to our bus. The bus takes us to school." As she talks, I write her words beneath the appropriate drawings.

"I've made a whole story! Look, it's like a real book!" Maggie says as she smiles.

"Yes, we can laminate it and put in on a ring and you can take it home."

"I love it. I wrote a story!"

These techniques of using visual books and individual photos are helpful to a child with autism. In addition, they help a child redirect her thoughts to what is happening at the moment. Maggie keeps her book by her bed in a box where she keeps all forty of her stories. The stories come from our conversations about what she does at school, at home, on play dates, and special events. Maggie's siblings love these books because they can use them to help their sister and share her life with them.

The small books also provide an opportunity to draw and to talk about abstract ideas. They are also motivators to the child who loves to show her work to others.

Strategy 68: Help the Child Watch Others Interact on the Playground by Pointing Out the Peers' Behaviors in the Interactions; Later Create Drawings with the Child to Talk about How to Read Subtle Language Cues Such as Facial Expression, Gestures, and Body Language

Christine, the child who had no language at age four and made her first contact with me when she tried to lift me out of the powder snow in phase one, is now age eight. She uses language to discuss her own ideas with peers and with some support retells past events. She is learning to talk about more abstract ideas that are hard for her to grasp when she first hears them in a social conversation; however, even in phase four it is difficult for Christine to draw inferences from people's subtle gestures used in conversation.

During school recess, I guide Christine as she watches two boys practice batting on the baseball diamond. The boys, Ricky and Danny, end up fighting over who is going to bat first. The school coach comes out on the field and takes the bat away from the boys. In order to use the situation to help Christine with her inferencing skills, I bring out a piece of paper and a marker to the field. We sit down on the baseball bench to talk. I draw the two boys with the bat between them. Christine starts to giggle.

I ask, "Christine, what do the think Ricky and Danny are feeling?"

"I don't know."

"Did you see their body language?

"Yes, Ricky slapped his hands down on his legs and Danny pouted like I do sometimes."

"What does that tell you?"

"They were both upset."

"Right." I draw a circle with a child's face that is sad.

"Why do you think that they were upset?"

"Because they just were mad at the teacher!"

"Why?"

"Because she's a dumb teacher."

"Why?"

"Well, she was dumb to take the bat away."

"Well, why do you think the boys felt upset?"

"Because they wanted to have the bat."

"Right. But, why did they want the bat?" I draw a picture of the bat and a baseball diamond and two boys on the diamond.

"Oh, they want to keep the bat so they could keep playing!"

"Yes, and they feel sad, disappointed, and angry."

"Yes they do. They both look down at the ground and they kind of growl at each other."

Christine sees the gestures and body language that match the boy's feelings and at the same time recognizes the causal link; the reason they are sad and angry is that they want to continue playing and not because the teacher is "dumb." Children need visuals and time to process information in order to draw inferences from social situations, particularly when the situation is not as clear as this one.

Strategy 69: Teach the Child about a Peer's Perspective in an Angry Interaction by Creating a Visual List of the Peer's Feelings As Well As the Child's Feelings

In another situation, Christine wants to keep Olivia's three-year-old brother, Jeremy, from using a big green marker to draw on her artwork while she's creating a picture.

She yells, "Get away!" and then feels bad that she exploded. Jeremy cries and goes to his sister, Olivia. Though Christine knows that she has a reason to be upset that Jeremy was about to draw on her picture, she is confused by the fact that he doesn't understand that her artwork is "hers" and not "his." She doesn't understand why he cries and runs to Olivia. Christine feels that she is the only person who should be crying at the moment.

We create a small book of drawings of Jeremy with his marker and her paper. Then we talk about his feelings and why he felt so upset. The first drawing is of Jeremy with big tears falling down his face. The next drawing is of Jeremy with his hand covering his face. The third drawing is of Christine with tears falling down her face into her lap. I acknowledge her feelings and her understanding about how Jeremy felt.

"Christine, it's okay to feel angry."

"Yes, I know, but I feel awful."

"It's okay to feel angry. That's okay. Did you see how Jeremy put his hands over his face when you got angry at him?"

"Yes, but why is he so sad. It's my paper!"

"Do you think that he might be feeling something about what he did?"

"No. It's my paper. I feel sad."

"Do you think Jeremy can feel sad because he was maybe thinking that he was helping you draw and he was surprised that he made you mad?"

"Oh, I didn't think of that."

"Let's ask Jeremy." We invite Olivia and Jeremy to visit Christine on the school playground.

Jeremy starts to cry again as Christine approaches him. He looks up at her; tears fall down his face.

"Christine, he's still very sad about the dinosaur drawing."

"Yes. Jeremy, why are you so sad?"

Jeremy answers, "Because I want to help you draw a dinosaur. I can draw really good dinosaurs. I see a mountain in your picture. My dino could be near the mountain!"

Christine kneels down next to Jeremy and whispers, "I didn't know that's what you wanted to do. I thought you wanted to ruin my picture."

"No, I wanted to draw a dino for you. I'm good."

Christine wipes away Jeremy's tears.

"Do you need some Kleenex?" she asks. He nods his head yes.

"I have lots of paper. Let's draw a dino together. Okay?"

"Okay."

Smiling, Jeremy takes Christine's hand, still holding the green marker in his other hand.

In the next session, Christine and I talk about ways to limit Jeremy. She learns to say, "Oh, Jeremy, this is special! Be careful!" or "You can draw on this paper, Jeremy. This one is yours. This one is my drawing." What is most important is that Christine learns to draw a new inference from a social situation and to see the other person's perspective. She is learning that children might have several ideas in their minds when they speak words or take action. Christine is learning to be more flexible, to search for more options in her own thinking, and at the same time, to think about what her peers might be thinking. She is also learning that she can hold onto more than one emotion. She can be disappointed and angry at Jeremy for interfering with her drawing and compassionate toward him because he wants to help her by adding to what she has drawn.

Strategy 70: Teach the Child with Autism to Interpret a Peer's Discomfort and Pain by Comparing the Painful or Sensitive Situation to the Child's Feeling in a Similar Incident

Unlike Jeremy, Michael, a four-year-old with autism, needs continual help on the playground or during unstructured activities because he is confused by the perspective/viewpoints of other children. I've been seeing Michael individually once a week for two hours for the past two years. During the last year, I've seen him an additional two hours a week at his school with classmates.

Michael is making significant progress in social language skills that are basic to communication. Now he can take turns, share toys, and create stories in play with objects. Despite his basic mastery of speech pragmatics skills, he still has difficulty understanding how a peer can see things differently than he does. He gets frustrated in conversations with peers even though he loves to play with them. Sometimes he misperceives another child's ideas and wants to collect all his toys and leave the situation so that he doesn't need to interact with him. Other times he looks at adults to help him decipher the message from his peer and continue an interaction.

During one outside recess session, I work with Michael and his class-mate, Angel, whom he loves to follow around the playground. They sit next to each other in class and talk during choice time activities. They are both sitting on a small hill surrounded by maples near the playground swings, creating a pretend campfire with twigs and leaves. I'm sitting next to them as a pretend camper.

I ask, "Can we cook marshmallows?"

Michael says, "Yes! Let's get some sticks!"

Angel says, "Okay! Let's get sticks over there!" She points to some twigs on the ground near the swings. She motions for Michael to follow her. He jumps up and follows her to the twigs. They find some pinecones and stick them on the twigs. They sit down in front of their pretend campfire and begin to roast their marshmallows. I join them with my own twig and pinecone. Michael's pinecone falls into the campfire and he giggles. All three of us laugh.

I ask, "Angel, can you tell us what you did last week on your va-cation?" After retrieving his marshmallow from the dirt and pushing it on the stick, Michael continues to focus on the campfire. He looks up at Angel as she speaks and then looks back at the campfire and at his marshmallow.

Angel says, "Well, I went to Disney World and I went on the roller coaster and I threw up!"

"You got sick on the roller coaster?" I ask.

"Yep, right in the roller coaster!" Angel covers her mouth with one hand and looks at Michael for a response. He continues to focus on his stick and the marshmallow as if Angel has said nothing. His marshmallow falls into the fire. Angel winces as she points at his marshmallow in the fire. He picks it up again and sticks it on the stick.

Angel says, "Isn't it hot? Your fingers will get burned!"

Michael looks up at her and keeps holding his marshmallow over the fire.

I ask, "Michael, that was nice of Angel to want to help you. She didn't want you to burn your fingers in the fire."

Michael says, "Oh, thanks, Angel."

I ask, "Michael, Angel got sick in the roller coaster at Disney World. How do you think she felt?"

Michael looks up at Angel. His marshmallow falls in the fire again. He lets it drop and he doesn't retrieve it this time.

I ask, "Michael, have you ever gotten sick?"

"Yes. I got the flu," he says, still looking at his marshmallow.

"How did you feel?"

"Okay. Well, not great."

"Did you want your mom to help you?"

"Yes and she did. She gave me ginger ale."

"Did you hear Angel when she said that she got sick on the roller coaster?"

"Yeah."

"Did you hear that she was real sick?"

"Well, no."

Angel looks sad and says, "I felt awful, Michael. I was real sick!"

I ask, "Michael, did you hear Angel?"

"Yes."

"How do you feel about Angel being sick?"

"Sick like me?"

"Yes, like you when you had the flu."

"Oh, that's awful, Angel. I'm sorry."

"Angel, did you feel awful?"

"Yep. Thanks, Michael."

"Are you okay?"

"Yes, I'm okay.

"Do you want any more marshmallows?" I ask.

Angel hands Michael her marshmallow stick saying, "This one is better. Your marshmallows will stay on it and you won't get burned." He slowly takes the stick and smiles at her.

"Let's get some more wood!"

"Okay. I see some wood over there near the slide!"

Michael leaves and uses his arm in a "come on" motion toward Angel, indicating that he wants her to follow him. Though he knows how to use gesture to get someone's attention, he's still learning to read another person's subtle gestures and facial expressions. In addition, once he understands what the gesture means, he needs to make the association to the peer's words and then respond with relevant words/gesture back to the peer. When the peer responds back again with a head nod or a smile, the therapist knows that Michael understands the perspective of the speaker, his peer.

Michael doesn't understand how Angel feels on the roller coaster at first, but he eventually learns that his experience is similar to hers. Even though he cries when another child cries and is sensitive to another child's feelings, he has difficulty interpreting his friend's story, her tone of voice, facial expression, and body language, all of which communicate her unhappiness about throwing up in a roller coaster. By relating Angel's discomfort to a situation that is familiar to Michael, I help him recognize and see her emotions. Michael will need many situations like this one to help him understand that he has to read and draw inferences from a peer's facial expression, body language, and tone of voice—all cues that explain another's perspective about her own experience.

DEVELOPING STRATEGIES FOR NEGOTIATION AND REASONING

Strategy 71. Help a child with autism illustrate and outline steps that will logically help him draw inferences from abstract texts as well as ambiguous words in classroom projects and concepts related to his curriculum.

Strategy 72. During a conflict or a negotiation, teach the child with autism to identify shared interests with others through six stages of negotiation by modeling and questioning both children in an interactive play situation.

Strategy 73. Introduce creative and high-interest activities in outside settings that are linked to the child's natural experiences with family and friends.

CREATING STRATEGIES FOR BEGINNINGS AND ENDINGS

Strategy 74. Create natural situations for play-dates/free time with peers and provide an "overall" structure that is predictable.

Strategy 75. Support the siblings as much as possible in natural situations.

Strategy 76. Create natural situations for ending therapy with children and help them to look forward to new relationships.

Strategy 71: Help a Child with Autism Illustrate and Outline Steps that Will Logically Help Him Draw Inferences from Abstract Texts As Well As Ambiguous Words in Classroom Projects and Concepts Related to His Curriculum

Another way in which drawing and writing help a child with autism is to create visuals that illustrate the steps of deductive reasoning so that the child can organize his thinking and draw logical conclusions about abstract information.

Patrick, the toddler who faced the corner and banged the wall with his trains and had no language at the age of two, is now ten years old. He is functioning well in a regular public school third grade classroom. I consult his teacher periodically to help her with curriculum modifications that make the language in the class texts clear and concrete for Patrick. He's doing well and requires no assistance in social interactions with peers. He had a reevaluation by a neuropsychologist who reports that Patrick no longer fits his diagnosis of autism. Patrick is in phase four, learning to negotiate with others and to draw accurate conclusions from what he hears in conversations or class discussions about texts he and his peers are reading.

During one particular geography lesson during class, Patrick becomes confused and wants to leave class. He asks his teacher if he can go on an errand. That is his signal to his teacher that he either needs some space from his peers or he is confused. She acknowledges his need for a break and sees his distress. She doesn't have the time to explain the text to him at the moment, but she knows that I will be there in class that day to observe and to help Patrick. When I arrive, Patrick brings me his text and he says,

"Wow! I don't get this! I'm confused!"

"Yes, Patrick, this is hard to understand at first. Let's draw out the ideas first."

"Okay."

We take out a large piece of white paper and the familiar markers, his favorite colors of green and blue. He smiles as we sit down to work. We read the problem together. There are several choices to the question in social studies: "The following areas of land exist in the United States. Which ones are not coastal?"

I say, "Patrick, first let's draw out a 'coastal' piece of land. What does it look like?"

Patrick promptly draws a linear piece of land with an ocean on the side of it. I nod yes and say, "That's right."

Patrick learns by seeing opposites, so I say, "Now draw a piece of land that is not coastal."

Patrick draws the state of Colorado. He looks up and smiles, saying, "I've skied in Colorado!"

I nod and say, "Yes, that's right."

"Now, if some land looks like this (I point to coastal land) and other pieces of land look like this (point to Colorado), then how do you decide what to do with these pieces of land (point to the test questions that include seven other pieces of land)?"

Patrick looks confused. I pull out a map of the United States and show him coastal land. We read a short book on coastal regions and where they are in the world. We talk about the characteristics of coastal land. Then, we go back to the text questions.

Patrick answers all seven questions correctly.

Children with autism often have difficulty deciphering the various meanings of abstract terms that allow them to logically infer the correct meaning of a particular word. The first part of this strategy is to define the abstract term, "coastal" in this case, and then figure out the opposite word to this concept of coastal. With a contrast, the child can usually understand the concept.

The following month, Patrick and I work on the definitions for the word "democracy" and how some countries have the opposite government system such as a "dictatorship" or a "hierarchy." Once he understands these opposite concepts, he begins to formulate the ideas underlying democracy. This discussion leads to more work on the abstract concept of "freedom." While we discuss, we also draw pictures and write down the abstract words, such as "democracy," "freedom," and "individual rights." Patrick keeps a special notebook with all of our drawings and writings about abstract concepts related to his curriculum.

Strategy 72: During a Conflict or a Negotiation, Teach the Child with Autism to Identify Shared Interests with Others through Six Stages of Negotiation by Modeling and Questioning Both Children in an Interactive Play Situation

Children with autism need to learn how to negotiate not only over concrete objects but also over abstract ideas, such as who will have the ultimate control over the play agenda. The strategy to teach negotiation to children in phase four is the same for all ages; however, the more verbal the child is, the more likely he will use this strategy and actually come to a final agreement with a peer.

The first principle of negotiation is to teach the child to look for the other child's interest in an interactive play situation.

Conrad, a four-year-old with a diagnosis of autism, has a fierce temper when things in play don't happen the way he thinks they should. I see Conrad at his preschool for two hours a week to help him as he plays with his peers. His expressive language is excellent and he loves to create pretend stories about dinosaurs and monsters. He builds forts out of twigs and mud and loves to use the hose to create a river of mud that sometimes flows into his classroom through the sliding door, unless it is closed. His favorite activity is to build a structure, create the stream, and then lead the dinosaurs and his peers down the river to find food. He also wants to control the pace and timing of when all of the dinosaurs get food like ice cream or pizza. His peers are reluctant to challenge him because if they do, he screams and pounds their dinos until all of the children do it his way.

Caroline, another four-year-old with a feisty temper, also wants to control the river and wants to be in the lead. She wants her dino to be eating pizza with extra cheese and chocolate ice cream and there's only one plastic pizza and one plastic ice cream at the end of the river. Caroline joins Conrad with two other four-year-old classmates.

When I enter the scene one morning I hold my own dinosaur in one hand and the hose in the other. The first step in teaching four children, one with autism, to negotiate is to introduce a story theme that encourages each child to move into the others' play area and to create a "shared space" that is smaller than the whole playground, a space where they both can hear each other talk and see each others' play.

"Who wants to turn on the hose?" I ask.

Conrad yells, "Me! Me!"

"But, Conrad, how about one of your friends?"

"Nope. I want to do it."

"Does anyone else want to turn on the hose besides Conrad?"

There is a stillness in the river and a resounding silence from the children, except some noise from water dripping from the hose. I wait and listen.

"Well, I do!" answers Caroline.

"Okay. So, now Conrad, why do you think Caroline wants to turn on the hose?" I ask.

"Oh, because she likes water! She always wants to be first in the sprinkler."

"Yes. She's interested in water. Right?" I say.

"Oh, but I want to turn it on!" Conrad complains.

"Well, what about Caroline? If she loves water, can't she be the one to turn it on?" I ask.

"No! I want to," Conrad yells.

"Caroline, what do you think Conrad likes to do out here on the playground?" I ask, looking at Caroline.

"Oh, he loves to eat the food with his dinosaurs and eat it all up before the other dinos get there!" she says.

"Oh, Conrad, do you like to do that?"

"Yep. I want to get the food and eat all the pizza and the ice cream!" he yells.

"Okay, then, if Caroline likes to play with the water, and you like to eat the pizza, how can we fix our problem? Remember how we are trying to listen to what each of our friends wants to do."

"Yes, but I don't care!" responds Conrad.

"But, Conrad, if you get to eat all the food first, for sure, and everyone agrees that you can be first and get to the food first for sure, wouldn't you be happy?" I ask.

"Yep. I would!" he says, smiling.

"Caroline, if you get to control the water in the hose for the rest of playtime, would you be happy, even if you don't get to eat pizza?" I ask.

"I guess so." Caroline whispers.

"Does everyone agree that Conrad gets to eat first and Caroline gets the hose?" I ask.

The group of three boys and one girl say yes in unison.

Conrad says, "Oh, I guess she can have one piece of pizza."

"Conrad, what about your other two dino friends?" I ask.

"What do you guys want?" he asks, remembering to ask what they are interested in from our practice negotiations last week.

Two of the four peers answer together, "I want to be first in line."

"Conrad, they both want to be first. What can we do?" I ask.

"Okay. What do you like the most when we play?" asks Conrad.

"Well, I like the biggest green dino. Can I have that one?" one peer asks.

I nod yes to signal to Conrad to give him that dino. He does in one quick action, saying "Here. It's yours."

"Have we solved our problems?" I ask.

"Yes. I get to eat all the food, except one piece for Caroline. Caroline gets to use the hose and the water. He points to a peer who gets to be the first in line and he points to another peer who gets the green dino. We are all ready to play!" says Conrad, smiling and grabbing his plastic pizza, placing it up to his dino's mouth.

All four children are engaged in a "shared experience" and are talking about the same play theme. This is the second principle of teaching negotiation after getting all four of them comfortable in a "shared space" to play together. Each child wants to be a "character" that is in the other child's story theme. They are sharing an experience in play.

The third principle of teaching of negotiation is to help them find some "shared interests." Children as well as adults often assume, according to Fisher and Ury (1981), that if there is opposition, there is no ground for a common interest. However, the authors propose that "interests motivate people" (Fisher and Ury, 1981, 41) and that finding "shared interests" leads to some common agreement.[2]

A child with autism usually assumes that if someone opposes him, he must first attack and win either by physical force such as grabbing or by threats such as yelling at the peer, "Give me that! No! You can't have it!" The therapist begins to teach this third principle of finding shared interests between the children by staying with the group and creating some peace within a conflict. Once the grabbing or yelling is under control, the child can talk to his opponents and share his feelings. Then, the child and the peers can begin to talk about what they have in common.

During play one morning on the playground at school, Conrad and Caroline are creating a fort for Caroline's doll figures and Conrad is the father and Caroline is the mother. The two children create a story about two kids wrecking the house while their parents go out to a movie. When the parents return, they get angry with the kids. Once a disagreement arises in how to narrate the story, the therapist uses this situation to draw out the negotiation and to teach the children how to see each other's shared interests.

A disagreement arises when Caroline says, "But I don't want the parents to get mad. I want them to laugh."

Conrad says, "Mothers and fathers don't laugh when you mess up a house!"

Caroline says, "This mother and father do!"

I ask, "What is the most important thing that you want to happen in your story?"

Conrad says, "Well, I want the house to be wrecked up!"

Caroline says, "I want the house to be beautiful because the kids clean everything up and the parents are happy."

I ask, "How can we have the house a mess and clean-up?" There is silence.

I ask again, "How do we both wreck the house for you, Conrad, since you love to see the house fall down and how do we keep it clean and have the kids fix it for you, Caroline? Can we do that?"

Both children answer together, "No."

"Can you play in the same house together?" I ask.

"No, but we WANT to play together in the same house." Conrad answers.

"Well, you both have a shared interest—you want to play together in the same place. Right?"

"Right."

"Okay, let's just have the kids wreck their rooms and not the whole house" says, Conrad.

"Okay, then we can have the kids clean it up. Right?" says Caroline.

"But what do we do about Conrad wanting the parents to be angry?" I ask.

"I don't know," answers Conrad.

"I know. The parents can get mad at first when they come home and then the kids can clean it all up. If we don't wreck too much, we can make the house look good!" says Caroline.

"Oh, no! I want the whole house to crash!"

"How about if the house is cleaned up and then later there is a tornado that crashes the whole house?" I ask.

"Yes! Is that okay, Caroline?" Conrad asks.

"No, I don't want a tornado. Well, how about a flood and I can use the hose!" Caroline answers with a grin.

"Yes. You love water. Okay!" says Conrad.

They play with each other for over forty-five minutes, carrying out their story theme and keeping each other to their agreements. There is a huge flood that comes with the help of Caroline's hose and the story ends. Fortunately, the sliding door to the classroom is closed.

The basic principles of negotiation are the same for typical elementary school children. The main difference is that children with autism need to learn to practice the hierarchical steps either in a quiet location with role-playing with figures before they engage in real social interactions or in the actual interaction on the playground. I usually teach children within the interaction, if I can get them to move beyond the physical grabbing state and talk to each other.

At age ten, Patrick is still working hard to draw conclusions from texts and oral information. At the same time, he is learning some basic principles of negotiation with a peer. The first principle is to teach Patrick that he is playing in a "shared space" with his peer or peers and is interested in being with others. The second principle is to develop a "shared experience" in which Patrick can feel a positive engagement with which he can relate a play theme. In this kind of play experience, they share ideas and talk not only about what they are doing, but also about what they are thinking about the play theme. Once these two principles are established then the therapist can begin teaching both children about how to find a "shared interest." In addition, Patrick has to learn that his and the other person's interests may differ and that difference is not necessarily a negative thing. Once he recognizes this, Patrick may be able to trade or share back and forth. In the whole process of seeing the peer's interests, he may find they do have a shared basic interest.

I list out the first steps of "Negotiation Practice for Children," on paper with Patrick and his peer:

1. Noticing stage:
   a) Notice your peer's play area and recognize that he's near you.
   b) Talk to your peer and ask him about his thoughts and ideas.
   c) Remember the rules of "no criticism," "threats," or "negative talk."
   d) Remember that once a problem arises, the solutions take time to uncover.

2. Questioning stage:
   a) Listen to what your peer is saying and ask him questions.
   b) Express your own ideas and opinion.

3. Looking for solutions stage:
   a) Brainstorm some solutions to the problem without requiring an agreement.

4. Writing stage:
   a) Take time to think of options and write them down.
   b) As you hear your peer's interests, think of what is common or shared between you.

5. Recognizing a shared interest stage:
   a) If you can see some shared interest, you can see some agreements.
   b) Remember that there is no one answer.
   c) Think about the fact that the peer may want something very basic such as a "feeling that he is a friend and that he can trust you."

6. The agreement stage:
   a) Develop an agreement that helps both children with their own interest.
   b) Acknowledge the agreement and talk about why this is the agreement.

In over thirty years of working with children, I've found that once a child knows that a peer really understands his interests as well as his own, he expresses more of a desire to come to an agreement. Children with autism and typical children have difficulty learning to negotiate and learning to see the other child's perspective.

I guide Patrick and his peer into practicing a "pretend negotiation." Patrick, who is Spiderman—a character that loves to save people from burning buildings, begins by asking Eric what he likes to do. Eric is GI Joe (a soldier doll), a lawyer who likes to go to court and win cases for people who have been robbed. They go back and forth fighting over who is going to be the hero of the day and who is going to do the first rescue. They yell at each other, insisting that their own superhero is the best and should be the first to rescue someone.

We write up a list of interests for each superhero and then find that they do share some common interests, the most important of which is that they want to be best friends. Eric and Patrick giggle when they both admit this to each other.

After working with the boys for two one-hour sessions about the same conflict, they decide on a more detailed shared interest: They both want to feel trusted by the other enough to be "best friends." The negotiation begins to be resolved when they realize that despite the arguing over who is going to be "first" to make a rescue, they both have a human need to have a good friend. With this new insight, they create a story in which both superheroes make rescues at the same time. The story ends as they set up a "rescue" camp together in the woods.

From that session forward, Patrick and Eric develop a friendship and a bond that is still strong today. They attend different schools, but their parents drive them to see each other once a week for a play date. During our last session on negotiation, the boys earn a real trophy for their work in their dyad. A couple of weeks ahead of time, I ask them what they want on the top of their trophy. Not surprisingly, Eric wants a superhero like GI Joe and Patrick wants Spiderman.

When I give them their trophies, Patrick looks at Eric and says, "Friends for life."

Eric takes his trophy and smiles at Patrick and says with a loud voice, "Friends for life." They give each other a "high-ten" and walk out the door of my office, talking.

With both pairs of children—Conrad and Caroline and Patrick and Eric—I first teach both children to see beyond the object or the idea for a story that they're arguing for by looking at the peer's interests and the interests they share. Then I prompt both children to ask the other what he's interested in and to tell his peer that he understands.

Once both children acknowledge and remember their peer's interest and feel more compassion for each other, they become more flexible and want to resolve the problem. Once Conrad embraces the idea that Caroline really loves water and why she wants the hose, he is less likely to negotiate against her and insist he get the hose. He becomes more flexible in his own thinking as a result of seeing her interests. In addition, Conrad learns that in a negotiation process he can give up something if he gets to follow his own strong interest in eating the pizza and ice cream. He learns that giving something not only helps his opponent but benefits him, too. In the other dyad, with Patrick and Eric, Patrick learns that he wants a best friend more than anything and is finally willing to allow Eric to make a rescue at the same time as his Spiderman. In the process of negotiation, Eric learns that having a best friend to trust is better than losing a friend because he wants to be first.

Sometimes children with autism cannot achieve this level of negotiation, but they can begin to reach a place where they share space and recognize a few of each other's interests.

Strategy 73: Introduce Creative and High-Interest Activities in Outside Settings that Are Linked to the Child's Natural Experiences with Family and Friends

One sports language session involves Patrick and three peers having lunch at MacDonald's and going bowling. This activity is a favorite for the boys and they never miss the opportunity to be with each other at MacDonald's. We arrive at MacDonald's for lunch and Patrick is in line with his three buddies. The place is noisy and he is anxious. Patrick turns to me and says, "I'll do this myself." He holds out his money. I nod yes and back away from the line.

The cashier person asks Patrick, "What'd ya like?"

He promptly answers, "The Red Sox!"

The cashier smiles and says, "I mean what would you like to eat?"

Patrick says, "A hot dog and a beer."

The cashier smiles and laughs and says, "I don't have those things here. Anything else?"

Patrick looks down and says, "Oh, I forgot where I was for a minute. I was thinking of my dad and me at the game. I'd like chicken McNuggets and milk, please."

Although Patrick has an acute memory for associations, he forgets the context of the situation. He does correct himself without any help and is proud of his ability to see what is happening to his cognitive thinking at that moment.

Later at the bowling alley, Patrick is thrilled to get a strike. His buddies cheer when the ball smacks the pins and they jump up and down.

"Nice going, Patrick!" one peer yells.

Patrick is so excited that he throws the next ball and releases it backwards instead of forward. It hits the floor and rolls across the bowling seating area. One of his buddies says, "Oh, Patrick, I'll get it. You're an awesome player. Don't worry."

Patrick sits down in the seat area and says, "Oh, I'm dumb!"

His buddy remarks, "Nope. You're not dumb. You are a walking encyclopedia! I can't remember all the things that you remember about some subjects in class!"

Patrick smiles and picks up the next ball to throw. He hits another strike. His buddies all pat him on the back. He laughs as they show him his scorecard.

Once the child's peers help, the therapist becomes an observer. In the simplest activities, such as lunch at MacDonald's and a game of bowling, a child with autism can learn that he is valued by others. He can improve his language disability, which is often an integral part of autism, through his peers' support and continual experience with social interactions in natural settings.

Strategy 74: Create Natural Situations for Play-Dates/Free Time with Peers and Provide an "Overall" Structure that Is Predictable

One of the most important interventions to make in helping children with autism become social is to assist them with a "play-date," an arrangement for the child to play with a peer during their free time at recess, in a neighborhood park, or even at a summer camp. The goal is to facilitate a relationship between the child and several peers in a natural situation. At first, the therapist works with the child and a typically developing peer. The peer may have some language disabilities, but he should be in at least phase two or three of Narrative Play. The peer should be available in the child's classroom or neighborhood so that the carryover is immediate. A child with autism will associate positive experiences with this peer and transfer the social skills to another setting, particularly if he meets the same child he practiced with in a play therapy setting.

Before a play date happens, the parent and the therapist set up a plan to talk about the structure of the play and the goal of the arrangement. The child may be in phase three of therapy and just moving into phase four of social engagement; therefore he'll need more adult support to be more reciprocal in his interactions. He may be able to take turns, but not sustain the interaction with a friend and stay on topic. The play date should be limited to one or one and one-half hours and set up in a familiar setting at first. The child's siblings may be included if they play well with their brother or sister, and if they won't become a distraction to the peer. In some families, the addition of a sibling is helpful, and in other families, a sibling may want to compete for the peer's attention and the child with autism is left out. If this happens, it is best for the family to bring another child to play with the sibling for the first few sessions. They can play together once the child with autism is socially connected to his peer. (see Appendix 1, p. 173).

In phase four of Narrative Play, social engagement, the therapist works closely with the child with autism and with the typical peers. The method of using peers as language models in Narrative Play therapy is similar to the Integrated Play Groups model (Wolfberg and Schuler, 1993).[3] Both models provide support for the child to reach his or her highest potential with a scaffolding approach (that is, supporting a child who is less skilled with a child who is more experienced to reach his highest potential). The more skilled peers have to become social models (Wolfberg, 1999). The role of the facilitator in the Integrated Play Groups is to guide and coordinate activities with both typical and "novice" children and to set the scene for a play scenario. In Narrative Play, the story theme is guided by the child more often than by the therapist; however, both models allow for spontaneous interactions in play that enhance social and play skills. In current research, the importance of peer play for children with autism is often not valued (Preissler, 2006).[4] When children with autism engage in play with peer models, they engage in more complex forms of play (Greenspan and Weider, 1997; Lord and Hopkins, 1986; Wolfberg and Schuler, 1993).[5]

In phase three or four of Narrative Play, the child with autism and his or her family and a peer may meet at a farm or a playground or at a sledding hill. It is best to pick a time of day when this particular place is relatively free of distractions and noise, and has few children. For example, I often take a child with a peer to Drumlin Farm in Lincoln, Massachusetts, in the spring when the animals have young babies and when the farm is quiet in the early morning. I avoid taking a child with a peer on a busy weekend. If I take them to a park, I look for a quiet corner of the park in the shade where I set up a small baseball diamond for play. I bring a thick heavy mat so that we can sit down outside together and work on the agenda for the session and talk about the goals. Even in winter, the first meeting should always begin in a quiet setting and the rules should be explained to each child.

I often meet with two families; each has one child with autism, and each of those children bring a peer who is of the same developmental age and has the same interests. All four children are verbal and able to use reciprocal language. One child, Lucy, age nine, was diagnosed with autism at the age of three and the other child, Julie, also age nine, was diagnosed with Asperger's Syndrome at the age of seven. Both children attend public schools and are well supported by their school team. They both engage in social skills groups with typical peers once a week. The school psychologist leads these groups and they work on speech pragmatics (turn taking, eye contact, initiating conversation, exiting conversation, sustaining an interaction, using language to express ideas). Both children have individual speech therapy once a week to work on receptive language and cognitive skills and to improve their sentence formulation skills. Both girls have an occupational therapist who works with them twice a week on sensory issues and provides on-going consultation to their schools.

Each Saturday morning, I join these two children for a one to one and one-half hour play therapy session outside with their parents and peers from the girls' classroom.

One morning, after a light snow, Lucy and Julie arrive at the sledding hill to practice their language skills during an activity they both love, sledding. They are seven years old at the time. Lucy runs down the snowy slope toward Julie, carrying her red plastic tube sled. Julie brings a classmate of hers, a typical peer who wants to go sledding with her. Lucy also brings a typically developing peer to join this playgroup on Saturdays. The peers are following each other down the slope to greet Lucy. Julie's dad and Lucy's dad are standing at the top of the hill talking and finishing a cup of Starbucks.

Lucy yells, "Hey, Julie, I got a new tube sled!"

Julie yells back, "Lucy, so did I! Look!" She holds up a blue tube sled.

I say, "Wow! That's great. You will be fast!"

Julie says, "Well, I'm a little scared."

I ask, "Julie ask Lucy how she feels."

Lucy says, "Oh, I'm a little scared, but not really."

I say, "Okay, let's go up to the top and sit on those logs. We need to figure out our goals for today." The two typical peers, Anna and Mary, also seven years of age, are from Julie and Lucy's classrooms. The parents and the peers walk over to join us on the logs. We sit down and face each other.

I ask, "Julie, can you introduce us to your friend?"

Julie says, "Oh, I forgot how to do it. I can't do it."

Lucy says, "I can. This is my friend Anna and this is Julie's friend Mary!"

I respond, "That was great, Lucy. Now you need to name each person you are introducing them to and then give that person eye contact and then look back at your friend. This is hard. Let's practice."

Julie says, "Oh, this is confusing!"

Lucy says, "Okay, I'll try." She continues, "Okay, Anna and Mary, this is Dr. Densmore and these are my parents, Mr. and Mrs. Kelly."

Julie says, "Okay, I'll try." She continues, "Okay, Anna and Mary, this is Dr. Densmore and these are my parents, Mr. and Mrs. O'Brien."

I model for them. "Watch me do this and watch my eyes as I look at Mary and Anna and then back to your parents and then back to Anna and Mary. It's hard."

I model several times. They watch and then imitate the introduction with the eye gaze shifts correctly.

We eat a small snack of water and crackers. In between taking small bites of crackers and sipping water, we talk about our goals. All four children need to understand the goals for the therapy session and help plan the activity schedule overall. Peer-mediated interactions, according to research, are effective in increasing participation by children with autism in natural settings (Kamps et al., 2002).[6] The goal for Lucy that day is to look back at her friends as she runs and to use better hand gestures. When she says, "Come on!" she needs to use her arm to motion to her friends to follow her. When she is sledding, she needs to turn and look at her peers when she gets up and smiles at them. Her goal is to let her peers know that she likes to be with them, and to let them know that she is noticing them in play. A simple glance over her shoulder will give Anna, her friend, that exact message. Lucy's parents know her language goals for today, and they will prompt her as they sled with her and watch her play.

The goal for Julie is to be more aware of her speaker-listener's distance in play and to monitor the loudness of her voice. Sometimes she speaks too loudly when she is next to her friends and other times, she speaks too softly and they can't hear her. She knows that she is to pay attention to her friend, Mary, and be aware of how loud she is speaking during interactions as she sleds.

The overall goal from our previous session that continues to be a goal for both girls is to use language to express their emotions instead of complaining and gesturing—for each child to say what she feels and to explain how she feels with words.

The parents of each child know the goals and agree to assist them in practicing the specifics of each goal during the session. I keep a small 3x5 card in my pocket to note how many times they each practice today's goal in the ninety-minute session of sledding. I explain to each family that the main objective is to have some fun and not to be too strict on the number of times they practice. When the opportunity comes up in the interactive play, both parents and children should remember to focus on the specific goals.

The sun is reflecting patterns on the snow as the girls line up to take their first downhill run. The slope is gentle and we agree to all go together. I have a tube sled and ride between the two girls. Their peers ride next to them. The parents are the "starters" and push us down at once. We all look at each other and one person is in charge of starting the group.

Lucy says, "Ready? Go!"

All five tube sleds slip down the hill with snow flying out the sides of each sled. The girls grip the handles of their sleds and try to stay together. They are all laughing at the bottom.

Lucy is the first to land at the bottom and looks back over her shoulder, yelling, "Nice ride. That's great, Anna!"

I make a mental note in my mind to praise her for remembering to practice her goals. Julie stands up and grabs her sled and in a soft voice says, "I'll race you back up to the top!" No one moves because no one can hear her voice. She repeats it again in a louder voice. They all laugh and race back up the hill.

As we begin the second run, Julie, who is in charge of this start, says, "Lucy, that was nice that you looked back at Anna. I saw that!"

When a peer reinforces another child with my prompting, I see progress. Lucy grins and said, "Thanks!"

Several runs later, we all convene on the logs for a second talk and snack. Lucy and Julie have accomplished their goal for the day. They each practiced over twenty times in this one session. My reminders and the parents' prompts were minimal. The parents ask questions about how to time their prompting when their child forgets to practice. Anna, Lucy's peer, remarks, "I'm having a blast! This is fun. Can we do this again?"

We take one last run for the morning and end up in a big pile at the bottom. The laughter can be heard through the trees.

Lucy and Julie worked in the group for a year and they all became friends with these peers. They still play together and now it is impossible to see who has autism and who is typical. This sport and language session of Narrative Play therapy is a way to begin the small steps toward socialization that will help a child with autism in other natural settings.

When the children with autism are younger or less high-functioning, with no spontaneous language except for a few imitated scripts, the sports and language session can be structured to accomplish smaller goals and more concrete goals. Sometimes, the goal is to say a word, such as the goal set for Christine, the child in the first chapter, who loved the snow. As Julie and Lucy make progress, their goals will include: imitation of social scripts during play interactions and creation of a story in play with a peer; watching a peer's action in play and just noticing each other; and tolerating one more person in the area, even if that person runs into their sled by accident.

For over two years, I worked with Patrick, the young boy in chapter one, phase one, who made his first statement to his parents as they drove past the town green. The Christmas lights on the green came on and Patrick said, "Look, it's a Christmas tree!" He also was the boy in chapter two, phase two, who wouldn't share his trucks and his trains, and screamed when anyone came near him. As Patrick progressed through the phases of Narrative Play, he reached phase three in kindergarten and learned to relate to adults and to some familiar peers. He began to work on being more reciprocal with a new peer. I became a consultant to his school district and I worked with him at his elementary school. He was in a public school kindergarten at this time and five years old. I received permission to take Patrick and his peer, Annie, outside to practice language on the small playground while recess was not in session. The overall goal was to help them develop a friendship that might carry over into a regular recess or into a natural play date at home. (see Appendix 4, p. 181)

It is June and the playground is empty in the morning at 9 A.M. Before we went out on the playground, we practiced some language by reading key-chain scripts (visual strips of language on a key chain) such as "Hey, look at me!" or "Watch this!" or "Wait for me!" or "Don't get too close!"

After practicing language in the school hallway for about ten minutes, we go outside to the playground. Patrick wants to learn how to hang upside down on the parallel bars and Annie has this skill. She is also five and in his kindergarten class. We approached the bars, and Annie immediately grabs both bars, scoops up her feet, and hangs upside down. I hold Patrick and he tries to swing his feet up to the bars and hang on with both hands at the same time.

As Patrick hangs on bars with my help, his peer, Annie, jumps off the bars saying, "The trick is to believe in yourself."

In order to be sure that Patrick heard Annie's comment, I said, "The trick is to what Annie? What did you say?"

Annie said, "The trick is to believe in yourself. I didn't even practice!"

I tapped her arm and moved her closer to Patrick as she balanced herself up on the parallel bars with both arms straight and her feet together.

I said, "Can you get really close to Patrick and tell him that?"

Annie looked at Patrick who was squatting on the ground with his arms reaching up to the bars, "Patrick, the idea is to believe in yourself. I didn't even practice on that."

Patrick turns away with a disappointed look. I place my hand on his arm, which is resting on the parallel bar. Annie and I are looking at him.

I ask, "Did you hear that?

Patrick whispers, "Yes" and continues to look away from us.

I ask, "What's it like to believe in yourself? What's it mean?"

Patrick turns toward me.

I say, "It means 'I can do it!'"

Patrick immediately responds by saying, "I can do it!"

He follows Annie to the low-balance beam that is appropriate for this age on the playground. He watches Annie walk the beam. He stands up on the balance beam and walks the beam half way with my help.

I prompt Annie, "What do you say, Annie?"

Annie takes my prompt and immediately shows Patrick how to balance, "You have to put your arms out like this!" Annie demonstrates by walking next to him as he walks the beam with her arms up like airplane wings. I help Patrick stand on the front of the beam again. "Keep your arms out."

Patrick says, "You run slow. Running fast is not good!" Patrick completes the walk down the whole beam.

Annie says, "And if you wiggle, just jump off." Annie is giving Patrick a way to abandon the beam if he feels off-balance.

Then I ask Patrick to watch Annie. Children with autism often have difficulty noticing others' actions. With one peer, in a quiet playground, I can facilitate this skill.

I kneel down next to Patrick's level and point to Annie and say, "Okay, you need to watch Annie and make comments when she does it." Annie steps up to the beam and steps out on one foot with her arms spread like an airplane.

I say, "Okay, Annie, we're watching."

I'm next to Patrick with one arm around his shoulder for support and also to keep him focused on what his classmate is doing. The therapist needs to stay close to the child who needs language facilitation, particularly at the point when he should make a comment about another child's action. Two things happen between a child with autism and a typically developing peer when a therapist stays close to both children. If the child is distracted by other stimuli in the environment, the therapist can redirect his attention by pointing or guiding him to face the child he needs to watch, and the child can hear the therapist when he needs a model for the language to use in that particular interaction.

Annie walks the beam, turns, and smiles at Patrick. I point toward Annie to help Patrick focus on her and say, "What do you say?"

Patrick says, "That's good!"

I prompt Patrick with a gesture, and point toward Annie. He responds again, "That's good, Annie!"

Without a prompt, Patrick steps up on the end of the beam at the opposite end of where he started, points forwards, and says spontaneously, "Let's go this way!" (This playground session with dialogue was taken from a film clip).[7]

He walks back the entire length of the beam with Annie following him.

After four months of working with Annie and Patrick in a dyad once a week for about thirty minutes each week, Patrick went out to regular recess and Annie became his partner, without any adult suggestions that she should be his friend. They played together for the whole year of kindergarten. I visited the school once a week at recess time and helped Patrick with language when he needed the help. By the fall of the second year, in first grade, Patrick needed little language facilitation. He was finally playing spontaneously with several classmates, including Annie. My role was to fade back my prompts and become almost invisible, a part of the peers.

I work with a child with autism during the first ten minutes of recess and allow him to play on his own the last half of the time. I believe that a child with autism who has to be prompted in class and who works so hard in school to stay focused, needs some time to be free at recess. There were some days when Patrick was confused and unhappy when he tried to play with others and needed time to be alone. During those days, he sat on the swing and sang songs to himself, now and then looking up at his peers.

Another child with a diagnosis of autism came to my office when he was four years old. He had tantrums, unintelligible language, and very little communication. His name was Chase. We worked in individual therapy for approximately six months and Chase began to talk with intelligible speech. When he entered phase three of Narrative Play, he participated in a dyad social therapy group with another child with autism, Ashley. Both Chase and Ashley had complex language by the age of four. However, they spoke to each other in monologues and wanted to talk and not listen to each other. They were both learning to play and to limit their repetitive behaviors. Chase was fixated on train wheels and Ashley was fixated on "being a doctor." Chase and Ashley worked together in the dyad in phase three of narrative play with the same goal—to use reciprocity (a back and forth exchange of ideas) with a peer.

For over a year, I consulted weekly with the occupational therapists for Chase and Ashley. On one particular day, a filmmaker was at the occupational therapy playroom, creating a film to teach pediatricians about how to recognize signs of autism in their pediatric populations. Chase and Ashley were the children with high-functioning autism and I was the clinician. This dialogue from the film provides an example of language facilitation in phase three between two four-year-old peers, both with autism. I was the therapist, trying to make the session "perfect" because we were being filmed.

The room had several toys and was distracting. I arranged a play mat and a train set in the center of the mat to help Chase stay in one area with his peer, Ashley, and play. I was not sure if they would play or stay near each other, given the situation with a camera, lighting cables, and several people watching. I sat down near the train track as Chase moved near the train track. He leaned his head down on the mat and began to watch the wheels of one train. He started to spin the wheels. Ashley found a doctor's kit and was wearing the stethoscope. She was seated with us on the mat next to a large stuffed dog. She moved the toy instrument near the stuffed dog saying, "I'm giving him a shot!"

"You're giving him a shot." I repeat.

"Yeah."

"Is the puppy well?" I ask.

"Yeah."

As I spoke to Ashley, I noticed Chase rolling the train along the track so that he can lie on the mat and watch the wheels move. His body was stretched out across the train track and his head was right next to the wheels of the engine. I reached over to try to stop the train.

I tapped Chase's arm and said "Chase, sit up a second."

Chase promptly said, "He's not" as he continued to fixate on the train.

I asked, "He's not well?" I was able keep him in the story dialogue of the puppy and the vet theme, but he was still fixated on his train.

I tapped his arm again and suggested, "Chase, ask Ashley, 'What do you want to do now?'"

Chase looked up for the first time since we started to play and asked, "What do you want to do now?

Ashley replied, "I'm the doctor."

I say, "Oh, she's going to be a doctor." I was surprised when Chase stopped rolling the train on the track and sat up. Ashley started to move close to Chase, so that he was within her reach.

Chase ignored the fact that she was so close to him and said, "Well, when I grow up I want to be a football player!"

Ashley looked directly at Chase and then tried to look in his ear with the odoscope again. He ducked and said, "Well, when I grow up, I wanna be a football player!"

I placed my hand on Ashley's hand lightly and suggested, "Ashley, you need to ask Chase if you can peek in his ear."

Ashley was holding a plastic medical doctor's kit and one item was in her hand. She wanted to look in his ear.

I said, "Chase, is it okay if I look in your ear?"

While Ashley was asking Chase this question, he was saying again, "Well, if I grow up I wanna be a football player!" Both children were talking at the same time.

I placed my hand between them and lightly tapped Chase's knee.

I ask, "Okay, Chase, listen to Ashley. She's going to ask you a question."

She said, "Can I look in your ear?"

Chase turned his head sideways to allow Ashley to put the odoscope in his ear.

I say, "Okay, Chase, say 'Sure.'"

While Ashley looked in his ear, she was quiet.

I prompt, "Is it all better?"

Ashley answers, "Yeah."

Chase was still fixated on his statement and said again, "Excuse me! When I grow up I want to be a football player! What do you want to be when you grow up?"

Ashley continued to play with the doctor kit and said, "Well, I'm going to *drink wine.*" (transcript from film clip 2001).[8]

At that point in therapy, on film, I laughed and lost the timing of what I was supposed to say next. Sometimes in therapy with peers, either one child with autism and a typical peer, or with two children who have autism, the session seems to include unscripted spontaneous language. That is the wonderful part of working in the context of play with two children.

During the summer, I accompany children to their summer camp and join with their peers in play when they have free time. This type of peer therapy is one of the best situations for helping a child socially engage and move into phase four. The child is free to experiment in the environment, and he can be taught to engage in language with several peers at once without disrupting the classroom structure. The child is also with these peers every day of the week for several weeks of intense play. It is an opportunity for the child to bring together language and storytelling with peers every day. Even typical children learn by telling stories in free play (Paley, 1992).

The therapist in this phase, working outside in the free play situation, needs to be able to run, change directions, climb ladders, slide through tube slides, or walk across "bumpy bridges" of rope that move, and at the same time, focus on the conversation between peers in order to give a verbal prompt or reminder when needed. The peers see the therapist as another "peer." In this role, the therapist can help facilitate the story that evolves between peers in interactive play. The stories may be pretend narratives about chasing a monster across the bridge or pretending to be a superhero, or saving children from a burning building. The story may be also a reenactment—pretend play that works through a real-life drama that the peers have experienced in real-life situations at home or at school.

The sun was hot on the first day of August when I joined Jonathan, a bright six-year-old, at his summer day camp in Massachusetts. At the age of three, Jonathan had tantrums, very limited language, and was not socially relating to anyone. With intensive therapy from several therapists, for over three years, several days a week, he moved into phase four of Narrative Play. I saw Jonathan in my office setting twice a week for fifty minutes each session for individual therapy and at his preschool for two hours twice a week for the majority of those three years. His brother, Jack, went to the same camp and was in the preschool group of four year olds. He was diagnosed with childhood apraxia of speech and was being monitored for autism. At times, he exhibited signs of autism with repetitive play and play that was centered around certain themes. His specialists were uncertain whether or not his behavior was because he was following his brother's earlier behavior of "stimming" on wheels and fixations with trains or because he was developing some autism-like issues.

When I visited his camp that last summer, I timed my visit of one hour to coincide with his free time at recess on the playground. Sixteen of his camper-classmates, including a small group of typical peers who played together the entire forty-five-minute play time were on the playground. I became another "peer," when I entered the playground, the children ran up to me, saying, "Ann, ya wanna play?" as they gestured for me to follow them. It was "Pirates Day" at camp and all of the activities were built around the pirate theme.

Here is how Narrative Play therapy developed and how I intervened to support the peers in order to develop the narrative.

Jack had just finished making a paper pirate hat and his friend, Andrew, was wearing his hat. Andrew started to prance around the play area, saying in a "sturdy, pirate-like" voice, "I'm a pirate!"

Jack was watching him. I moved to Andrew's eye level and crouched close to him and in front on him so he could hear my prompt.

I said, "Are you a pirate?"

Andrew answered, "Yeah! I'm a pirate!"

He used his hands to pretend to capture me and growled.

I reacted as a pirate might and said, "Oh, you're scary!"

Jack walked up to his counselor and said, "I'm a pirate! Walk the plank!"

The counselor said, "I don't understand why I have to walk the plank. Did I steal the treasure?"

Jack said, "Yeah" and nods his head to mean "yes."

Jack's aide, Molly, reinforced the story by saying, "Oh, no, is she a bad pirate? So, bad pirates have to walk the plank?"

Jack again said, "Yeah!" and turns to look directly at his aide, Molly.

He was engaged in the narrative with his peer and his counselors, using eye-gaze shifts, body language to show emotion, and appropriate facial expressions and gestures.

Molly says, "Do you wanna walk the plank? Is it kinda like a diving board?"

Jack smiled and nodded his head again.

I encouraged another peer to move close to Jack and position him so that he was looking at Jack. I prompted Ryan, "Ask Joe, 'Do you want to walk the plank?'"

I said, "Okay, take his hand. Tell him how you walk the plank!"

Ryan shouted, "How do you walk the plank?" and looked at Jack.

Jack looked back and counted, "1-2-3- and jump!" as he walked in a steady pace toward the end of the walk area. His peer followed him.

I asked, "You want to do that again?"

Jack nodded yes.

We invited a second peer, Jerry, to walk the plank with Jack and Ryan. All three boys held hands and lined up to walk the plank.

I prompted Jack, "Ask Jerry if he wants to walk the plank."

Jack asked, "Jerry do you want to walk the plank?

They ran to the end and jumped up as if they were diving into the water.

Jack was thrilled and said, "There are fish in there!" (This dialogue of "Pirates' Day" was taken from the transcript of a film clip taken at the camp, August 8, 2006.[9])

In this simple example of using Narrative Play during a free-play time at camp, the child with the language delay was totally engaged with his peers in a story theme about pirates. He was not stuck on objects or busy with repetitive play or looking at lines in the walkway. There were several opportunities for him to use language with support and to practice what to say in a natural setting with peers. His language had to be prompted, but his gestures matched his words. He was engaged in using language, narrative, and play with more than one peer.

That afternoon, I worked with Jack's brother, Jonathan, at camp in a free-time situation on the camp playground. Jonathan is six years old and in the same camp. He has a diagnosis of autism; however, he has progressed through the four phases of Narrative Play and he is now in phase four. He can be socially engaged, with support from the therapist, with more than one peer. The goal of this camp session was to keep Jonathan with his peers, and to help him use language to sustain a narrative in play.

Typical five- and six-year-olds talk fast, run fast, and make quick decisions about where they are going on the playground. They climb, jump, skip, and move in and out of play structures as if they are in flight. They stop talking now and then and use gestures, but when they stop, they talk again to plan, to include others, and negotiate. In this setting, a child with autism has to learn how to manage and become a part of this social scene. It is not easy for the child or for the therapist. (The following example is taken from a film clip during Narrative Play therapy on the playground, August 8, 2006.) Jonathan is playing with a typical peer, Blake, and they are on the swings. The playground is filled with campers of all ages. The noise level is high. The day is hot and sunny.

Both boys are sitting on the swings, their feet on the ground and I am standing behind them, but close to them. I prompt, "Jonathan, ask Blake, 'Can you swing high?'"

Jonathan repeats my verbal prompts, "Can you swing high?" He looks at Blake who is looking at him. Both boys have joint attention skills and are ready to work in phase four. They talk back and forth, laughing and saying who is higher than the other.

I slow them down and say, "Okay, let's practice. Here's what I want you to do."

Both boys know that their goal that day is to stay in the same physical proximity, in the play area with each other, to make comments, and to use gestures and language together.

I say, "Okay, Blake, I want you to run that way and Jonathan is going to say, 'Wait for me!'"

Blake runs and Jonathan says immediately, "Wait for me!" We practice several times and have Jonathan run and Blake say "Wait for me!"

I say, "Okay, now watch this!" I run away from them and use a hand gesture and say, "Follow me!" The model seems to be clear, but Jonathan has difficulty executing the arm movement while running away from his peer and saying the request, "Follow me!' Some children with autism have to practice using language and gestures to create meaning in their play as they run and talk. Jonathan practiced several times and did acquire the skill. After practicing the talking while running, as well as the other skills and the gestures, we returned to swing so that the boys could relax and feel the freedom of the swing movement. This activity often helps children with autism and gives them a break from the work of practicing social skills.

The next skill we practice happened naturally. Blake was following Jonathan down the slide and they both came to a stop at the end, but almost on top of each other. I knelt down to their eye level and asked them to listen.

I prompted, "Jonathan, I want you to turn around this way (I gestured) and tell Blake, "Blake, you're too close!""

Jonathan repeated, "Blake, you're too close!"

I prompt again, "Move back please!"

Jonathan responded, "Move back please!" Children with autism have difficulty reminding peers that they need more room or space. They usually have sensory integration needs and being crowded by another child is a problem for these children (Ayers, 1994; Kranowitz, 2003).[10] When they have the language to limit a peer in their play area and realize that they won't lose the friendship by limiting a friend, they feel more in control of their play. A child with sensory issues wants to be social and play, but he needs to feel confident that he can limit another's action and protect his own space.

I prompt, "Okay, follow me! I'm going over there!"

Jonathan prompts with a smile, "I'm going over here!" (He ran toward the trolley and Blake followed him).

I prompt Blake, the peer, to say, "I'm coming!"

It is as important to focus on the peer as it is to attend to the child with autism. When the peer knows what to do, the child will imitate him and follow him.

At the trolley, both boys line up with the trolley. They each have a trolley next to each other. I ask, "Do you want to go together?"

I prompt, "Ask Blake, if he'll start with you."

Jonathan turns to look over at Blake, with his hands on the trolley, and says, "Would you start with me?"

This is an advanced social skill, to be able to talk and set up an action at the same time with a peer and use the appropriate eye contact to engage the peer.

At the end of the play session, the boys come together to say goodbye until the next day at camp.

With the boys facing each other and about a foot away from each other, I kneel sideways next to Jonathan and prompt, "I had fun!"

Jonathan giggles and jumps up and down saying, "I had fun!"

Blake says, "I had fun!"

I ask, "What was the best part?'

Jonathan spontaneously says, "Swing!"

I ask Blake, "What did you like the best?"

Jonathan says, "What did you like the best?"

Blake says, "Jumping off the swing!"

I tap Blake on the shoulder and say, "Ask Jonathan what he liked the best."

Blake asks Jonathan, "What did you like the best?"

Jonathan answers, "Holding onto the swing, then jump, then I put my body onto the ground!" Jonathan runs off.

I say, "Jonathan, we need a high-five!" (The previous dialogue was taken from a transcript of a film clip taken at the camp, 2006.[11])

Both boys connect with a high five and run back to their camp classroom to end their day.

The following week, I returned to observe Jonathan and Blake on the playground and they were connected. They were using gestures appropriately, language for commenting, and engaged in a real camp friendship. Jonathan, at the end of phase four of play therapy, was able to follow a peer model, and use language to express his ideas and emotions while interacting. He needed to increase his repertoire of playground language and gestures. He practiced with his aide, who was with us during the therapy sessions, every day during free time. Two weeks later, when I observed, I had difficulty finding him because he looked like a typical peer at camp on the playground. He was not stuck on the trolley wheels or the small details of the structure or picking up small chips of wood from the ground. He was socially engaged and experiencing the thrill of play.

A child with autism needs help with learning the social skills of play and how to interact with peers. If left alone, this child may look like he is "playing" with peers; however, he may be only engaging in parallel play, following his peers on the playground, imitating their actions, but not having conversations. According to research, "A child with ASD (autism spectrum disorder) may be interested in other children but lack the ability for spontaneous social engagement and therefore play next to others without communication or reciprocity" (Preissler, 2006, 237).

One of the encouraging outcomes in current research is that "peers can be invaluable for offering support, reinforcing social interactions, and helping to elicit social initiations" (Preissler, 2006, 245).[12] The therapist must prepare the typical peers and give them the skills to help the child with autism. Through play, a child with autism can learn to distinguish between what is fantasy in play and what is reality. One of the most important skills for a child with autism to learn is to recognize what is an invading thought in their own mind and what is a real event in life. "Play bridges the gap between real events in the changing world and imagination in one's head" (Preissler, 2006, 233). Children with autism can develop symbolic thinking and practice the dynamics of social interaction. They can learn to tell stories, pretend or real, and participate in something that builds confidence. Play with peers is a self-regulating experience where a child can learn to manage his own emotions with others and see the perspective of another child. (see Appendix 2, p. 177)

Strategy 75: Support the Sibling As Much As Possible in Natural Situations

For several years, I worked with two siblings from the Roberts family—a wonderful family with two boys. Ten-year-old Chase has autism, and five-year-old Jimmy, a kindergartener, is developing typically. When Chase was eight years old and Jimmy was only three, I worked with them once a week for a year in sessions lasting an hour and a half, sometimes at the playground. Chase has a treatment team at his school that included a speech therapist, an occupational therapist, and a reading tutor that met with him each week. In addition, he came to my office for private speech therapy twice a week and to a private occupational therapy office once a week. Jimmy learned to occupy himself in the waiting room while Chase was in his private speech or OT sessions. Jimmy was doing well in preschool and adjusting to having a brother with autism. Once in a while, Jimmy complained to his father about the long car rides. During a recent parent consultation, Mr. Roberts reported that his son Jimmy was wearing "magic glasses." I asked, "What are magic glasses?"

He smiled and said, "I took Jimmy to see the ophthalmologist because he has been complaining about his vision. He told my wife and me that he couldn't see his letters well and he was seeing some letters backwards. I immediately thought that he could have the same biological predisposition to carry dyslexia like his brother" (father's interview, January 8, 2007).[13]

At the ophthalmologist, Jimmy performed exactly like a child with some visual perceptual disorder, perhaps dyslexia. Jimmy went up to the letter chart and said, "This letter is funny and it's blurry!"

The ophthalmologist said, "Well, we may have to give you a referral to a specialist. But, I can try one more thing—magic glasses." He handed the magic glasses to Jimmy. Jimmy smiled and carefully placed them over his nose with both hands. He read every letter perfectly with 20-15 vision. The interesting thing was that the lenses in these glasses were made of pure glass. There was no correction. Jimmy wore these glasses to school everyday and read his kindergarten grade level primers. He was happy. He was like his brother and he got the attention he wanted.

Perhaps the only way Jimmy could see how to gain that attention that he perceived to be the "best" kind of attention was to develop a visual disability like his brother, Chase. Jimmy's father felt that in some way, Jimmy believed that he had this disorder. The current research on the social and emotional adjustment of siblings of children with autism is surprisingly positive and finds them well-adjusted considering the social stresses they face (Pilowsky et al., 2004).[14] However, other studies found an increased risk of negative outcomes such as depression when compared to control groups of siblings to children of other disabilities (Bagenholm and Gillberg, 1991; Fisman et al., 2000).[15] Some siblings suffer from the idea that they have "lost" a playmate when their brother or sister isn't responding to their initiations and interactions or noticing them in play. They may suffer a loss and grieve this loss throughout their childhood. Some seek positive ways to compensate for their grief and loss of a typical brother or sister who could play with them. In general, current research confirms that children with siblings with autism manage to keep a positive self-concept and they have social competencies that are equal to their peers who are siblings to children without disabilities or with other disabilities. In my experience, siblings who are adjusted to their brother or sister with a disability are good language facilitators in social interactions.

With modeling and training, a child whose sibling has autism can learn how to initiate conversation, how to support an interaction and keep it going, and how to wait for his or her sister or brother to respond. Phase two of Narrative Play, Joint Attention, provides an opportunity to work with siblings. In this phase, the child with autism needs contact with both the therapist and his sibling. This contact creates a dyad where the siblings are encouraged to attend to one another and to share during play. As the siblings become familiar with how to interact with each other in a dyad in the office setting, the therapist can help them shift to a less structured, natural setting such as a small playground with a few children or a quiet park or farm. In this kind of setting, both children are free to run, make comments, and follow each other as they play. During the first year of sibling therapy, the therapist should avoid a large playground that may be filled with many children and distractions. The typical children need direct training on how to support their siblings before they move to an outside environment. The child with autism needs help attending to the sibling's language modeling and also needs help sharing toys and the events in play. The first few sessions with both children need to be more structured, in a quiet office setting or small quiet playground, with specific goals for each child. Some studies found that children with autism may have executive dysfunction in the area of planning and set shifting (flexibility) (Szatmari et al., 1990; Liss et al., 2001), whereas other studies found no correlation between executive dysfunction and socialization, except that participants with autism showed difficulty with expressive grammar, figurative language, planning, and spatial working memory (Landa and Goldberg, 2005).[16] In my experience, children with autism need some structure to create predictability and a plan for their play sessions. They have difficulty shifting when they need to formulate a plan or change a direction in their agenda, especially in the outside environment. They often need social scripts (verbal or visual) to use to practice the more abstract terms that children use in conversation.

Children with autism needs visual scripts to remind them what to say and how to sustain joint attention. I create scripts that are appropriate for each child. If the child is at the "requesting" level of conversation (asking for things), I create scripts and put them on a key chain. If the child who has autism needs help with making comments about another's actions, I create those scripts (e.g., Look at what Chase is doing! Look at that!). If the child who has autism has sensory integration issues and needs to limit his sibling in his space, I create scripts to limit his sibling in his space (e.g., "I need more room, please. More space, okay?"). Then, I give the scripts to the child's sibling, his teachers, aides, and the parents. The scripts for the typical child may be language to use to prompt their brother or sister with autism (e.g., Jimmy, watch me! Look at what I'm doing! Or "Watch this!"). I often practice with the typical sibling first and then show him how to move to his brother's or sister's eye level and prompt him with the script, either visual or verbal or both (see Appendix 4, p. 181).

Both children need *daily* practice on the language that they may use in social interactions with each other in natural settings. Usually the siblings use these scripts in practice for approximately a month; they don't need them during play. The social scripts are for cueing before they play together or they can be used if they need reminders. The social scripts should be faded out of the social situation as early as possible.

After I work with siblings in a quiet setting, I join them on the playground or a familiar park in the child's neighborhood at a time of day when there are fewer distractions. I encourage the parent or teaching assistant to join us in order to teach them how to facilitate language. After approximately one year, the siblings are usually ready to work together at school (if they are at the same school) on the busy playground with adult support. Sometimes I see a child with autism in a typical after-school program at his school or in his preschool class during choice time. If the child with autism has a sibling that attends the same school, I work with both children at school. In my experience, the average time for sibling therapy to be effective is approximately two years from the first session in the quiet setting to the busy playground with adult support. After two years, the typical child can help his sibling without adult support and is usually proud of his accomplishment. In some cases, this sibling work enhances the typical child's self-concept and improves his social skills with his own typical peers.

Current research on children whose siblings have autism has shown that their social competencies are equal to those of their peers who have typical siblings, and they also have good self-concepts. However, some younger children (like Chase and Jimmy) exhibit attention-seeking behaviors (Pilowsky et al., 2004).[17] Other research is targeting the behavioral problems, social competence, and self-concepts of siblings of children with autism (Hastings, 2003; Verte, Roeyers, and Buysse, 2003).[18] According to one study, "siblings of children with autism did not differ significantly from siblings of children with Down syndrome or normal development on measures of self-competence or social competence" (Rodrique et al., 1993, p. 671).

A limited number of outcome studies on peer modeling show that training the sibling is helpful to the child with autism (Goldstein and English, 1997; Goldstein et al., 1992; Harrower and Dunlap, 2001; McConnell, 2002; Kamps et al., 2002).[19] One study suggests that a "prerequisite skill for all observational learning is imitation" (Jones and Schwartz, 2004, 187).[20] This research has some implications for teaching a child with a disability. In order to learn, the child with autism needs some other person to relate to and then to imitate for language interactions. In addition, the typical sibling needs direct training on the specific skills of social interaction (e.g., shifting eye gaze while playing; making comments about each other's actions in play, etc). Without that training, the typical sibling and his or her brother or sister do not interact as long or as often, and there is less spontaneous commenting between the children (Jones and Schwartz, 2004,192). It is interesting to note the social skills acquired through work with adults did not generalize to their peers (Rogers, 2000).

Since many of these typical siblings are socially competent and seem to maintain a strong self-concept (Verte et al., 2003), they are good candidates for training in natural language situations. Some siblings may not be available to help and may not respond to this support. The temperament of the typical sibling may influence how much he can tolerate if his brother or sister has an outburst or doesn't respond to him. The therapist, the teacher, and the parent must consider all of these factors when helping siblings work together (see Appendix 3, p. 179).

When I work with a child with autism, I invite the typical sibling to join his brother or sister in therapy whenever it is possible in that child's schedule—or at least once a week for an hour to an hour and a half session. Sometimes the typical sibling joins the social language session at the end for the last fifteen minutes. One of the main concerns about siblings, in my experience, is that siblings need to understand that their brother's inability to notice them, or reach out for them, is not their fault. They need to understand what autism is and how it can affect a child's social relationships. They need a safe place with a therapist to express their feelings. Typical siblings need help with what language to use to explain to friends what their brother or sister is like and why. They also need encouragement to develop their own lives and create time with friends away from their brother. When the typical sibling is the older child, I often invite her or him to help with language facilitation no matter what phase the child is in. If the typical sibling is younger, I wait until he is verbal and socially engaged and then introduce some sibling therapy.

The next case, the older sister, Sarah, is typically developing and her younger brother, Evan, is nonverbal. He has limited speech sounds and gestures, and is in phase one of Narrative Play. He is learning to watch his sister, to play with objects, and to relate to her with an object in play. Although the younger child doesn't have social language, he has facial expressions and body language that communicate to his sister that he cares about her and wants her to play. In one of our early sessions, Sarah started to make a list of things that she loved about Evan and other things that were frustrating to her about her brother. She worked on this list for several sessions in therapy and at home with her mother, Dorothea Iannuzzi, a mother and a clinical social worker. Sarah drew pictures illustrating her list of ideas and her feelings about her brother. This project became a wonderful published book, *All about My Brother* (Sarah Peralta, 2002). She created a positive way to talk about the difficult situations and the more positive situations that she got into with her endearing brother, Evan. Through this process, Sarah developed a strong sense of her role as a helper and as his sister. She learned to laugh with him and to tolerate his mood swings and generally help him communicate.

Once a week for almost two years, Evan came for speech therapy and Sarah joined us. It was Sarah's choice to choose whether or not she joined us. Sometimes she did join Evan in therapy and other times she chose to be with her mother and do something special. I spent time alone with Sarah to train her how to increase joint attention with her brother. According to a recent study, children with autism increased their frequency of joint attention with their sibling during play sessions after the siblings were trained to "stay in the physical proximity of the child, get the child's get the child's attention, find a conversation topic, create chances to share toys, give opportunity for turn-taking, give ideas about play, negotiate play, ask questions, understand what the child wants, and provide verbal comments" (Tsao and Odom, 2006, 109).

The first sibling session with Sarah and Evan is in my office setting. Evan loves to tap long sticks. While Evan plays, I teach Sarah how to relate to her brother and to use a neutral and clear tone of voice. I model for her and show her what my "neutral, but clear" voice sounds like. I give Sarah one goal—to help her brother notice her actions as he plays. I suggest that she first notice what her brother is doing—tapping his long stick on the floor as he giggles. Sarah practices her voice tone and watches her brother tap his stick. She moves closer to him and tries to show him a toy car. Evan pushes it away.

I say, "That's okay, Sarah. Keep trying. Don't give up. Try showing him the car another way. He will notice you."

Sarah smiles. She lies on the floor near him as he sits in a bean-bag chair and Sarah moves the car toward his feet. She taps his foot with the toy car. He looks up at her and moves his toes to push the car away. She looks back at me and nods her head. They are connecting. I coach Sarah to continue to follow him and move into his play area. She continues to move the car near him and moves it up and down a small car track. He watches the car.

I say, "Evan! Watch! Sarah is moving the car! Watch!" I encourage her to keep going and soon Evan is giggling and watching her move the car toward him. I praise Sarah for reaching her goal today.

Sarah says, "I think he knows me now."

I respond, "He knows who you are. Keep going at home. He will notice you more and more."

Ten weeks later, after nine sibling sessions, Evan and Sarah come to my office for a tenth session. Evan is tapping the railing of the staircase. I hear Sarah's soft-spoken words as she follows her brother up the stairs to my small office. I watch her help him take off his jacket and hang it up on the coat hook. I see her caring touch on Evan's shoulder as she asks, "Evan, do you want to play?" She pulls out the train box in my office and starts to set up the track. Evan responds and his eyes twinkle at his sister. He reaches for a train. Sarah sets up the track. She moves her train along the track making the sounds of a train whistle. Evan moves his train.

I say, "Ready?" as I place my train car on the top of the bridge.

Evan follows with a loud, "Go!" (I recorded this transcript from a film clip 2001).[21] He looks up at Sarah with a big grin. His stick is on the floor. Sarah smiles.

Evan's mother is in the room, filming our therapy session. She places the camera down and says, "Did you hear that?"

Evan shrieks with laughter and pushes his train car along the track. Sometimes children with autism who are nonverbal will say a word or two, but with some children this is rare and often unrelated to the actions in play. Evan knew that "Go!" meant to let the train go down the track. For Evan, making the connection of placing the car action on the car track was one accomplishment, and making the connection to his sister by looking at her was an even bigger accomplishment.

Sarah knows the frustration of waiting for her brother to respond, but endures and waits and waits. She encourages him, imitates his sounds, and gives him short phrases with various intonation patterns. He laughs and giggles at her. He calls his sister, "Sa-Sa." We work together, prompting Evan with words, gestures, and visuals. Sarah rephrases every sound he makes. I introduce new receptive language concepts to keep developing his cognitive skills.

"Put the train under the bridge, Evan." I say.

Evan promptly places his train car underneath the bridge and giggles at me. He knows that he is right. He leaves his stick on the floor while he plays with the train. He stops the tapping and he tries to play. Evan and Sarah work together once a week for a fifty-minute session each week (although Sarah misses some sessions) for almost three years. Evan does not develop expressive language, except for one-word comments now and then and gestures and facial expressions that indicate that he wants to relate to his sister. Sarah is pleased. She has learned to connect in some way to her brother. Evan also has a speech therapist at school who works on his expressive and receptive language every week, twice a week. He makes slow steady progress. The sibling therapy is in addition to his regular school speech therapy. After our last session, Sarah, her mother, Dorothea, Evan, and I went to a nearby restaurant to say goodbye. Evan was not talking to his sister, but he was relating.

Evan sits in the restaurant seat, tapping the menu with his stick.

She turned to him, pushed his stick away from the table, and said, "Oh, Evan, how about some hot dogs?"

Evan dropped his stick. He made a sound, smiled at her, and made the approximated hand sign for more hot dogs. We all laugh and giggled. He was proud of his communication even though he couldn't use spoken words. Sarah learned how to relate to her brother through pictures, simple sign language, and facial expressions with gestures and, eventually, with a programmed augmented device. Evan is still nonverbal, but smiles and giggles when he sees his sister.

As a therapist, I spend as much time with the sibling as I do with the child with autism. My attention is divided but always sensitive to who needs me at the moment. The sibling, younger or older, will need the therapist's undivided attention, training in how to facilitate language, and praise as much as possible. Sometimes the use of video modeling can help both children practice the social skills they need. For a typical sibling, teaching a brother or a sister with autism to communicate is a long frustrating task. Research in general supports some "direct sibling-to-sibling instruction" and support and then practice in natural settings (Taylor et al., 1999).[22] Siblings must know that you understand the challenges of this relationship.

As the sibling reaches adolescence, the task of adjusting to a brother with a severe disability like autism becomes more difficult. They must explain to their friends that their brother can't help it when he lines up toys, or when he throws a tantrum at the school playground. Sarah learned to relate and be helpful to her brother, but she has a new task in middle school with her older classmates who may tease her about her brother.

Some siblings never show any obvious signs of depression or attention-seeking behavior to their parents or teachers. They become "little troopers" that follow their parents' directions and often work hard to be the best at school. Once in a while, they may show some signs of needing more attention from those who care for them. When a sibling complains about something that seems to be unrelated to the real issue of coping with a brother or sister who cannot relate to them like they expected, the sibling may be seeking help in some way or just attention from adults.

Chase's younger brother, Jimmy, who suddenly developed "visual problems," was seeking some attention from his parents. He is currently in a sibling therapy group and so far, he still needs to wear his "magic" glasses.

Strategy 76: Create Natural Situations for Ending Therapy with Children and Help Them to Look Forward to New Relationships

It was July—the end of baseball season for kids in summer camp in New England and one month before the end of therapy for a young boy I had treated for social language disorder for more than nine years. Noah was three years old when he played on our T-ball team on Saturdays. He hit his first ball and ran to third base instead of first. He loved baseball and he never stopped talking about the Red Sox. He finally learned to play well enough to be on a town team, but that took many hours of practice and special help from his coach. So many children with disabilities never have the opportunity to be on a "real" town team and win a trophy. He was now twelve and in middle school.

Noah was a high-functioning three-year-old who ran fast, talked fast, and ignored his peers. Through the years, he had struggled to overcome years of a social language disability and no friends. He worked with me in a dyad with one other boy who also had a similar social language delay. Both boys were diagnosed with nonverbal learning disability, a disorder that neuropsychologists sometimes place on the autism spectrum and other medical experts sometimes place on a separate scale of language disabilities.

Noah was talking, but he was not 100 percent intelligible because he spoke so fast and had limited eye contact and no interest in finding out what his peers were doing. His teachers complained that he wanted to pace the playground and he would engage in a game of tag when he could be chased. He loved to be chased because he was a natural runner and he could outrun any child in his preschool. This way he could also avoid social communication. Pacing was a coping strategy for Noah.

Noah and Connor worked together in my office, learning social strategies and language scripts to solve social situations. When they were four, I took them out to a nearby ball field with their dads and taught them T-ball. They learned how to run bases, compliment each other, and stay connected on the field. They learned to relate as peers through the game of baseball and with the help of their dads. We played baseball from the time Noah was three until he was six. Both boys were natural athletes, but they lacked the skill of interacting with a peer in an activity.

Connor graduated from the dyad speech sessions and went on to a private school. Noah stayed with me for three years on a monitor basis (once a month) for speech therapy and support with social situations at school. I visited his school and helped the staff work with him on the playground. He learned to play games instead of tag and he learned the abstract rules of several sports. As time went on, Noah became his "own" coach. He would monitor his own volume and lower his voice when he knew he was being too loud. He would smile at me when he said something that was inappropriate and corrected himself immediately. He often came to our session with a school social problem and he would set up the options of solving it on his own. He even went to my computer and wrote out his solutions. I was not giving him suggestions or social scripts by this time. I became a silent listener. I could see the signs that he was ready to graduate from our language/sports group. His social skills were in his mind intellectually and emotionally in his heart. He was connected to his friends.

Saying goodbye after all these years was a serious process. I introduced the idea in a session six months before his last speech session. We talked about how to do the ending and how he was okay and could do these things on his own. He wanted to leave, and at the same time, he was afraid. We decided to see each other every two weeks and then not in the summer. The first summer was hard for Noah. He missed our speech sessions and he wrote postcards to me from camp.

For the next few months, we talked about what it would be like to not see each other and how he might feel. We made our final plans for the last session. I asked Noah if he wanted a reward for his hard work in language/sports group. I suggested that he may want a hot-fudge sundae or some cookies or a present or even an engraved trophy that said, "For outstanding performance in speech." Noah looked down and pulled his baseball cap over his eyes.

He said, "Oh, no, not that stuff."

He paced back and forth across the room, nodded his head left and right, and said, "Nope, I wanna play baseball with you alone on a real field for two hours. That's what I want to end my social group with you."

"Okay, that's fine. But, remember that you're a good baseball player now and I don't know if I can catch you!" I remember Noah when he ran the bases so fast that even the dads couldn't catch him.

"Oh, I'll run slower for you. I'll let you get one out." We set the date in our calendar for his last session.

His last session arrived, the day after the Fourth of July. Noah came to my office with his baseball mitt, some plastic bases, and his baseball hat.

"Did you have a good Fourth?" I asked.

"No. It was boring. I hate firecrackers," he answered as he looked away from me. I could feel his sad response and his need to be heard. I smiled at him to let him know that I heard him. I collected my mitt, a new ball that I was giving him as a transitional gift, and some bats and stuffed them in a duffle. We drove to a nearby field after saying goodbye to his mother, Ellen. She waved as we walked out the door. Noah was silent on the way to the field.

As my VW Beetle swerved into the driveway of the field, I glanced down the dirt path from third to home and realized that this was not Fenway Park, but it was a big field. We each took one side of the duffle bag of bats and dragged it toward the field.

As we walked toward the field, he said, "Okay, I play two-man baseball with my sisters and my friends, so I can teach you."

"Okay," I said.

I placed the third base on the field and Noah moved it in line with home plate. He placed each base on the correct spot.

He announced, "Okay, I'll bat first. You can pitch."

I asked, "Noah, can I pitch underhand?"

He hesitated, "Well, okay, if you want to." I was afraid that if I pitched a hard ball overhand that I wouldn't be steady enough to keep the ball over the plate.

He practiced swinging his bat several times over the plate. We forgot a helmet. He pushed his baseball cap around so the brim was facing backwards. Noah took a swing at the first pitched ball. He connected. The sound of the ping on the metal bat rang as the ball spun past my head out to center field. I ran after the ball, breathing hard. I realized that the full field created long runs and that two hours would be a challenge. Noah made it to third base. He returned to home plate to bat again. The rule of two-man baseball is that you bat until you get three outs, and then the pitcher is up to bat. You keep score by keeping track of the base hits and then add them up at the end.

I stepped up to bat, exhausted from running the bases, trying to tag Noah out. I hit my first pitched ball from Noah. He stuck out his glove and grabbed the ball. I didn't get to first base. The second pitch was low, so I grounded it to second. I ran to first. My third hit was to the outfield and I ran to third.

It was a hot summer day and the dust from the field was flying as we ran the bases. I was sweating and panting by the end of the two hours.

On our way back across the schoolyard, Noah whispered, "I slammed you. I won. But, you're not bad at running!"

"So, what did you learn in speech all these years?" I asked.

He said, "Oh, eye contact, turn your shoulders to listen, listen to your friend, try to let him choose what to do, before you get angry, listen to what he is saying."

I was impressed that he remembered all those skills. Then he turned toward me, lifted up his Red Sox baseball cap, and said, "You know what I learned the most?"

"I'd love to know," I answered.

"Most of all I learned that I was a good person."[23]

Tears streamed down my face as I drove home, realizing that Noah had beaten the odds and he would be okay.

SUMMARY OF STRATEGIES IN PHASE FOUR

Elsie, by age nine, talks about her own feelings, reflects back on how she felt in the past, and connects with her current peers. She is no longer suicidal. Anna, another nine-year-old who has learning disabilities and who doesn't fit in socially with her classmates, learns to read subtle social language. She learns to read facial cues and body language and to follow the fast pace of conversation with her peers. With a peer, Anna learns to play tag and to navigate around the busy playground, creating narratives and talking to others. She becomes connected to her friends.

Nathaniel, a ten-year-old with Asperger's, learns social language with a peer and practices limiting his monologues in a special visual technique that allows him to connect with his peers.

The use of visual materials helps several children with autism focus on social skills and relate to their peers. Nicky, an eleven-year-old with autism, also practices social skills with a classmate through the use of visual materials. He learns to listen to the keywords in conversation and to interact with his peers. Another child with Asperger's, Abby, an eight-year-old, also learns social skills through the use of small books of photographs. Maggie, a first grader with obsessive thoughts, also learns how to control her own thinking through drawing and the use of small books. Even Christine benefits from the use of visuals and drawings when she needs to express her feelings about her friend's brother.

The most difficult strategies in this method are the ones that involve teaching a child to see the perspective of another child. In phase four, Michael, a four year old with autism, learns perspective taking with a peer and begins to see the discomfort of Angel, his peer. He struggles over heating his marshmallow over a pretend campfire that he built with Angel on the playground. His marshmallow falls off the stick several times while Angel is describing her plight at Disney World on the rides. She shows her distress on her face as she tells her story. At first, Michael doesn't see or feel her distress and her perspective on being in a fast-moving roller coaster. I encourage Angel to show her concern for him and his hands that could get caught in the campfire. Then I introduce Michael to Angel's distress over getting sick in the roller coaster. When he can't see her distress, I remind him of a moment when he had the flu. He was able to make the association between his pain and her pain. When Angel gives Michael her marshmallow stick at the end of the session, they are looking at each other, both with compassion.

Patrick, the young child who bangs his trains in the corner in phase one, is now in phase four. He learns to understand abstract terms and draw accurate inferences from his peer's conversation. Patrick learns to negotiate in play with a peer over a Spiderman narrative. He also learns to negotiate in a game of bowling with his peers and his peers begin to appreciate who he is. Patrick learns that he may not be the best in bowling, but he has his own talents—he remembers details that his peers can't remember and he helps them in class discussions. His peers love him. Patrick hits a great "strike" in bowling and wins in his own search for genuine social relationships with his peers.

Conrad, a four-year-old with autism, learns to control his temper with his peer, Caroline, as they eat pizza. He learns to see the interests of his peer, to allow the peer to change the agenda of the narrative, and to be more compassionate in a peer relationship. He learns the steps of negotiation and how to come to an agreement, the most difficult skill for a child with autism.

When a child with autism comes to a real agreement, seeing the perspective of an opponent, the therapist's job is over. The ending process of therapy is to help the child reflect on his performance and to congratulate the child and his family on completing the long, tedious journey toward communication. When Conrad graduates from this play therapy language group, he hands the trophy I'd given him for outstanding work to his peer, Caroline. I smile and hand Caroline a trophy, too. I say, "Oh, the peers work just as hard as you do. Caroline gets one, too." As they leave the play yard for the last time as partners in play therapy, I smile. They are both going on to kindergarten. I see Conrad point to the hose and stop to ask Caroline if she wants to turn it on one more time. She giggles and nods her head no. They leave the preschool yard holding hands, hugging their trophies against their chests with their other hands.

Even with the severe limitations of autism, all children need the support to do the best they can to be more social. Not all children with autism can reach this potential. Some children manage to see the perspective of others. Some children become more aware and loving. Some children struggle and do not learn to sustain relationships with peers, but they may learn to notice others. Some learn to play baseball with a peer and find that the fourth base is called "home." Children with autism can learn to be social and connect with peers. Some children with language and social disabilities, like Noah, discover in the process of play therapy that they are good people.

Facilitating Language in Play Dates for Younger Children: Suggestions for Parents, Specialists, and Teachers

1. At the beginning of the play period, create a plan in writing/drawing along with two children. Draw pictures of each activity as you discuss it with them. They may want to help you draw or write.

2. Explain "sensory breaks" and write them in the plan to meet the needs of the particular child you are treating. Consult with the child's occupational therapist for specific suggestions. These breaks are for sensory activities such as

   - bouncing on a therapy ball
   - blowing horns
   - tossing a ball (Gertie soft) back and forth
   - getting "squished" under a beanbag
   - swinging (outside or inside if available)
   - using musical instruments such as a small drum or the ocean drum
   - playing with fuzzy stuffed animals
   - listening to music under headphones

3. Plan a snack break at the end of a thirty-minute play period if the whole play date is one hour. Be aware of the dietary needs of both children.

4. Explain one goal for the play date. Make it concrete such as

   - looking at your friend
   - noticing what your friend is doing

- giving your friend a compliment
- making a comment about what you're doing
- making a comment about what your friend is doing
- using your gestures to help you tell your friend what to do next
- noticing your space between yourself and your friend
- watching out for a "loud" voice that is too loud because you are close
- watching out for a "soft" voice that is too soft when you're far away
- thinking about how your friend is feeling
- thinking about how to make your friend feel needed
- allowing your friend to set the agenda or play theme

5. Set the play objects out on a small rug or mat to define where the children will play and explain to them where they can play. Keep the play area organized. Too many objects may be confusing or disorganizing for young children.

6. Observe the children as they begin to play with objects and figures and help them set up the play set, if needed.

7. Suggest a story theme by asking them what they like to do. Create a beginning to the story by naming the time of day, the place, and the characters in the story.

8. Give them one or two play actions with an object (one that you have) and model for them, if needed. Vary the play actions so they don't get stuck on one theme.

9. Narrate your actions and the actions of each child. Talk about what they are doing at first. They should continue to narrate their own actions.

10. Identify a specific speech goal if the child who is being treated has speech issues such as apraxia (developmental verbal dyspraxia). Work on the syllable sequencing or a specific set of sounds as you play with the two children.

11. Help each child continue the story in a sequence of actions and help them come to an ending.

12. Observe and let them play.

13. Use music and art that is set up for the sensory child.

14. Give them five-minute warnings before the play date ends.

15. Ask them to sit on a beanbag and face each other to say goodbye. Ask each child to tell the other child what he/she liked about the play date. Plan for the next one and ask them what they want to do next time.

16. Praise them for the things they did well and positively reinforce each time a child uses language to request, to express emotions, or to just narrate the play actions.

17. Have them check off the activities on their plan.

18. Keep the play date to an hour or an hour and a half for the first few weeks. After the first few weeks, the play date can be extended to two hours.

19. When you take them outside, make a plan and follow the rules necessary for a particular activity.

A Playground Program for Peers at Recess in School: Suggestions for Teachers and Specialists

1. Identify a peer to work with the child who has difficulty with language.

2. Create a picture that will show the child his/her choices of available activities (in the classroom or at recess).

3. Preteach the plan with the picture. For example, set goals with the child each day to

   • Remember how to invite a friend.

   • Pick a friend.

   • Choose three things you want to do today outside.

   • Ask your friend what he/she wants to do.

   • Decide on a plan of action.

   Make the play experience successful by

   • Teaching the child and the peer skills with both visual and verbal prompting and modeling.

   • Allowing them to play together without prompting.

   • Helping them end their play period. Show them how to say goodbye to a friend.

   • Planning a play date or time to play at recess next time.

4. Provide activities that are concrete and require hands-on materials. Have a duffel bag ready with supplies (chalk, jump rope, Gertie ball, soccer ball and

cones, games for quiet play, a white board for explanations, a few fidget toys, a baseball that is soft, a soft bat, a soft mitt).

5. Allow other peers to join in when the child understands the game.

6. Adapt regular baseball, soccer, kickball, and tag games to allow the child with a language disability to play (e.g., keep bases and the pitcher close, the baseball soft, and the bat large).

7. Always be aware of the child's sensory and gross motor needs. He/she may need help moving across the trolley or getting up on the play structures or throwing a ball. Give him/her homework to practice these skills.

8. Ask the occupational therapist or physical therapist to help you with a plan if the child needs extra support.

9. Write a short note or report for the teacher, the aide, and others who work with the child so that the skills can be practiced during the school week.

10. Meet with your team, weekly at first, to discuss what is working at recess and how everyone can help the child.

APPENDIX 3

Working with Siblings: Suggestions for Parents, Specialists, and Teachers

1. Create a safe, quiet play space with some organization of toys.

2. Develop a plan with the sibling with one to two objectives per session.

3. Teach the sibling the particular method that their brother/sister responds to best. If he/she needs to learn Applied Behavior Analysis prompting, teach the exact cues that are used by the child's teacher or home trainer. This can be incorporated into a play scheme. If he/she needs to learn Floor Time or Narrative Play, teach the strategies in an individual session and model all techniques with figures first.

4. Connect with all specialists on the child's team each week, even if it is through e-mail.

5. Model the voice intonation pattern, rate, and volume for the sibling.

6. Ask questions that suggest ideas for conversation between siblings.

7. Suggest a story to go along with actions of figures.

8. Keep them on the narrative of the play scheme. Be a character. Move with them.

9. Gesture/verbal prompt both siblings to notice each other and make comments.

10. Keep verbal prompts consistent and short in length.

11. Engage in well-timed sensory integration breaks and gross motor activities.

12. Maintain eye contact equally with both siblings.

13. Acknowledge both siblings for appropriate gesture, facial expression, and sounds that show some reciprocity.

14. Be aware of emotional responses and support both siblings.

15. Be available for any questions. Be honest and clear.

16. Giggle and use gesture frequently. Engage 100 percent in all interactions.

17. Laugh hard when appropriate!

18. Teach the more verbal sibling to wait for responses. Teach breathing techniques.

19. Be yourself each moment.

20. The more verbal sibling needs to know that you understand.

Social Language Scripts for Unstructured Time in Situations at Playgrounds/Parks: Suggestions for Teachers, Specialists, and Parents

These are a few examples of social language scripts for an elementary school student (grades 3–5) with a social language disorder. Additional social scripts may be downloaded from www.child-talk.com. The teacher or assistant may write these scripts on a small white board to remind a student during recess or they may be used as practice scripts for home or in a quiet setting before a child goes into the social situation. The scripts may be made into laminated strips on a key chain that can be stored in the child's backpack. The best way to use the scripts is to "preteach" the language before the child enters the social situation. Encourage the child to create his/her own scripts. As they learn these scripts, children often vary them and create their own as they play. After a few practice sessions with one peer, a child may not need them at all.

Recess

Initiating a conversation:

Hey, what did you do last night?

What are you reading?

What are you doing this weekend?

Do you watch videos? Which ones?

What did you do last weekend?

Are you going on vacation?

Soccer:

What do I do?

What are you doing?

Can I play?

Nice kick!

I scored!

You scored!

What team can I be on?

Tag:

Let's play tag.

Who's it?

Can I be it?

I'm out. Oh, bummer!

Hurry!

Hey, wait!

Okay, I'm it.

Okay, I'm out again.

Classroom

Commenting:

Hi, what are you doing?

That's cool.

How did you make that?

That's awesome.

I like that!

That's cool.

Encourage a child to:

Try out scripts with one peer in a quiet setting.

Practice every day at home or in a quiet setting.

Try out a few scripts (without the visual) with one peer.

Try out recess or a game or entering the classroom.

Allow the child to experiment on his/her own with social scripts.

Fade prompting when you can.

Let him/her make mistakes.

Encourage the child to use words instead of getting too close or jumping up and down and giggling.

Notes

PREFACE

1. O. Sacks, 1995, *An Anthropologist on Mars*, New York: Vintage Books, A Division of Random House, Inc.; T. Grandin, 2005, *Animals in Translation*, New York: Scribner; T. Grandin, 1995, *Thinking in Pictures*, New York: Vintage Books. Temple writes from the experience of being a person who has grown up with autism. She is a brilliant writer who has the insight to understand what it is like to think in pictures. She writes, "I think in pictures. Words are like a second language to me. I translate both spoken and written words into full color movies complete with sound, which run like a VCR tape in my head" (Grandin, 1995, 1). Temple also writes, "Social interactions that come naturally to most people can be daunting for people with autism" (Grandin, 1995, 132). Temple emphasizes two ideas—that a person with autism thinks in the visual modality, in full color; and, that acquiring the skills of social interaction do not come naturally. Children with autism need help learning to become social in all settings.

American Psychiatric Association, 2005, *Diagnostic and Statistical Manual of Mental Disorders, Fourth Edition (DSM-IV-TR)*. The definition of autism or "autistic disorder" states "the essential features of Autistic Disorder are the presence of markedly abnormal or impaired development in social interaction and communication and a markedly restricted repertoire of activity and interests" (DSM-IV, 70). Pervasive Developmental Disorders include impairment in social interaction, communication, and present with stereotyped behaviors, interests, and activities. Autistic Disorder, one of the Pervasive Developmental Disorders, includes

Pervasive Developmental Disorder Not Otherwise Specified. Specific diagnostic criteria may be found in detail in this reference. The qualitative impairment of autism includes social interaction that has two of these four impairments: impairment in eye-to-eye gaze, facial expression, body postures, and gestures; failure to develop peer relationships; lack of seeing shared interests; lack of social and emotional reciprocity. In addition, further qualitative impairment includes at least one of the following: delay or lack of spoken language; impairment in ability to initiate or sustain a conversation; stereotyped and repetitive use of language; lack of spontaneous make-believe play or social imitative play. Finally, autism has at least one of the following: preoccupation with one or more stereotyped and restricted patterns of interest; inflexible adherence to specific routines; repetitive motor mannerisms; or preoccupation with parts of objects (DSM-IV, 75).

S.E. Bryson, L. Zwaigenbaum, and W. Roberts, 2004, "The early detection of autism in clinical practice," *Paediatrics and Child Health*, April, 9(4): 219–221; S. Bryson, L. Zwaigenbaum, and W. Roberts, 2005, "Understanding autism—what every family doctor needs to know," adapted from April 2004 article in *Paediatrics and Child Health*. These authors distinguish between ASD, otherwise known as autism spectrum disorder, and PDD, otherwise known as pervasive developmental disorder and Asperger's syndrome. These authors include Asperger's syndrome in ASD (autism spectrum disorder), but distinguish Asperger's from ASD by saying that Asperger's syndrome has "relatively strong cognitive and language skills" (Bryson et al., 2004, 1). These authors, Bryson, Zwaigenbaum, and Roberts (March 2005) define autism:

- Autism or autistic disorder: the classical type of autism with onset prior to age three, which encompasses a group of neuropsychiatric disorders characterized by deficits in social interaction and communication, and unusual and repetitive behavior.
- Asperger's syndrome: impairments in communication and social development, and by narrow interests and repetitive behaviors. Unlike typical autism, individuals with Asperger's syndrome have no significant delay in language or cognitive development.
- Atypical autism or PDD-NOS: conditions don't quite fit autism and specifically, while there are impairments of social communication, interaction and imagination, intellectual impairment is seen less often.
- Childhood disintegrative disorder: condition occurring in three and four year olds characterized by deterioration of intellectual, social, and language functioning from previously normal functioning.

2. S. Baron-Cohen, 2001, *Mindblindness*, Cambridge, MA: MIT Press. The main idea behind Baron-Cohen's theory is that a person must have competence in four things to read the minds of others: social understanding, behavioral predictions, social interaction, and communication. The theory of mind mechanism (ToMM) developed from Alan Leslie's theory (1994) and then redefined by Simon Baron-Cohen (2001) refers to a system in which an individual can read the behavior of

others in terms of volitional mental states (desire and goal) and can read eye direction and predict some intention by this eye gaze. The theory is complex. Simon Baron-Cohen revealed that children with Autism Spectrum Disorder (ASD) are poor at following another person's gaze (Baron-Cohen, 1995), have difficulty recognizing facial expressions, and have more difficulty understanding what the other person might be thinking.

S. Pinker, 1997, *How the Mind Works*, New York: W.W. Norton & Company. Steven Pinker says that "anything we can think is also something we can think someone else thinks (Mary knows that John thinks that there are unicorns)." These are what Pinker calls "onionlike thoughts-inside-thoughts . . . " (Pinker, 1997, 330). Pinker says that we can't really read other people's minds, but we can make good guesses from "what they say, what we read between the lines, what they show in their faces and eyes, and what best explains their behavior." He writes clearly, "It is our species' most remarkable talent" (Pinker, 1997, 330).

D. Premack and G. Woodruff, 1978, "Does the chimpanzee have 'a theory of mind?'" *Behavior and Brain Sciences*, 4: 515–526. Typical children have what is called a "theory of mind" because they can "attribute mental states to oneself and to others and interpret behavior in terms of mental states" (Premack and Woodruff, 1978). Children with autism need help in understanding that others have mental states similar to or different from their own mental ideas. Some children need help in drawing inferences from the other person's eye direction, body language, and facial expression in order to conclude that the person is in a similar mental state or perhaps a different one. Often children with autism misperceive what another person is thinking and become frustrated because they think that the other person doesn't understand them or intends to do something that is the opposite of the expected behavior. Some children become so angry that they respond with negative comments, and behaviors that look aggressive; however, they are frustrated because they don't understand why the person reacted in a particular way. The behaviors are not "against" the other person. They may cry out or throw something, but usually not at another person.

"Around the age of 18–24 months human toddlers begin to pretend and recognize the pretending of others, and this seems to mark a qualitative change in their play" (Leslie, 1987; Dunn and Dale, 1984). Leslie argues that the mental state "pretend" is probably one of the first epistemic mental states that young children come to understand" (Simon Baron-Cohen, 2001, 53). In Baron-Cohen's studies of young children he found that "if a person is looking at something, this is interpreted as an object that he or she may desire, or plan to act upon next. This is not a quirk in early development either: It remains a powerful way that we interpret another's gaze, even in adults (Argyle, 1972)" (Baron-Cohen, 2001, 105).

3. H. Tager-Flusberg, 1993, "What language reveals about the understanding of minds in children with autism," in *Understanding Other Minds: Perspectives from Autism*, ed. S. Baron-Cohen et al., Oxford University Press. Tager-Flusberg has done extensive research on the theory of mind concept and children with autism and how this affects the child's language.

INTRODUCTION

1. S.I. Greenspan and S. Wieder, 2006, *Engaging Autism*, New York: The Perseus Books Group, DaCapo Lifelong Books. The cornerstone of Dr. Greenspan's work is the following: "Language and cognition, as well as emotional and social skills, are learned through relationships that involve emotionally meaningful exchanges; children vary in their underlying motor and sensory processing capacities; and progress in all areas of development is interrelated." Based on these ideas, Dr. Greenspan created the Developmental, Individual-Difference (DIR) model (Greenspan and Wieder, 2006, 40), an overarching framework for the general theory behind play therapy with children. The Floortime model is a part of the DIR model and focuses on creating emotionally meaningful interactions that connect to several basic mental capacities. These key components that relate to Narrative Play therapy are the stages of emotional development in Floortime:

- Regulation and interest in the world
- Engaging and relating; intentionality and two-way communication
- Social problem-solving, mood regulation, and formation of a sense of self
- Shared problem-solving, and regulating mood and behavior
- Creating symbols and using words and ideas
- Emotional thinking, logic, and a sense of reality
- Multicausal and triangular thinking
- Gray-area, emotionally differentiated thinking
- A growing sense of self and reflection on internal standard (Greenspan and Wieder, 2006, 43–47).

Families and caregivers are active participants in using Floortime techniques, which are similar to Narrative Play therapy. The parents are always invited to engage in play, to relate to the child, and to engage with the child. Siblings are encouraged to participate in play as they learn how to help the child with "circles of communication" or reciprocal interacting, and extending communication in a two-way experience. In Narrative Play therapy the goals are the same as in Floortime during the first part of play; relating and engaging are critical to the whole therapy method. Once the child is engaged, the therapist in Narrative Play suggests ways to incorporate speech production, language, play themes, and story telling within the play. Both methods can be used in natural settings and both methods enhance the family relationships.

S. Greenspan and D. Lewis, 2002, *The Affect-Based Language Curriculum (ABLC)*, Bethesda, MD: Interdisciplinary Council on Developmental and Learning Disorders (ICDL). This program combines Floortime and systematic instruction to track language and oral-motor progress and sensory skills and affect in a therapeutic setting. The program is designed with specific core areas that are taught systematically, such as engagement, coregulated reciprocal interactions, pragmatics, imitation, receptive language, and expressive language. The book includes several checklists for families and therapists to define where the child is and how to proceed in the program. The program is similar to Narrative Play in that they both encourage peer play and begin this interaction after the child is engaged with family members and familiar adults. Both models include Floortime methods to engage the child in a relationship with affect and to make contact with the child. Both models are helpful for the child with autism and language delay.

2. B. Prizant, A. Wetherby, E. Rubin, A. Laurent, and P. Rydell, 2002, "The SCERTS model: Enhancing communication and socioemotional abilities of children with autism spectrum disorder," *Jenison Autism Journal*, 14(4): 2–19; B. Prizant, A. Wetherby, E. Rubin, and A.C. Laurent, 2003, "The SCERTS model: A transactional, family-centered approach to enhancing communication and socioemotional abilities of children with autism spectrum disorder," *Journal of Infants and Young Children*, 16(4): 296–316; A. Wetherby and B. Prizant, 2000, *Autism Spectrum Disorders: A Transactional Developmental Perspective*, Baltimore, MD: Brookes Publishing Company. The SCERTS Model (Prizant et al., 2003) is a comprehensive, multidisciplinary developmental model for enhancing communication and socioemotional abilities of young children with ASD. This model is derived from a theoretical as well as an empirically based foundation on communication and socioemotional development in young children. The SCERTS model prioritizes social communication, emotional regulation, and transactional support as the primary developmental dimensions that must be addressed to support the development of children with ASD. The model provides strategies for the child to develop symbolic play skills that are similar to the strategies used in Floortime, Replays, and in Narrative Play. All of these developmental play-based models provide therapeutic strategies to relate to the child while including the family and to assist him or her in managing his or her emotional reactions to particular situations and events. Like Floortime and Narrative Play, SCERTS uses interpersonal supports across partners to develop the child's emotional development and social skills (Prizant et al., 2003).

3. S. Gutstein and R.K. Sheely, 2002, *Relationship Development Intervention with Young Children*, London: Jessica Kingsley Publishers. Relationship Development Intervention (RDI) was developed by Gutstein and Sheely and "is an adult-led model that applies a remedy, a gradual systematic process of correcting a deficit to the point where it no longer constitutes an obstacle to reaching one's potential. RDI's work is a cognitive intervention with the goal of remediation. A primary focus for RDI consultants is helping parents and their children restore the critical Intersubjective Relationship (IR) that is inherently damaged by ASD. The IR is perceived by developmental psychologists as the primary lab for learning to function in dynamic environments. We (RDI) quote Barbara Rogoff: There is general agreement . . . that early childhood involves transformations in the nature of the sharing of meaning between partners. . . . By its nature, communication presumes intersubjectivity—that is, shared understanding based on a common focus of attention and shared presuppositions that form the ground for communication" (Rogoff, 1990). According to Rachelle Sheely, "failure to develop intersubjectivity is the most documented deficit in the autism research. It has also been found to be the most persistent and resistant to change over time. Our hope is that through

reengaging the IR, the child, through parental guidance, can begin to develop on the pathway of dynamic learning opportunities and can internalize the complex mental processes that are essential to attaining a quality of life" (Sheely, 2007). RDI teaches specific techniques to the child with autism, and focuses on the nonverbal and gesture system of communication. This model is successful when the child with autism is unable to attend, to join others, or to focus on the perspective of the other person. RDI is complex with several levels of achievement built into the method. RDI activities are designed for a range of AS, PDD, and autism and for low- and high-functioning children. Activities are presented from age two onward.

I have several children who work with me in Narrative Play Therapy and at the same time work with an RDI therapist. Both methods work together well if the providers communicate the intent of each session and support the work of the other therapist. There are several ways to use a car in Narrative Play to teach a child to play and to narrate his own actions, and at the same time, to work on RDI Level II, Stage 5, Activity 56, called "Car Crash Variations" (Gutstein and Sheely, 2002, 152). The child has a toy car and the therapist or peer has another car. In RDI, the child at this level is practicing degrees of speed changes with a small car, and adapting to the activity variations. In Narrative Play this activity includes a peer, and the child with autism is in Phase Three. The activity helps that child attend to another's actions and to regulate his actions along side of his peer. In the RDI activity, the child is asked to deliberately pass the other person's car or, alternately, to "crash" into the car. The child is asked to regulate the speed of his car with cues like "Let's crash them slower now." In Narrative Play the child and his peer are asked to create a story theme and then continue playing by making the cars pass each other until they reach a destination. They are asked to narrate their own actions, the actions of the other child, and then to talk about how the story ends when they reach where they are going. Both methods work together well and accomplish more than one goal in the same therapy session.

4. P. Wolfberg, 1999, *Play and Imagination in Children with Autism*, New York: Teachers College Press. Integrated Play Groups Model: This play therapy model is based on the concept of "guided participation," and draws from Vygotsky and "apprenticeship in thinking," a theory developed by Barbara Rogoff (1990). Barbara Rogoff writes about the cognitive development of the mind in a sociocultural context. In her book *Apprenticeship in Thinking*, she explains the core value of her theory of guided participation developed from Vygotsky's theory on "interpsychological processes." She quotes Leont'ev (1981) who writes about Vygotsky, saying that "higher psychological processes unique to humans can be acquired only through interactions with others, that is, through interpsychological processes that only later will be carried out independently by the individual" (Leont'ev 55–56 in Rogoff, 1990, 13). Rogoff developed her model of "apprenticeship" based on Vygotsky's concept that the active role of children and support of others in social interactions promote cognitive development. Her theory is based on "shared problem solving," which means that a new learner participates with a more skilled learner—the central theme of Apprenticeship. She writes that "children's cognitive

development is an apprenticeship—it occurs through guided participation in social activity with companions who support and stretch children's understanding of and skill in using the tools of culture" (Rogoff, 1990, vii).

Wolfberg created a similar model of observation and guided participation in play. She described her model "as the process through which children learn and develop while actively participating in culturally valued activity with the guidance, support, and challenge of partners who vary in skills and status" (Wolfberg, 1999, 49). Wolfberg's model is unique because she not only draws on the ethnographic tradition, but also provides a model for keen observation and interpretation of how children play independently of other children, beside them, and with them. This model offers tools for observation, and it teaches the adult how to "scaffold" interactions between two children. Rogoff first developed the term "scaffolding" to describe how the adult adjusts the support for the interactions between children, and guides children based on their need during play. When the children become more comfortable the adult fades away and gradually lessens support. This "fading" of support is also the therapist's responsibility in Narrative Play therapy, and usually occurs in Phase Three and Four. The adult remains on the sidelines and provides some help, modeling play initiations, if needed. Wolfberg's model provides "play guidance," which means that the less-skilled players are matched with more capable players. The "novices gain practice and skill while guided by an adult and more capable peers" (Wolfberg, 1999, 52). This play-based model takes place in natural, integrated settings where a child would naturally play. In Narrative Play therapy the child is also matched with peers and encouraged to engage with them in such natural settings as schools, parks, playgrounds, and various other environments.

5. K.A. Quill, 2000, *Do-Watch-Listen-Say*, Baltimore: Brookes Publishing Inc.; K. Quill, 1995, *Teaching Children with Autism: Strategies to Enhance Communication and Socialization*, New York: Delmar Publishers. Kathleen Quill's books are comprehensive tools for assessing, implementing strategies, and developing curriculum for children with autism. She explores creative ways to assess and support specialists in teaching children skills of socialization. Her book (2000) includes specific charts for assessment, checklists, and activity sheets that correspond with a skill list. The book is highly organized and provides suggestions to build nonverbal social interactions, imitation, and organization. The book has a comprehensive list of resources and references that are essential for specialists, parents and teachers.

6. S.J. Roger, D. Osaki, T. Hall, and J. Reaven, 1998, *The Denver Model: An Integrated Approach to Intervention for Young Children with Autism*, Denver, CO: JFK Center for Developmental Disabilities. This model is a treatment program for young children that places families at the core of the treatment and acknowledges that each child with autism and family is unique. The goals are individualized. The model was developed to treat toddlers through preschool children with autism. The model consists of an interdisciplinary treatment team that is directed by a parent along with one core professional. The treatment occurs within the family routines, within the preschool settings, and in 1:1 direct teaching sessions. The program includes twenty hours of planned instruction focused on concrete objectives and

goals. The emphasis is on relationships, shared control, and positive emotion. These skills are addressed within six content areas: social interactions, play skills, fine and gross motor development, cognition, and personal independence. The Denver Model is similar to Narrative Play in the area of play skills. Both models develop play skills in natural settings at preschools or in play activities. Both models incorporate specific goals and strategies for the child to acquire language and social skills.

7. K. Levine and N. Chedd, 2006. *Replays: Using Play to Enhance Emotional and Behavioral Development for Children with Autism Spectrum Disorders*, London: Jessica Kingsley Publishers. Replays is a play-based approach that can also help children with behavioral difficulties, who have rapid, intense, and negative emotional reactions to seemingly small events. The therapist suggests that the child "practice" reexperiencing such an event and guides the child within the context of playful, exaggerated, and symbolic reenactment. The child takes on different roles in the play and the overreactions diminish over time. This method is based on the concept of "systematic desensitization" that has been used by therapists to help children overcome phobias and fearful events. In Replays the child experiences small amounts of stress in a safe context and eventually forms more positive experiences with this fearful event by being with a trusted adult. The child begins to experience control and feels that the event is less frightening. This method works well with Narrative Play. I often integrate "replays" (Levine and Chedd, 2006) into my play therapy method, particularly in the second phase, joint attention, when the child is most likely to refuse to change an agenda or allow a child in their play area. Through this method, the child can replay his anxiety and desensitize himself to the situation. Dr. Levine and I have treated a child together using the Replays method and with Narrative Play in the same play therapy session.

8. C. Maurice, G. Green, and S.C. Luce, 1996, *Behavioral Intervention for Young Children with Autism*, Austin, TX: Pro-ed. This book is based on the concept that autism is a syndrome of behavioral deficits with a neurological basis and that the behaviors may be changed through constructive interactions that are carefully programmed. Behavior analytic treatment focuses on teaching in small, measurable units of behavior systematically. This book includes teaching guides with curriculum and very specific skills to teach the child. ABA was originally developed by Lovass (1987) and is based on operant conditioning. This method is adult directed and relies on structure and responses in small incremental units. The child is reinforced for reaching a target behavior with positive reinforcement and the therapy is usually administered in quiet and controlled environment with visuals and adult support. The problem with this approach is that if the child executes these skills in this controlled environment, he may not be able to transfer the skills to a more natural setting with unfamiliar adults (Tager-Flusberg, 1981). The goal of ABA is to provide direct examples of positive behavior. In my experience, despite the contrast to Narrative Play methods, a child can be in both therapies at once, if the clinician collaborates on cues and provide consultation time each week to go over the goals of both sessions.

9. J. Ayers, 1994, *Sensory Integration and the Child*, Western Psychological Services; C.S. Kranowitz, 2003, *The Out-of-Sync Child Has Fun*, New York: Perigee Book; J. Koomar and A. Bundy, 2002, "Creating intervention from theory," in *Sensory Integration Theory and Practice*, Philadelphia, PA: FAA David Company. "Sensory integration is the organization of sensation for use. Our senses give us information about the physical conditions of our body and the environment around us. Sensations flow into the brain like streams flowing into a lake. Countless bits of sensory information enter our brain at every moment, not only from our eyes and our ears, but also from every place in our bodies" (Ayers, 1994, 5). Ayers believes, as I do, that a vestibular disorder may cause a child to run in the wrong direction on a busy playground. This behavior will interfere with social relationships. The child has trouble judging whether he is too close or too far away and often bumps into peers. He has difficulty visualizing space and may not know how to move to one play or another, particularly on a busy playground at recess. These difficulties are a part of a sensory integration disorder. Kranowitz's book is a sequel to *The Out-of-Sync Child: Recognizing and Coping with Sensory Integration Dysfunction* (1998). This book includes many activities that help children with this disorder. These activities also help a child with language disabilities. I have spent many years cotreating with occupational therapists and I believe in what they do. The methods they use are similar to my work on the playground with children in phase three and four. Children need respect and help with sensory integration problems. They may become overwhelmed if they are exposed to loud noises outside, unpredictable objects, open spaces, or children running into them. In addition, while addressing these needs during play, therapists can encourage language within the session. Cotreatments between occupational therapist and speech therapists are valuable to a child with autism. I have learned to integrate the activities of occupational therapy within Narrative Play therapy because I have had the opportunity to work with many wonderful OTs at OTA, Watertown, and OTA, Wakefield, both in Massachusetts. It is important to collaborate with a child's occupational therapist every two weeks to plan activities that will help him or her at school and in therapy.

PHASE ONE: FIRST CONTACT

1. M. A. Preissler, 2006, "Play and autism: Facilitating symbolic understanding," in *Play=Learning*, ed. Dorothy Singer, Roberta M. Golinkoff, and K. Kathy Hirsh-Pasek, New York: Oxford University Press; M.A. Preissler and S. Carey, 2004, "Do both pictures and words function as symbols for 18 and 24 month children?" *Journal of Cognition and Development*, 5: 185–212. Early longitudinal research indicates that play is essential to language development and that in autism, play is a long-term outcome (Sigman et al., 1999). Melissa Allen Preissler writes, "There is a critical link between the development of symbolic play and the use and understanding of symbolic language. . . . many children with ASD appear to have an associative learning style, reflected in scripting, contextual based responding, and difficulties in generalization" (Preissler, 2006, 233). Kanner (1943) defined autism as a deficit

in pretend play. Other studies show how play is compromised in children with autism as their play is "less innovative, less symbolic, and more developmentally immature than normally developing peers (Sigman and Ungerer, 1984 in Preissler, 2006, 237). The repetitive and unimaginative play in children with autism was called "echoplaylia" (Schuler and Wolfberg, 2000). This type of limited play may be an imitation of a video story that a child with autism enacts. A child with autism may have a limited repertoire of play themes (They repeat one theme or ask endless questions about this theme). Current research has found that children with autism may not see that a picture represents an actual object. When developing toddlers are asked to pair a word (e.g., whisk) with a picture (a real whisk), they will learn the label for the picture; however, when asked to pair the word with the object, they will return to selecting the picture (Preissler and Carey, 2004). Many children with autism fail to see that a real object can represent a picture of that object. Vygotsky (1978) suggested that abstract thought is unattainable for young children and they must develop this ability to create meaning for objects in the real world. In my clinical work, children with autism have difficulty seeing that once the object is removed and the picture is present with the name (e.g., truck), the picture represents the actual toy truck. These children can be encouraged to develop symbolic play as the therapist models the agent (object) and actions in play with the child. At first, they may imitate one play action with one object (e.g., mommy doll goes to bed); however, as they accumulate a larger repertoire of play actions and objects, they begin to create their own representational play. When this happens, in my experience, children develop more complicated language and narrate their actions in play. There is an integral link between a child's ability to use representational (symbolic) play and language. The experience of play and finding meaning in objects allows children to create narratives and develop language as they narrate and play.

2. A. McCabe and C. Peterson, 1991, *Developing Narrative Structure*, Hillsdale, NJ: Lawrence Erlbaum Associates Publishers; A. McCabe and L. Bliss, 2003, *Patterns of Narrative Discourse*, Boston, MA: Allyn & Bacon Press; V.G. Paley, 1990, *The Boy Who Would Be Helicopter: The Use of Storytelling in the Classroom*, Cambridge, MA: Harvard University Press. A child's early learning includes developing symbolic play and storytelling about actions in play or narrative. Allysa McCabe (McCabe and Peterson, 1991) follows the Labov (1972) tradition and defines narrative as "two temporally ordered clauses in the past tense" (McCabe, 1991, ix). Although definitions of narrative differ in detail, they include a "recounting of events that follow each other in time" (Labov, 1972; Peterson and McCabe, 1983; Polanyi, 1985). Polanyi suggests that a story must include not only main events, but also "contextualizing clauses" that describe the participants, explain the setting, or evaluate the situation. Narratives from children that are typical in language development narrate from the age of about 27 months (McCabe and Bliss, 2003). Preschoolers lengthen their stories and at first tell events in leap frog structure (Peterson and McCabe, 1983). They may leave out events or tell events out of sequence. They may produce many actions that are about only one event. Four-year-olds use abundant

conjunctions (and, but, when, so). It is not unusual for a child of four to use dysflu-
encies ("and . . . ahh . . . so . . . we . . . well). According to McCabe and Bliss (2003),
a child of five can narrate events in sequence and by six tell a complete narrative. By
six years, the child can orient a listener to who, what, where, and when something
happened, give some actions, and build to a high point in the story. Then they
resolve the event and even evaluate what happened. However, in some cultures, the
sequence of the event may not be the main focus for a child's story. The therapist
must inquire about the nature of storytelling traditions in the family culture in
which the child experiences narratives. The general definition by McCabe is that
narrative or storytelling "is the oral sequencing of temporally successive events, real
or imaginary" (McCabe and Peterson, 1991, ix). This definition may be restricting
as seen in the research by James Gee (1991, 1990) who suggests that a narrative is
shaped by personal history and the culture of the child and the social interactions
with the child's family. Labov (1972) described narrative structures as including
several parts:

- Abstract function: the speaker informs the listener of the main idea of the story
- Orientation: the speaker informs the listener who the participants are and
  where they are and when the events happened
- Complicating action: there is a chronology of events and actions that lead up
  to one action that is the "high point" of the story
- Evaluation: the speaker lets the listener know why the story was told
- Resolution: the events and problems are solved
- Codas: formal endings.

In 1991, Alyssa McCabe and I developed a study to look at the narratives
of children who suffered from abuse and wrote a paper presented at American
Psychological Association. We used a prompt developed by McCabe that recorded
the child's narrative structure for these elements: Orientation, Action, High Point,
Resolution or Ending, Coda. This particular structure has been a guideline for
developing stories within the Narrative Play model. The child is encouraged to
decide who is in the story and where it takes place. As the child plays, the therapist
rephrases the child's descriptions of sequential actions in the story. Then, when
a high-point occurs in the narrative, the therapist can help the child see the excitement of the story. Finally, the ending of the story happens and the child can
explain why the story happened. The narrative structure provides an overall frame
for encouraging language and play and storytelling. Vivian Paley (1990) shows with
compassion, the real world of using narratives in the classroom to bring a special
child together with his classmates.

Vygotsky (1987) devised the concept that play is a resource, a place for the
development of narrative skills. James Paul Gee, sociocultural linguist, writes, "Narrative is fundamentally a perspective that human beings take on the way in which
certain themes fall into a satisfying pattern, a perspective stemming from social
identity and the resources social groups make available to them" (Gee, 1991, 13).

It is the use of narratives in play that helps a child recognize his own identity and become more socialized through storytelling with others. The child begins to practice telling stories in the socialization of play and eventually writes these narratives. Other researchers have provided evidence that a child's acquisition of narrative skills in preschool years is important for early literacy (Dickinson and Tabors, 2001; McCabe and Bliss, 2003; Feagans and Applebaum, 1986; Snow, 1983). In my doctoral work at Clark University, I worked on the Home School Study Project (Harvard University and Clark University) with Dr. Dickinson and Dr. Snow and studied the effects of language, literacy, and the development of forms of discourse that children construct. These forms of discourse often include narratives. Researchers confirm that developing narrative skills in play prepares a child for school as well as forming literacy skills and oral language skills in social contexts. Parents can help children with their narratives by listening, asking leading questions, and following the child's conversational lead (McCabe and Bliss, 2003, 133).

P. Uccelli, L. Hemphill, B. Alexander, and C. Snow, 2006, "Conversing with toddlers about the nonpresent: Precursors to narrative development in two genres," in *Child Psychology: A Handbook of Contemporary Issues*, 2nd ed., ed. Balter Lawrence, Tamis-Monda, Catherine Snow, New York: Psychology Press, xv, 679. These researchers found that in typically developing toddlers, precursors to narrative development can be identified in the language of exchanges of young children. The authors argue that there are individual differences that emerge in a child's early development and while some children make gains in fantasy, others develop personal narrative about real experience. The relationship between a child's early experience with social interaction and their later narrative development is explored. This is new research that may have some impact on how young children develop narratives and play.

A. Nicolopoulou, J. McDowell, and C. Brockmeyer, 2006, "Narrative play and emergent literacy: Storytelling and story-acting meet journal writing," in *Play=Learning*, ed. Dorothy Singer, Roberta Michnick Golinkoff, and K. Hirsh-Pasek, New York: Oxford University Press, xvi, 272. Although this study is about typically developing children, the authors provide evidence that storytelling, along with journal writing and story-acting, promote learning and development in low income families. The study advocates for more child-centered activities that also combines several educational activities. In Narrative Play, the therapist includes many types of educational activities, including storytelling, are a part of the method.

3. Patrick's dialogue: Unpublished film clip taken in Lexington, MA, in my office when he was two years of age on October 5, 2000. His mother was present.

4. H. Seung, 2006, "Intervention outcomes of a bilingual child with autism," *Journal of Medical Speech-Language Pathology*, March, 14(1): 53–63; V.F. Gutierrez-Clellen, 1999, "Language choice in intervention with bilingual children," *American Journal of Speech-Langauge Pathology*, November, 8: 291–302. Both studies found that a child who is diagnosed with autism at a young age and lives in a bilingual family would benefit from intervention that is given in the child's primary language first and then may be transitioned to a secondary language later, after twelve months.

The study supports the practice of providing services in the primary language when English is not the language used at home to "establish linguistic foundation of the primary language" (Seung, 2006, 53–63).

5. Sonia's dialogue: unpublished film clip taken in Lexington, MA, in my office in 2000 while she was visiting from a country in Europe with her family. She understood three languages and she had autism. Her expressive language was unintelligible at first, but she began to put some one–two word phrases together when she saw objects and real-life animals. I worked with her in Narrative Play for seven hours a day for ten days.

6. A. McCabe (see note 2 above).

7. This was a parent quote, a mother, during a parent conference at the end of a speech therapy session in my office in Lexington, MA, 2003. The statements were recorded in clinical notes following the session.

8. D. Hatton, "Early intervention and early childhood special education for young children with neurogenetic disorders." In *Neurogenetic Developmental Disorders*, edited by Michele M.M. Mazzocco and Judith L. Ross. Cambridge, MA: MIT Press. C. Solot, C. Knightly, S. Handler, M. Gerdes, D.M. McDonald-McGinn, E. and Moss, 2000, "Communication disorders in 22q11.2 microdeletion syndrome," *Journal of Communication Disorders*, 33: 187–204. Current researchers recognize that a child's receptive language may be higher and his/her expressive language during toddler and preschool years; therefore, it is important to recognize that the intellectual capabilities of the child may be higher because of early language delays that frequently occur in children with disabilities.

9. M.J. Baker, 2000, "Incorporating the thematic ritualistic behaviors of children with autism into games: Increasing social play interactions with siblings," *Journal of Positive Behavior Interventions*, 2(2): 66–84. When children with autism were taught a play interaction based on their thematic repetitive behavior (e.g., a child who perseverated on themes, movies, or videos), the percentage of social interactions and joint attention skills increased. The rate of ritualistic behaviors decreased to a minimum or did not occur at all. In Narrative Play therapy in phase two, joint attention, when the child is encouraged to play with another child and develop stories in play, the desired object, a train car, for example, may be incorporated into the story and the play. In my experience, when the child does include his object into a play theme, he does not perseverate on the object and instead creates a role for that object in the narrative. He begins to feel the need to notice his siblings and to join them instead of focusing on a particular object.

PHASE TWO: JOINT ATTENTION

1. R. Landa, 2005a, "Assessment of social communication skills in preschoolers," *Mental Retardation and Developmental Disabilities Research Reviews*, 11: 247–252; R. Landa, 2005b, "Language, social, and executive functions in high functioning autism: A continuum of performance," *Journal of Autism and Developmental Disorders*, 35(5): 557–573; R. Landa and E. Garrett-Mayer, 2006, "Development in

infants with autism spectrum disorders: A prospective study," *Journal of Child Psychology and Psychiatry*, 47(6): 629–638; K.E. Nichols, N. Fox, and P. Mundy, 2005, "Joint attention, self-recognition, and neurocognitive function in toddlers," *Infancy*, 7: 35–51; P. Mundy and J. Stella, 2000, "Joint attention, social orienting, and nonverbal communication in autism," in *Autism Spectrum Disorders: A Transactional Developmental Perspective*, ed. Amy M. Wetherby and Barry M. Prizant, 55–77. Dr. Rebecca Landa, Ph.D., also defines joint attention as crucial and pivotal skills in social communication. She writes, "One of the most important types of communication for children to understand and initiate is joint attention. Joint attention refers to the ability to coordinate attention with a social partner around an event or object" (Landa, 2005a, 248). Pointing to an object and showing an object to another person, using body language that communicates the intent to share, is basic to social communication with peers. Later, pointing is often replaced by the linguistic means of sharing information, according to Landa. "Joint attention . . . is believed to be a pivotal aspect of the development of intersubjectivity and a precursor to the development of theory of mind" (Landa, 2005a, 248). In addition, joint attention predicts future language development (Mundy, Sigman, and Kasari, 1990; Nichols et al., 2005). The absence of joint attention skills appears to be an early marker for signs of developmental disabilities, such as autism (Charman, 2003 in Landa, 2005a, 248). One of the difficulties of measuring this skill is that children may be able to point and share a toy; however, they may lack the subtle skills of using eye gaze shifts (to person and back to object) and vocal expression with a variety of intonation patterns to gain the other person's interest. In my clinical work with children with autism, I've seen these children share toys and appear to have the basic joint attention skills; however, they lack the subtle cues that sustain the interaction with others. For example, a child may have the basic pragmatic skills of initiating and greeting others with "Hi, how are you?" or "Let's play." But, they do not respond with relevant comments and voice intonation and gestures that communicate their own intent to sustain the interaction.

G. Dawson, A.N. Meltzoff, J. Osterling, J. Rinaldi, and E. Brown, 1998, "Children with autism fail to orient to naturally occurring social stimuli," *Journal of Autism and Developmental Disorders*, 28(6): 479–485. Children with autism in this study failed to orient to social stimuli (name called, hands clapping) and were unable to share attention and follow another's gaze or a point. They exhibited impairments in shared attention. Children with autism have difficulty following the social stimuli in the natural environment with the rapid shifting of attention between different peers and social stimuli in a natural setting. The author found that shared attention impairment in autism may be a result, in part, of a failure to attend to social stimuli such as a person's facial expression or eyes.

2. Sandy and therapist dialogue: Clinical notes taken during therapy in my Lexington office in the summer of 2002.

3. John and Jim and mother and therapist dialogue: unpublished film clip of twin boys, filmed at a local farm, Drumlin Farm in Lincoln, MA, in June 2002 and clinical notes taken on site at the farm.

4. Christine and Olivia and therapist dialogue: Clinical notes and observation data from doing narrative play therapy at the beach in the summer of 2003.

PHASE THREE: CHILD INITIATED RECIPROCITY

1. T. Attwood, 1998, *Asperger's Syndrome*, London: Jessica Kingsley Press. Tony Attwood does a wonderful job of writing about a person with Asperger's who has difficulty in understanding and using the subtle cues of language. He explains how these individuals tend to have a literal interpretation of what another person says. He talks about how children are confused by teasing. He explains how clinicians must teach language prosody (stress, rhythm, pitch) and how they can, with the use of *Social Stories* (Gray, 1994a) and "*Comic Strip Conversations*" (Gray, 1994b), help these children understand social interactions. The author points out how "there is natural tendency to imitate the posture, gestures, and mannerisms of the other person" (Attwood, 1998). The person with Asperger's or autism may have difficulty synchronizing his movements without appearing false. In general, it is difficult for a child with social language disabilities to coordinate facial expression, voice tone, body posture, and language in a social interaction. This book is an excellent resource for specialists and parents with children with social language disorders.

2. R. Landry and S.E. Bryson, 2004, "Impaired disengagement of attention in young children with autism," *Journal of Child Psychology and Psychiatry*, 45(6): 1115–1122. Children with autism have atypical responses to visual stimuli and have marked difficulty shifting their attention or disengaging attention. In this study, children with autism remained fixated on certain visual stimuli when two stimuli were presented for the entire eight-second trial. Although this study has a small sample size, the research recognizes the importance of children with autism having difficulty orienting to visual events when they are fixated on some other visual stimuli. Further research is needed in this area of visual fixation and attention.

3. Justin and Mark and Erik (ice sculptor) and therapist: Clinical notes and observation notes taken at Justin's elementary school during the early spring of 2004.

4. Elsie and therapist: Clinical notes taken over a time period of two years of therapy at Elsie's school from 2000 through 2002.

5. Sarah's transcript: Transcript from clinical notes taken in Lexington, MA, in my office on June 6, 2004.

6. D.J.: a preschooler in a preschool class—clinical notes taken on site at a preschool in Boston, MA, in April 2004. The children were playing in a box of real "squirmy" worms with mud. They used small plastic spoons to dig up the worms. The dialogue was taken exactly as shown in the text from clinical notes.

7. Jamie and therapist: dialogue from official progress notes written by the therapist and given to Jamie's preschool team each week for over the period of a year. I visited his recess and free-choice time most weeks in 2003 to help him make social connections with his peers. By the end of therapy he was relating and he was a part of his class. Jamie made it through all the phases of Narrative Play, even to

phase four. He became the school's best kickball kicker and he stopped eating tree bark.

8. Eddy and Tim and therapist: Clinical notes taken during our language/sports group while playing T-ball and baseball on Saturdays with their parents from 2002 to 2004. Eddy graduated to phase four and became involved in school plays. He learned to act, to dance, and to relate to his peers and make good friends. He didn't give up baseball with his friends.

9. Jacob and Michael and therapist: Clinical notes and tapes of speech sessions for a period of two years. Jacob progressed to phase four of Narrative Play.

10. Second-grade class in Massachusetts elementary school with the teacher and the therapist: direct transcript from a film clip taken on January 15, 2007, in the classroom.

PHASE FOUR: SOCIAL ENGAGEMENT

1. K. Stewart, 2002, *Helping a Child with Nonverbal Learning Disorder or Asperger's Syndrome*, Oakland, CA: New Harbinger Publications, Inc. Early researchers thought that Nonverbal Learning Disability (NLD) was a dysfunction of the right hemisphere of the brain and that social skills were affected. Rourke (1989) published *Nonverbal Learning Disabilities: The Syndrome and the Model*, and described the characteristics of these children, such as, difficulties with tactile perception, psychomotor coordination, visual-spatial orientation, nonverbal problem solving (knowing how something goes together) and the ability to use humor. The current list of criteria, "NLD and Related Conditions Symptom List," was developed by Kathryn Stewart and Darlene Sweetland (Stewart, 2002) The list includes social/emotional indicators: poor ability to read facial expression and cues; literal interpretation of language in social situations; concern over "fairness"; black and white interpretation of rules; rigid thinking; inconsolableness; obsessive compulsive disorder; frustration; sudden outbursts; poor grooming; history of sleep difficulties. In the language area, the child has no history of language delays, a high output of language, distorted prosody (rhythm), excellent verbal production, problems in pragmatics, and development of expertise on a topic. In terms of cognition, the child has an inability to pretend, disorganization, difficulty telling time, confusion, deficits in learning, difficulty finding a main idea, and dependence on auditory information. Also, the child has several sensory-motor indicators of tactile sensitivity, auditory sensitivity, tendency to "get lost in space," and motor skill problems. Stewart says, "Both disorders (NLD and Asperger's) involve similar difficulties processing information and engaging in social interaction, a high level of verbal skills, and a need for a specialized learning environment" (Stewart, 2002, 15). Stewart believes that children with either NLD or Asperger's benefit from the same interventions.

2. R. Fisher and W. Ury, 1991, *Getting to Yes*, New York: Penguin Books. I took a course with Roger Fisher at the Harvard Project on Negotiation in 1989 at Harvard Law School. One of Fisher's principles that helped me the most with my work with children with autism was the rule that participants always "focus on

interests, not positions." The basic idea is for each participant in a negotiation to learn that each side has needs, desires, concerns, and fears. If the two sides can find a shared interest it is possible to come to an agreement. When helping children with autism form friendships, the person who is facilitating language should focus on the particular interests of each child in a negotiation. It may take time, but once two children realize that they each have needs and that they can be friends and still disagree, they come together in a negotiated agreement.

3. P. Wolfberg, 1999, *Play and Imagination in Children*, New York: Teachers College Press; P. Wolfberg and A.L. Schuler, 1993, "Integrated play groups: A model for promoting the social and cognitive dimensions of play in children with autism," *Journal of Autism and Developmental Disorders*, 23: 467–489. See note 4 of Introduction.

4. M. Preissler, 2006, "Play and autism: Facilitating symbolic understanding," in *Play=Learning*, ed. Dorothy G. Singer, R. Golinkoff, and K Hirsh-Pasek, New York: Oxford University Press. According to Melissa Allen Preissler, "Speech and language skills are typically paramount in therapeutic interventions and the importance of peer play is frequently underrated" (Preissler, 2006, 244).

5. S. Greenspan and S. Weider, 1997, "Developmental patterns and outcomes in infants and children with disorders in relating and communicating: A chart review of 200 cases of autism spectrum diagnoses," *The Journal of Developmental and Learning Disorders*, 1: 87–141; P. Wolfberg and A.L. Schuler, 1993, "Integrated play groups: A model for promoting the social and cognitive dimensions of play in children with autism," *Journal of Autism and Developmental Disorders*, 23: 467–489; C. Lord and J.M. Hopkins, 1986, "The social behavior of autistic children with younger and same-age nonhandicapped peers," *Journal of Autism and Developmental Disorders*, 16: 249–263. These studies show that when peers are taught to become social models for children with autism, the children with autism engage in more complex forms of play. These researchers support the concept that children with autism may be supported through their interactions with peers in natural play situations. The peers need training to develop the skills of how to socially interact with children with autism.

6. D. Kamps, J. Royer, E. Dugan, T. Kravits, Gonzalez-Lopez, J. Garcia, K. Carnazzo, K. Morrison, and L.G. Kane, 2002, "Peer training to facilitate social interaction for elementary students with autism and their peers," *Council for Exceptional Children*, 68(2): 173–187. These studies support research that says that peer-mediated interventions for students with autism are effective in increasing participation in natural settings. Recommendations include (1) training for students with autism in the use of language in social settings, perhaps in dyads initially and (2) training peers to prompt and reinforce language, and to use specific strategies such as time delay and incidental teaching (Kamps et al., 2002, 185).

7. Patrick: Transcript from unpublished film, *Narrative Play Therapy*, presented to Harvard Medical School faculty, a course on "Autism, PDD, and Other Disorders across the Spectrum" with a paper, "The Relationship of Autism, Language, and Narrative play" on January 8, 2005. The particular film clip was taken in Massachusetts at a public elementary school in May of 2004.

8. Ashley and Chase: transcript from unpublished film clip taken at OTA, Wakefield, by Sid Levin and Nancy Mauer, videographers of First Frame in Concord, MA, for *First Signs, Inc.* Nancy Wiseman, author of *Could It Be Autism?* (2006), produced a film to educate pediatricians about autism (2001) called *On the Spectrum* (First Signs, Inc. 2001). This particular film clip was not used in the film.

9. Jack and peers: transcript from unpublished video film clip taken at Beaver Country Day Camp, Chestnut Hill, MA, in August 2006, during a day camp event called "Pirates Day."

10. J. Ayers, 1994, *Sensory Integration and the Child*, Western Psychological Services. "Sensory integration is the organization of sensation for use. Our senses give us information about the physical conditions of our body and the environment around us. Sensations flow into the brain like streams flowing into a lake. Countless bits of sensory information enter our brain at every moment, not only from our eyes and our ears, but also from every place in our bodies" (Ayers, 1994, 5). Ayers believes, as I do, that a vestibular disorder may cause a child to run in the wrong direction on a playground, will interfere with social relationships. The child has trouble judging whether he is too close or too far away and often bumps into peers. He has difficulty visualizing space and may not know how to move to one play or another, particularly on a busy playground at recess. These difficulties are a part of a sensory integration disorder.

11. Jonathan and Blake: transcript from unpublished video film clip taken at Beaver Country Day Camp, Chestnut Hill, MA, on August 8, 2006 with the preschool group on the playground.

12. M. Preissler, 2006. "Play and autism: Facilitating symbolic understanding." In *Play=Learning*, edited by Dorothy G. Singer, Roberta M. Golinkoff, and Kathy Hirsh-Pasek. New York: Oxford University Press, Chapter 12, 231–250 (see Chap. 4, n. 21). Several therapy treatments are available to children with autism and early detection is critical according to these authors (Lord and McGee, 2001). The most effective mode of treatment is a specific, intense program of intervention administered as soon as possible to the child (Weisman, 2006; Preissler 2006). Preissler (2006) says that even though there are many behavioral treatment interventions that increase speech and cognitive skills for children with autism, "these skills are not generalized to novel settings and stimuli and lack a certain social quality" (Preissler, 2006, 245). Therefore, the child needs some play therapy as a part of his or her overall intervention program. With some structure and peer models, the child with autism can develop social skills with peers. Wolfberg and Schuler (1993) found that children with ASD (Autism Spectrum Disorder) are more capable of interacting in play than typically observed and that intervention programs that leave out play are limited in scope. Peers can offer support and provide social initiations that will teach the child with autism to imitate and to begin to use language of their own to communicate.

13. The father of a patient with autism told me this story. His words are included from a transcript in a counseling session with the parent on January 8, 2006. Both children are doing well; the child with autism is happy in a private school and

relating to his peers, participating in karate and in car track races designed for young adults; his typical sibling is doing very well in his preschool and although he is still wearing his "magic glasses," his self-esteem is fine and he is socially connected to his own peers and his family.

14. T. Pilowsky, N. Yirmiya, O. Doppelt, V. Gross-Tsur, and R. Shalev, 2004, "Social and emotional adjustment of siblings of children with autism," *Journal of Child Psychology*, 45(4): 855–865. Other researchers found that "siblings of children with autism are, for the most part, surprisingly well adjusted, considering the genetic, familial, and social stresses they face" (Pilowsky et al., 2004, 863). This particular study was limited by the absence of a comparison group of siblings of children with normal development; however, the study points out the need for further research on not only the social and emotional adjustment of siblings, but on the quality of their social relationships. The authors suggest research be done on theory of mind abilities to compare siblings of typically developing children to siblings of children with diagnoses other than autism. Despite these limitations, the authors agree that the current findings suggest that children with siblings who have autism are not necessarily "associated with vulnerability for social and emotional difficulties" (Pilowsky et al., 2004, 863). Therefore, if this is the current thinking by the majority of researchers, then these typical children are good candidates for training on how to assist their siblings with autism in social language interactions.

15. A. Bagenholm and C. Gillberg, 1991, "Psychosocial effects on siblings of children with autism and mental retardation: A population-based study," *Journal of Mental Deficiency Research*, 35: 291–307; S. Fisman, L. Wolf, D. Ellison, B. Gillis, T. Freeman, 2000, "A longitudinal study of siblings of children with chronic disabilities," *Canadian Journal of Psychiatry*, 45: 369–375. Some studies suggest that siblings of children with autism "may be at increased risk of negative outcomes such as depression when compared to control groups but also to siblings of children with other disabilities" (Bagenholm and Gillberg, 1991; Fisman et al., 2000).

16. R.J. Landa and M.C. Goldberg, 2005, "Language, social, and executive functions in high functioning autism: A continuum of performance," *Journal of Autism and Developmental Disorders*, 35(5): 557–573. Children with high-functioning autism (HFA) have both verbal and nonverbal communication impairments according to these authors. Often grammatical markers are impaired (Scarborough, Rescorla, Tager-Flusberg, Fowler and Sudhalter, 1991) in children with autism. These studies have looked at the relationships between HFA and impairment in language, and social and executive functions. Although this study found a mixed profile of impaired abilities, they did find children with autism have problems shifting sets (flexibility).

17. Pilowsky et al. 2004, "Social and emotional adjustment of siblings of children with autism," *Journal of Child Psychology*, 45(4): 855–865. See note 14 above.

18. S. Verte, H. Roeyers, and Buysse, 2003, "Behavioural problems, social competence, and self-concept in siblings of children with autism," *Child: Care, Health & Development*, 29: 3, 193–205, Blackwell Publishing, Ltd. The question addressed in this sibling research was whether having a brother or sister with HFA (high-functioning autism) is associated with a disadvantage or a benefit for the

siblings in psychological adjustment. Overall, the research found that "siblings of children with HFA are not more susceptible to adaptation problems than siblings of children without a disorder (Verte et al. 2003, 202). In addition, this research found that "younger children show more behavioural problems because of attention seeking" (Verte et al. 2003, 202).

19. H. Goldstein and K. English, 1997, "Interaction among preschoolers with and without disabilities: Effects of across-the-day peer intervention," *Journal of Speech, Language, and Hearing Research*, 40: 33–49. Four sibling dyads participated in this study; four of the children had autism, and four were the typically developing siblings. The children were between three to six years of age. The framework for training was on the three steps of "Stay-Play-Talk" (Goldstein and English, 1997). The typical child was asked to move in proximity to the child with ASD while calling his name and to maintain this proximity while talking or playing. The child was also taught that he should expect some rejections by his sibling and he should not give up. All four children with ASD increased their frequency of joint attention with siblings during play sessions. Their social behaviors (positive social initiations and positive social responses) toward their siblings also increased; J.K. Harrower and G. Dunlap, 2001, "Including children with autism in general education classrooms: A review of effective strategies," *Behavior Modification*, 2: 262–284; McConnell 2002.

20. C.D. Jones and I.S. Schwartz, 2004, "Siblings, peers, and adults: Differential effects of models for children with autism," *Topics in Early Childhood Special Education*, 24(4): 187–198. The most effective modeling for children with disabilities needs four factors—attention to the model, model competency, nature of the model/learner relationship, and length of the model/learner relationship" (Jones and Schwartz 2004,187).

21. Evan: Transcript from unpublished film clip taken in Lexington, MA, by his mother, Dorothea Peralta, holding my camera during a speech session with his sibling, Sarah Peralta. Sarah is the author of a book about her sibling: *All about My Brother*, 2002, Shawnee, KS: Autism Asperger Publishing Co. Evan said the word "Go!" on the tape.

22. B.A. Taylor, L. Levin, and S. Jasper, 1999, "Increasing play-related statements in children with autism toward their siblings: Effects of video modeling," *Journal of Developmental and Physical Disabilities*, 11, 253–264. Some researchers have found that "direct-sibling-to-sibling instruction" can be useful as an educational method (Taylor, Levin, and Jasper, 1999). Of course, if the child's sibling has autism, then it may not be possible to meet these four criteria for learning. For example, if the child has completed phase one of Narrative Play and he can make contact and relate with some gestures or sounds to his sibling, then he will attend to the sibling and pay attention to a model from his brother or sister. Otherwise, the child may struggle to make contact with his sibling unless he is given full support from an adult. Bringing a child into phase one with his disabled sibling is possible, but requires more time in the outside environment to make a connection between them, and it also requires giving 100 percent support to the typical child who may be rejected by

his sibling. In addition, when the child has a severe social language delay and rejects playing with partners, the therapy process may take longer, more than two years of sibling therapy. It is also difficult for many children with autism to learn the abstract concepts underlying human interaction. The therapist may need to incorporate some direct teaching of each social skill with visuals (e.g., responding back to another person with relevant information) in order for the child to understand the concepts (e.g., that if you respond with relevant language, your listener will know that you're interested in the conversation and even the relationship.) A child with autism may take time to acquire such concepts in social language. However, if the child with autism is high functioning, has good long-term memory and the social skill is concrete, he will associate the language script (e.g., Wow! Look at this!) with a particular social skill (e.g., eye-gaze shift: looking at your sibling and then gazing at the object and then back to the sibling). In that case, he might retain the skill in one or two sessions. The third factor to consider is the type of relationship that the typical child has with his sibling. The relationship may affect the progress of the sibling work on language facilitation and joint attention, particularly if the child with autism has multiple "melt-downs" or rejects his sibling and wants to play alone. Regarding the fourth factor for learning, some researchers have found that the modeling needs to occur on multiple occasions. Since siblings are together a high percentage of their day, a sibling who can model social skills for his brother or sister, helps to create one of the best situations a disabled child can have for learning.

23. Noah and therapist: Clinical notes taken after our last language/sports session at an official baseball field in Massachusetts on July 5, 2006.

References

American Psychiatric Association. 2005. *Diagnostic and Statistical Manual of Mental Disorders, Fourth Edition (DSM-IV-TR)*. American Psychiatric Association.

Argyle, M. 1972. *The Psychology of Interpersonal Behavior*. Pelican: University of Chicago Press.

Ashwood, P., Willis, S., Van de Water, J. 2006. "The immune response in autism: A new frontier for autism research." *Journal of Leukoc Biology*, 80(1): 1–15.

Attwood, T. 1998. *Asperger's Syndrome*. London, England: Jessica Kingsley Press.

Ayers, J. 1994. *Sensory Integration and the Child*. Western Psychological Services.

Baker, M.J. 2000. "Incorporating the thematic ritualistic behaviors of children with autism into games: Increasing play interactions with siblings" *Journal of Positive Behavior Interventions*, 2(2): 66–84.

Bagenholm, A. and Gillberg, C. 1991. "Psychosocial effects on siblings of children with autism and mental retardation: A population-based study." *Journal of Mental Deficiency Research*, 35: 291–307.

Baron-Cohen, S. 1991. "Do people with autism understand what causes emotion?" *Child Development*, 62: 385–395.

———. 1993. "From attention-goal psychology to belief-desire psychology: The development of theory of mind and its dysfunction." In *Understanding Other Minds: Perspective from Autism*, edited by Simon Baron-Cohen et al. London: Oxford University Press.

———. 2001. *Mindblindness*. Cambridge, MA: MIT Press.

Baron-Cohen, S., Campbell, R., Karmiloff-Smith, A. Grant, J., and Walker, J. 1995. "Are children with autism blind to the mentalistic significance of the eyes?" *British Journal of Developmental Psychology*, 13(4): 379–398.

Baron-Cohen, S., Spitz, A., and Cross, P. 1993. "Can children with autism recognize surprise?" *Cognition and Emotion*, 7:507–516.

Bauman, M.L. and Kemper, T. 1985. "Histoanatomic observation of the brain in early infantile autism." *Neurology*, 35: 866–874.

———. 1988. "Limbic and cerebellar abnormalities: Consistent findings in infantile autism." *Journal of Neuropathology and Experimental Neurology*, 47: 369.

———. 1994. *The Neurobiology of Autism*. Baltimore and London: The Johns Hopkins University Press.

Bauman, M.L., Anderson, G., Perry, E., and Ray, M. 2006. "Neuroanatomical and neurochemical studies of the autistic brain: Current thought and future directions." In *Understanding Autism: From Basic Neuroscience to Treatment*, edited by Moldin Steven and John Rubenstein. CRC/Taylor & Francis: Boca Raton, Florida, 303–322.

Bell, Nanci. 1991. *Visualizing and Verbalizing*. Paso Robles CA: Academy of Reading Publications.

Bryson, S.E., Landry, R., Czapinski, P., McConnell, B., Rombough, V., and Wainwright, A. 2004. "Autistic spectrum disorders: Causal mechanisms and recent findings on attention and emotion." *International Journal of Special Education*, 19: 14–22.

Bryson, S.E., Zwaigenbaum, L., and Roberts, W. 2004. "The early detection of autism in clinical practice." *Paediatrics and Child Health*, April, 9(4): 219–221.

Bryson, S.E., Zwaigenbaum, L., and Roberts, W. 2005. "Understanding autism— What every family doctor needs to know." *Paediatrics and Child Health*, 2(1): 1–6.

Dawson, G., Meltzoff, A.N., Osterling, J., Rinaldi, J., and Brown, E. 1998. "Children with autism fail to orient to naturally occurring social stimuli." *Journal of Autism and Developmental Disorders*, 28(6): 479–485.

Densmore, A. 2000. "Speech on location: A narrative play technique to teach expressive language and communication to children with PDD/autism/language delay." *The Journal of Developmental and Learning Disorders*, 2: 216–217. International Universities Press, Inc.

Dickinson, D. and Tabors, P. 2001. *Beginning Literacy with Language*. Baltimore, MD: Brookes Publishers.

Dunn, J. and Dale, N. 1984. "I a daddy: 2 year olds' collaboration in joint pretense with sibling and mother." In *Symbolic Play. The Development of Social Understanding*, edited by L. Bretherton. Orlando, FL: Academic Press.

Feagans, L. and Applebaum, M.I. 1986. "Validation of language subtypes in learning disabled children." *Journal of Educational Psychology*, 78: 358–364.

Fisher, R. and Ury, W. 1981 [2nd ed. 1991]. *Getting to Yes*. New York: Penguin Books.

Fisman, S., Wolf, L., Ellison, D., Gillis, B., and Freeman, T. 2000. "A longitudinal study of siblings of children with chronic disabilities." *Canadian Journal of Psychiatry*, 45: 369–375.

Gee, J.P. 1990. *Social Linguistics and Literacies: Ideology in Discourses*. London: The Falmer Press.

———. 1991. "Memory and myth: A perspective on narrative." In *Developing Narrative Structure*, edited by Allyssa McCabe and Carole Peterson. Mahwah, NJ: Lawrence Erlbaum Associates, p. 13.

Goldstein, H. and English, K. 1997. "Interaction among preschoolers with and without disabilities: Effects of across-the-day peer intervention." *Journal of Speech, Language, and Hearing Research*, 40: 33–49.

Goldstein, H., Kaczmarek, L., Pennington, R., and Shafer, K. 1992. "Peer-mediated intervention: Attending to, commenting on, and acknowledging the behavior of preschoolers with autism." *Journal of Applied Behavior Analysis*, 25: 289–305.

Garfinkle, A.N. and Schwartz, I.S. 2002. "Peer imitation: Increasing social interactions in children with autism and other developmental disabilities in inclusive preschool classrooms." *Topics in Early Childhood Special Education*, 22: 26–38.

German, D. 2001. *It's on the Tip of My Tongue*. Chicago, IL: Word Finding Materials, Inc.

Gerber, S. and Prizant, B. 2000. "Speech, language, and communication assessment and intervention for children, Chapter 5." In *Principles of Clinical Practice for Assessment and Intervention. The ICDL Clinical Practice Guidelines*, edited by S.I. Greenspan and S. Wieder. Bethesda, MD: Interdisciplinary Council on Developmental and Learning Disorders (ICDL) Press, 109.

Grandin, T. 1995. *Thinking in Pictures*. New York: Vintage Books.

———. 2005. *Animals in Translation*. New York: Scribner.

Gray, C. 1994a. *The Original Social Story Book*. Arlington, TX: Future Horizons.

———. 1994b. *The New Social Story Book*. Arlington, TX: Future Horizons.

Greenspan, S. I. 1995. *The Challenging Child*. Reading, MA: Addison-Wesley Publishing, Inc.

Greenspan, S. I. and Lewis, D. 2002. *The Affect-Based Language Curriculum (ABLC)*. Bethesda, MD: Interdisciplinary Council on Developmental and Learning Disorders (ICDL).

Greenspan, S. I. and Weider, S. 1997. "Developmental patterns and outcomes in infants and children with disorders in relating and communicating: A chart review of 200 cases of autism spectrum diagnoses." *The Journal of Developmental and Learning Disorders*, 1: 87–141.

———. 2006. *Engaging Autism*. New York: The Perseus Book Group.

Gutierrez-Clellen, V.F. 1999. "Language choice in intervention with bilingual children." *American Journal of Speech-Language Pathology*, November, 8: 291–302.

Gutstein, S. and Sheely, R.K. 2002. *Relationship Development Intervention with Young Children*. London: Jessica Kingsley Publishers.

Harris, P., Johnson, C., Hutton, D., Andrews, G., and Cooke, T. 1989. "Young children's theory of mind and emotion." *Cognition and Emotion*, 3: 379–400.

Harrower, J.K. and Dunlap, G. 2001. "Including children with autism in general education classrooms: A review of effective strategies." *Behavior Modification*, 2: 262–284.

Hastings, R.P. 2003. "Brief report: Behavioral adjustment of siblings of children with autism." *Journal of Autism and Developmental Disorders*, February, 33: 1.

Hatton, D. 2007. "Early intervention and early childhood special education for young children with neurogenetic disorders." In *Neurogenetic Developmental Disorders*, edited by Michele M.M. Massacco and Judith L. Ross. Cambridge, MA: MIT Press.

Herbert, M.R. 2005a. "Autism: A brain disorder, or a disorder that affects the brain?" *Clinical Neuropsychiatry*, 2(6): 354–379.

———. 2005b. "Large brains in autism: The challenge of pervasive abnormality." *The Neuroscientist*, 11(5): 417–440.

Herbert, M.R., Russo, J.P., Yang, S., Roohi, J., Blaxill, M., Kahler, S.G., Cremer, L., and Hatchwell, E. 2006. "Autism and environmental genomics." *NeuroToxicology*, 27: 671–684.

Herbert, M.R., Ziegler, D.A., Deutsch, C.K., O'Brien, L.M., Kennedy, D.N., Filipk, P.A., Bakardjiev, A.I., Hodgson, J., Takeoka, M., Makris, N., and Caviness, V.S. Jr. 2005. "Brain asymmetries in autism and developmental language disorder: A nested whole-brain analysis." *Brain*, 128: 213–226.

James, J.S., Melnyk, S., Jernigan, S., Cleves, M.A., Halsted, C.H., Wong, D.H., Cutler, P., Bock, K., Boris, M., Bradstreet, J.J., Baker, S.M., and Gaylor, D. 2006. "Metabolic endophenotype and related genotypes are associated with oxidative stress in children with autism." *American Journal of Medical Genetics* Part B (Neuropsychiatric Genetics) 141B: 947–956.

Jass, J.R. 2005. "The intestinal lesion of autistic spectrum disorder," *Eur Journal of Gastroenterol Hepatol*, 17(8): 821–822.

Jones, C.D. and Schwartz, I.S. 2004. "Siblings, peers, and adults: Differential effects of models for children with autism." *Topics in Early Childhood Special Education*, 24(4): 187–198.

Kamps, D., Royer, J., Dugan, E., Kravits, T., Gonzalez-Lopez, Garcia, J., Carnazzo, K., Morrison, K., and Kane, L.G. 2002. "Peer training to facilitate social interaction for elementary students with autism and their peers." *Council for Exceptional Children*, 68(2): 173–187.

Kanner, L. 1943. "Autistic disturbance of affective contact." *Nervous Child*, 12: 217–250.

Koomar, J. and Bundy, A. 2002. "Creating intervention from theory." In *Sensory Integration Theory and Practice*. Philadelphia: FAA David Company.

Kranowitz, C.S. 1998. *The Out-of-Sync Child: Recognizing and Coping with Sensory Integration Dysfunction*. New York: Perigee Book.

———. 2003. *The Out-of-Sync Child Has Fun*. New York: Perigee Book.

Labov, W. 1972. *Language in the Inner City*. Philadelphia: University of Pennsylvania Press.

Landa, R. 2005a. "Assessment of social communication skills in preschoolers." *Mental Retardation and Developmental Disabilities Research Reviews*, 11: 247–252.

———. 2005b. "Language, social, and executive functions in high functioning autism: A continuum of performance." *Journal of Autism and Developmental Disorders*, 35(5): 557–573.

Landa, R.J. and Goldberg, M.C. 2005. "Language, social, and executive functions in high functioning autism: A continuum of performance." *Journal of Autism and Developmental Disorders*, 35(5): 557–573.

Landa, R. and Garrett-Mayer, E. 2006. "Development in infants with autism spectrum disorders: A prospective study." *Journal of Child Psychology and Psychiatry*, 47(6): 629–638.

Landry, R. and Bryson, S.E. 2004. "Impaired disengagement of attention in young children with autism." *Journal of Child Psychology and Psychiatry*, 45(6): 1115–1122.

Leont'ev, A.N. 1981. "The problem of activity in psychology." In *The Concept of Activity in Soviet Psychology*, edited by J.V. Wertsch. Armonk, NY: Sharpe.

Leslie, A. 1987. "Pretence and representation: The origins of 'theory of mind.'" *Psychological Review*, 94: 412–426.

———. 1994. "ToMM, ToBy, and Agency: Core architecture and domain specificity." In *Mapping the Mind: Domain Specificity in Cognition and Culture*, edited by L. Hirschfeld and S. Gelman. Cambridge: Cambridge University Press.

Levine, K. and Chedd, N. 2006. *Replays: Using Play to Enhance Emotional and Behavioral Development for Children with Autism Spectrum Disorders*. London: Jessica Kingsley Publishers.

Liss, M., Fein, D., Allen, D., Dunn, M., Feinstein, C., and Morris, R. 2001. "Executive functioning in high-functioning children with autism." *Journal of Child Psychology and Psychiatry*, 42: 261–270.

Lof, G.L. 2006. *Logic, Theory, and Evidence against the Use of Non-Speech Oral Motor Exercises to Change Speech Productions*. Presentation paper at ASHA Convention, November 17, 2006. MGH Institute of Health Professions.

Lord, C. and Hopkins, J.M. 1986. "The social behavior of autistic children with younger and same-age nonhandicapped peers." *Journal of Autism and Developmental Disorders*, 16: 249–263.

Lord, C. and McGee, J.P. 2001. *Educating Children with Autism*. Washington D.C.: National Academy Press.

Lovass, O.I. 1987. "Behavioral treatment and normal educational and intellectual functioning in young autistic children." *Journal of Consulting and Clinical Psychology*, 55: 3–9.

Maurice, C., Green, G., and Luce, S.C. 1996. *Behavioral Intervention for Young Children with Autism*. Austin, TX: Pro-ed.

Mazzocco, M.M. and Ross, J.L. 2007. *Neurogenetic Developmental Disorders*. Cambridge, MA: MIT Press.

McCabe, A. 1996. *Chameleon Readers*. New York: McGraw-Hill Companies, Inc.

McCabe, A. and Bliss, L. 2003. *Patterns of Narrative Discourse*. Boston, MA: Allyn & Bacon Press.

McCabe, A. and Peterson, C. 1991. *Developing Narrative Structure*. Hillsdale, NJ: Lawrence Erlbaum Associates Publishers.

McConnell, S.R. 2002. "Interventions to facilitate social interaction for young children with autism: Review of available research and recommendations for educational intervention and future research." *Journal of Autism and Developmental Disorders*, 32: 351–372.

Mundy, P. and Stella, J. 2000. "Joint attention, social orienting, and nonverbal communication in autism," In *Autism Spectrum Disorders: A Transactional Developmental Perspective*, edited by Amy M. Wetherby and Barry M. Prizant. New York: Brookes Publishing Co., Inc., 55–77.

Mundy, P., Sigman, M., and Kasari, C. 1990. "A longitudinal study of joint attention and language development of joint attention and language development in autistic children." *Journal of Autism Developmental Disorders*, 20:115–128.

Murch, S. 2005. "Diet, immunity, and autistic spectrum disorders." *Journal of Pediatrics*, 146(5): 582–584.

National Institute of Mental Health (NIMH). 2006. "Suicide in the U.S.: Statistics and prevention." *NIH Publication* no. 03-4594. Revised December 2006.

Nichols, K.E., Fox, N., and Mundy, P. 2005. "Joint attention, self-recognition, and neurocognitive function in toddlers." *Infancy*, 7: 35–51.

Nicolopoulou, A., McDowell, J., and Brockmeyer, C. 2006. "Narrative play and emergent literacy: Storytelling and story-acting meet journal writing." In *Play = Learning*, edited by Dorothy G. Singer, Roberta Michnick Golinkoff, and Kathy Hirsh-Pasek. London: Oxford University Press, xvi, 272.

Paley, V.G. 1990. *The Boy Who Would Be Helicopter: The Use of Storytelling in the Classroom*. Cambridge, MA: Harvard University Press.

———. 1992. *You Can't Say You Can't Play*. Cambridge, MA: Harvard University Press.

Peterson, C. and McCabe, A. 1983. *Developmental Psycholinguistics: Three Ways of Looking at a Child's Narrative*. New York: Plenum.

Peralta, S. 2002. *All About My Brother*. Shawnee Mission, KS: Autism Asperger Publishing Co.

Pilowsky, T., Yirmiya, N., Doppelt, O., Gross-Tsur, V., and Shalev, R. 2004. "Social and emotional adjustment of siblings of children with autism." *Journal of Child Psychology*, 45(4): 855–865.

Pinker, S. 1994. *The Language Instinct*. New York: HarperCollins Publishers.

———. 1997. *How the Mind Works*. New York: W.W. Norton & Company.

Polanyi, L. 1985. *Telling the American Story*. Norwood, NJ: Ablex.

Preissler, M.A. 2006. "Play and autism: Facilitating symbolic understanding." In *Play=Learning*, edited by Dorothy G. Singer, Roberta Michnick Golinkoff, and Kathy Hirsh-Pasek. New York: Oxford University Press, 231–250.

Preissler, M.A. and Carey, S. 2004. "Do both pictures and words function as symbols for 18 and 24 month children?" *Journal of Cognition and Development*, 5: 185–212.

Premack, D. and Woodruff, G. 1978. "Does the chimpanzee have 'a theory of mind?'" *Behavior and Brain Sciences*, 4: 515–526.

Prizant, B., Wetherby, A., Rubin, E., Laurent, A., and Rydell, P. 2002. "The SCERTS model: Enhancing communication and socioemotional abilities of children with autism spectrum disorder." *Jenison Autism Journal*, 14(4): 2–19.

Prizant, B., Wetherby, A., Rubin, E., and Laurent, A.C. 2003. "The SCERTS model: A transactional, family-centered approach to enhancing communication and socioemotional abilities of children with autism spectrum disorder." *Journal of Infants and Young Children*, 16(4): 296–316.

Quill, K. 1995. *Teaching Children with Autism: Strategies to Enhance Communication and Socialization*. New York: Delmar Publishers.

Quill, K. A. 2000. *Do-Watch-Listen-Say*. Baltimore, MA: Brookes Publishing Inc.

Rodrigue, J.R., Geffken, G.R., and Morgan, S.B. 1993. "Perceived competence and behavioural adjustment of siblings of children with autism." *Journal of Autism and Developmental Disabilities*, 23: 665–674.

Rogers, S.J. 2000. "Interventions that facilitate socialization in children with autism." *Journal of Autism and Developmental Disorders*, 30: 399–409.

Rogers, S.J., Osaki, D., Hall, T., and Reaven, J. 1998. *The Denver Model: An Integrated Approach to Intervention for Young Children with Autism*. Denver, CO: JFK Center for Developmental Disabilities.

Rogoff, B. 1990. *Apprenticeship in Thinking*. New York: Oxford University Press.

Ross, P. and Cuskelly, M. 2006. "Adjustment, sibling problems, and coping strategies of brothers and sisters of children with autism spectrum disorder." *Journal of Intellectual & Developmental Disability*, 31(2): 77–86.

Rourke, B. 1989. *Nonverbal Learning Disabilities: The Syndrome and the Model*. New York: Guilford Press.

Rutter, M. 2000. "Genetic studies of autism: From the 1970s into the millennium." *Journal of Abnormal Child Psychology*, 28: 3–14.

———. 2005. "Incidence of autism spectrum disorders: changes over time and their meaning." *Acta Paediatrica*, 94: 2–15.

Sacks, O. 1995. *An Anthropologist on Mars*. New York: Vintage Books Random House Inc.

Scarborough, Rescorla, Tager-Flusberg, Fowler, and Sudhalter. 1991. "The relation of utterance length to grammatical complexity in normal and language-disordered groups." *Applied Psycholinguistics,* 12: 23–45.

Schuler, A. and Wolfberg, P. 2000. "Promoting peer play and socialization." In *Autism Spectrum Disorders: A Transactional Developmental Perspective*, edited by A. Wetherby and B. Prizant. Baltimore, MA: Paul H. Brooks, 251–278.

Seung, H. 2006. "Intervention outcomes of a bilingual child with autism." *Journal of Medical Speech-Language Pathology*, March, 14(1): 53–63.

Sheely, R. 2007. Interview data obtained by phone about the RDI program (Gutstein, S. and Sheely, R.K. 2002. *Relationship Development Intervention with Young Children*. London: Jessica Kingsley Publishers.

Sigman, M., Ruskin, E., Arveile, S., Corona, R., Dissanayake, C., Espinosa, M. et al. 1999. "Continuity and change in the social competence of children with autism, Down syndrome, and developmental delays." *Monographs of the Society for Research in Child Development*, 64: 1–114.

Singer, D., Golinkoff, R.M., and Hirsh-Pasek, K. 2006. *Play=Learning*. New York: Oxford University Press.

Snow, C. 1983. "Literacy and language: Relationships during the preschool years." *Harvard Educational Review*, 53: 165–189.

Solot, C., Knightly, C., Handler, S., Gerdes, M., McDonald-McGinn, D.M., and Moss, E. 2000. "Communication disorders in 22q11.2 microdeletion syndrome." *Journal of Communication Disorders*, 33: 187–204.

Spezio, M.L., Adolphs, R., Hurley, R.S.E., and Pivan, J. 2007. "Analysis of face gaze in autism using 'Bubbles.'" *Neuropsychologia*, 45(1): 144–151.

Stewart, K. 2002. *Helping a Child with Nonverbal Learning Disorder or Asperger's Syndrome*. Oakland, CA: New Harbinger Publications, Inc.

Strand, E. and Caruso, A. 1999. *The Clinical Management of Motor Speech Disorders in Children*. New York and Stuttgart: Thieme Publishers.

Szatmari, P. Tuff, L., Finalyson, M.A., and Bartolucci, G. 1990. "Asperger's syndrome and autism: Neurocognitive aspects." *Journal of the American Academy of Child and Adolescent Psychiatry*, 29: 130–136.

Tager-Flusberg, H. 1981. "On the nature of linguistic functioning in early infantile autism." *Journal of Autism and Developmental Disorders*, 11: 45–56.

———. 1993. "What language reveals about the understanding of minds in children with autism." In *Understanding Other Minds: Perspectives from Autism*, edited by S. Baron-Cohen et al. New York: Oxford University Press.

Taylor, B.A., Levin, L., and Jasper, S. 1999. "Increasing play-related statements in children with autism toward their siblings: Effects of video modeling." *Journal of Developmental and Physical Disabilities*, 11: 253–264.

Tomasello, M. 1988. "The role of joint-attentional processes in early language acquisition." *Language Sciences*, 10: 69–88.

Tsao, L.L. and Odom, S.L. 2006. "Sibling-mediated social interaction intervention for young children with autism." *Topics in Early Childhood Special Education*, 26(2): 106–123.

Uccelli, P., Hemphill, L., Alexander, B., and Snow, C. 2006. "Conversing with toddlers about the nonpresent: Precursors to narrative development in two genres." In *Child Psychology: A Handbook of Contemporary Issues*, 2nd ed., edited by Balter Lawrence, Tamis-Monda, Catherine Snow. New York: Psychology Press, xv, 679.

Vargas, D.L., Nascimbene, C., Krishnan, M.H.S., Zimmerman, A.W., and Pardo, C.A. 2005. "Neuroglial activation and Neuroinflammation in the brain of patients with autism." *Annals of Neurology*, January, 57, 1: 67–81.

Verte, S., Roeyers, H., and Buysse. 2003. "Behavioural problems, social competence, and self-concept in siblings of children with autism." *Child: Care, Health & Development*, 29: 3, 193–205. Blackwell Publishing, Ltd.

Vygotsky, L.S. 1978. *Mind in Society: The Development of Higher Mental Processes*, edited and translated by M. Cole, V. John-Steiner, S. S. Scribner, and E. Souberman. Cambridge, MA: Harvard University Press. (Original work published 1930–1935).

———.1987. *The Collected Works of L.S. Vygotsky, Vol. I: Problems of General Psychology*, including the volume Thinking and Speech, edited by R.W. Rieber and A.S. Carton. New York: Plenum.

Weisman, N.D. 2006. *Could It Be Autism?* New York: Broadway Books.

Wetherby, A. and Prizant, B. 2000. *Autism Spectrum Disorders: A Transactional Developmental Perspective*, Baltimore, MD: Brookes Publishing Co., Inc.

Wolfberg, P. 1999. *Play and Imagination in Children with Autism*. New York: Teachers College Press.

Wolfberg, P. and Schuler, A.L. 1993. "Integrated play groups: A model for promoting the social and cognitive dimensions of play in children with autism." *Journal of Autism and Developmental Disorders*, 23: 467–489.

Index

About the Author

ANN E. DENSMORE has been a speech and language consultant at private and public schools for more than thirty years. She has also served as a consultant internationally, helping children with autism, and has taught graduate seminars for professionals and students at Harvard Medical School and the University of Canterbury, New Zealand. Densmore holds an Ed.D. in education with a specialization in child discourse from Clark University. She is board-certified in speech and language pathology and audiology.